BERLITZ®

BUDAPEST

By the staff of Berlitz Guides

Library of Congress Catalog Card Number
81-70089.

Printed in Austria.

Deluxe Guide
1989/1990

How to use our guide

- All the practical information, hints and tips that you will need before and during the trip start on page 102.

- For general background, see the sections Budapest and the Hungarians, p. 6, and A Brief History, p. 15.

- All the sights to see are listed between pages 24 and 74, with suggestions on daytrips from Budapest from page 74 to 85. Our own choice of sights most highly recommended is pinpointed by the Berlitz traveller symbol.

- Entertainment, nightlife and all other leisure activities are described between pages 85 and 94, while information on restaurants and cuisine is to be found on pages 95 to 101.

- Finally, there is an index at the back of the book, pp. 126–128.

Although we make every effort to ensure the accuracy of all the information in this book, changes occur incessantly. We cannot therefore take responsibility for facts, prices, addresses and circumstances in general that are constantly subject to alteration. Our guides are updated on a regular basis as we reprint, and we are always grateful to readers who let us know of any errors, changes or serious omissions they come across.

Photography: Eric Jaquier
Layout: Doris Haldemann
We wish to express our thanks to Vue Touristique I.P.V., Budapest and in particular to Prof. Joseph J. Hollos for their decisive roles in guiding this project to fruition.

 © Cartography: Cartographia, Budapest

Contents

Cover picture: Houses of Parliament
Photo, pp. 2–3: Széchenyi Baths

Budapest and the Hungarians

The Danube cuts through the heart of the city, distancing the historic Buda Hills from the elegant boulevards of Pest, yet linking and enhancing the beauty of the whole. And in part it's the dramatic setting that helps make Budapest one of Europe's most romantic cities. For romantic it undoubtedly is—you'll feel it, sense it, see it all around you. Love is in the Budapest air. Maybe it's those gypsy violins.

With a population above two million—ten times the size

of the country's next biggest town—Budapest is Hungary's economic and cultural capital as well as the political power-house. And it enjoys the lion's share of the tourist attractions and general excitement. In spite of its size and such metropolitan complications as the rush-hour traffic jams, the people of Budapest maintain a relaxed good cheer. They find time to smile, help a stranger, watch the city lights sparkling on the Danube.

Danube panorama with St. Gellért statue. Agriculture Hungarian-style keeps markets well-stocked.

The mighty river is crucial to Budapest's fascination; it also explains the city's very existence. Since prehistoric times, the Danube has provided settlers with plentiful fish and a means of communication. The Romans made it official nearly 2,000 years ago, when they chose the readily defensible hills of Budapest as the site for an important military garrison and provincial capital. They drew the line along the Danube, establishing the river as the last frontier between civilization and the barbarians. Inevitably, the barbarians won. But Budapest rose again... and again and again.

Since the Dark Ages, due to the tragic recurrence of invasion, war and revolution, the city has had to be rebuilt with disheartening frequency. The excavated vestiges of imperial Rome maintain a low profile on today's skyline. There are a few monuments to be approached with awe, but many restored buildings of advanced age, as well as admirable experiments of the 19th and 20th centuries. The most compelling slice of cityscape, in the Castle District of Buda, boasts a massive palace begun in the Middle Ages, the soaring barbed tower of an often-rebuilt 13th-century church, a joyous Gothic folly less than a century old, and a glassy Hilton hotel filling the gaps in an ancient monastery.

For all its familiar comforts, Budapest belongs, for a visitor from the West, to another world. The Ladas and Skodas jockeying for parking meters are just one reminder. But if your preconceptions about life in a People's Republic entail intrusive bureaucrats, ideological slogans, queues and surly waiters, you'll certainly find Budapest a surprise. Nobody will bother you; the slogans are just as likely to advertise T.V. sets or soft drinks; food and consumer goods are in plentiful supply; and when the waiter hands you the menu, he may actually click his heels! In Budapest, as ever, *joie de vivre* comes first.

But for visitors interested in politics and economics, Hungary offers a look at the workings of a different social system. There are big state-run factories and collective farms, but also an area of private initiative—family-operated restaurants and shops, and a

Shoppers throng bustling Kígyó utca, a pedestrian street in Pest.

8

cornucopia of home-grown produce in the marketplace. The school-children wear red Pioneer kerchiefs, but they also don jeans and buy the latest western pop records. And, in a country where the role of religion in society has caused pain and controversy, you'll find the churches packed every Sunday.

Budapest became the sum of its parts in 1873 with the amalgamation of the cities of Pest, Buda and Óbuda (Old Buda). The modern metropolis is divided into 22 administrative districts. As in Paris with its arrondissements, the number of the district tells you what kind of neighbourhood to expect. The first zone is historic, the second is rich in hillside villas, the third has Roman ruins and row after row of housing projects....

Because of architectural achievements old and new, and the profusion of trees, parks and gardens—and above all because of the Danube—the citizens love to look at Budapest from its many vantage points. Is the view of Buda from Pest more magnificent than the view of Pest from the heights of Buda? Is the grace of Elizabeth Bridge more fetching by day or by night? The people of Budapest are

crazy about their bridges, perhaps because of their relative novelty. The first permanent span didn't go into service until 1849; the Chain Bridge was a great engineering achievement, for it crosses the Danube at a point where the river is wide and swift and prone to break up into ice-floes in the spring. Also, the older generation remembers Budapest at the end of World War II, when German demolition squads had blown up all the bridges and people had to rely on ferries and pontoons. So the sight of a hydrofoil skimming beneath the arching bridges rates a special sigh of appreciation.

Many an admiring glance is dedicated to the chic women of Budapest. Not all of them can look as glamorous as those ageless Hungarian exports, the Gabor sisters, but that same vivacity and flair often shines through. The government, aware of the importance of this natural resource, makes sure the city is well supplied with modern hairdressing establishments. They open as early as 6 a.m. for the convenience of customers who need a pick-me-up on the way to the factory.

The Hungarians conform to no stereotype in their

physical appearance. There are high-cheekboned blondes and round-faced brunettes, swarthy men with droopy moustaches and blue-eyed red-heads to confuse the issue. But, with middle age, most show the toll of all those strudel snacks and feasts, thickening around the middle in spite of the calisthenics classes so prominent on TV.

Visitors soon understand that in Budapest—as in Paris or Peking—good food plays an exceptionally important role in life. With all the gourmet restaurants and pastry shops, this is a perfect place to abandon a diet. But to sharpen the appetite, a stroll through the city is in order. You have to stay alert for architectural curiosities and surprises: colourful mosaics or sculpted ornaments on otherwise prosaic buildings; fountains and statues, historic and modern; an outdoor café just when you need it.

The more formal sights of Budapest are scattered all over the city's 200 square miles, so you can't expect to accomplish a lot on foot. Fortunately, public transport is highly developed and cheap. Peppy yellow tram-cars supplement the bright blue fleet of buses; and below ground, the metro system manages to be both hygienic and efficient. The taxi service is good, with reasonable fares, but here as elsewhere it's the same old story: when it rains, there never seems to be a cab for hire.

However you get around, you'll find revered relics that tell the story of the city's development. There are the remains of the Roman town of Aquincum and authentic Turkish baths, still in operation. (The Ottoman Turks controlled Budapest for a century and a half.) A few Gothic churches have been restored, along with fine Baroque mansions. Under the Habsburgs, avenues of Baroque, neo-Classical and Eclectic buildings were laid out, and delightful experiments in Art Nouveau followed.

Budapest's many museums cover history, art and science, as well as such offbeat subjects as pharmacology and philately. Incidentally, the Budapest Fine Arts Museum may have the best collection of El Grecos and Goyas this side of Madrid. Theatres and concert halls maintain a busy programme of the performing arts. Though the language barrier blunts the appeal of the plays, you can take advantage of the abundance of good music. What other city of this size supports **11**

Figures from the past line up to form an imposing backdrop to the Heroes' Square.

two opera companies and four professional symphony orchestras? Not to mention chamber music, operetta and folk groups. In the land of Liszt and Bartók, music holds a special place of honour.

For a notoriously intellectual country, Hungary has a surprisingly big reputation in sports. This is based on many Olympic feats as well as memories, alas ever more distant, of a golden age of soccer. For the visitor there's plenty to watch, with international competi-

tions in sports ranging from archery to wrestling. The big matches take place in the 73,000-seat Népstadion (People's Stadium), a sight in itself. In the same part of town are the racecourses—one for trotters, the other for flat racing. Hungary's famous horses also star in shows put on for tourists in the *puszta* or prairie. And horse-riding package holidays can be arranged.

Since prehistoric times a mystique has surrounded the hot springs of Budapest, of which there are well over 100. Locals and visitors plunge in for relief of various medical problems, or merely to unwind after a gruelling day. Aside from the steam, the baths have plenty of atmosphere, especially the Turkish ones, architectural monuments from the 16th and 17th centuries.

Some of this thermal energy has been utilized to provide the central heating for whole areas of Budapest. Warm radiators and double-glazed windows are essential defences against winter here. Officially, the January average is just below the freezing point, which is cold enough to ice the Danube and bring down the ear-flaps on fur hats. In July the mean temperature is a perfect 20°C (68°F). But it's never monotonous. The weather in summer is temperate but temperamental—subject to heat waves and sudden thunderstorms. Vacationers at Lake Balaton, Hungary's substitute for a sea, watch out for colourful rockets which the authorities launch to warn of approaching tempests.

Balaton, called the biggest lake in central Europe, attracts throngs of holiday-makers for swimming, boating and fishing. The south shore, with its endlessly shallow slope toward waist-deep water, is popular with parents of small children. The nearby villages and vineyards add to the picturesque appeal of Balaton, which makes for a busy day-trip from Budapest—or a relaxed week or two. Other organized excursions from Budapest go to the Danube Bend, the beautiful and historic area where the river changes its direction from eastbound to southerly. Closer to town, coach tours cover the Buda Hills; or you can do it yourself by public bus, cog railway and ski-lift.

Another popular excursion is called "Budapest by Night". You may be surprised to learn that nightlife tours are a standard feature of the tourist circuit. Budapest, "the Paris of the East", really does have a number of nightclubs, statuesque showgirls and all, plus various nightspots with live music and dancing. The guided tours promise to return celebrants to their hotels around 1 a.m., but the revelry continues around town until 5 in the morning. There are also a couple of gambling casinos, open until about 2 a.m., where roulette, baccarat, blackjack and one-armed bandits are played in deutsche marks only.

For more sedate evenings out, there are Budapest's ma- **13** ny fine restaurants. Hungarian cuisine is first class, and much more varied than its reputation for paprika might indicate. Headed by the world-renowned Tokay, the roster of Hungarian wines is ample and attractive. And the after-dinner fruit brandies must be tried—and taken seriously.

Almost all of Budapest's restaurants come equipped with gypsy violin ensembles, strolling or stationary. The gushing music, under the influence of the wine and candlelight, may sound like an overdose of romance. But most visitors survive it, and many vow to return to Budapest to recapture the spell of the city that loves life.

Hungary: Facts and Figures

Geography: Area 35,919 square miles, slightly larger than Austria, but half the size of Oklahoma or Missouri. Landlocked Hungary borders on Austria, Czechoslovakia, the Soviet Union, Rumania and Yugoslavia. Most of the terrain, a fertile plain, lies less than 655 feet above sea level.

Population: 10,500,000 (in 1987), of which one-fifth lives in Budapest. Aside from the Hungarians, there are small minorities of Germans, Slovaks, Southern Slavs and Rumanians.

Government: People's Republic led by the Hungarian Socialist Workers' Party. The National Assembly has executive powers, a Presidium fulfills the functions of head of state and the Council of Ministers carries out policies. Hungary is a founder-member of the Council for Mutual Economic Assistance (Comecon) and the Warsaw Pact.

Economy: Socialist with decentralized management, incentives for profitability and private operation of some consumer service outlets and supplementary production units. Principal exports: agricultural and food products, bauxite, buses, consumer goods, machinery, pharmaceuticals.

Religion: No official statistics are kept, but Catholics are clearly the strong majority.

Language: Hungarian. A widely understood second language is German, while the favourite of the younger generation is English.

A Brief History

By European standards the Hungarians are newcomers. They've lived in the Carpathian basin for less than 1,100 years—though they've invested that relatively brief tenure with a full quota of suffering, struggle and achievement.

As for the history of the land, the preamble goes back hundreds of thousands of years. Less than 40 miles west of Budapest, at the village of Vértesszőlős, human traces thought to be half a million years old have been excavated. The bones of these early men are displayed at the Hungarian National Museum.

The tribes that migrated to the area in prehistoric times brought new skills and tools which improved a hunter's odds, made farming feasible and permitted the rise of primitive industries. And tenuous trade routes were established which linked Hungary with more sophisticated societies thousands of miles away. At the start of the Iron Age, when the Scythians rode onto the scene, local workshops were producing weapons, pottery and jewellery.

In the 3rd century B.C. Hungary was occupied by Celtic warriors, retreating from defeat in Greece. They established a tribal centre atop Budapest's Gellért Hill, commanding the Danube. The Celts were responsible for major artistic advances and industrial innovations.

But the full benefits of western civilization didn't reach Hungary until the 1st century A.D. with the conquering legions of the Roman empire. The strategy of the Emperor Augustus (27 B.C.—A.D. 14) pushed the north-east frontier of the empire to the Danube. By the 2nd century perhaps 20,000 Roman soldiers were deployed along the river between Vienna and Budapest alone, manning the main line of defence against the barbarians.

To command and coordinate this long, exposed perimeter, the Romans built Aquincum, a military camp which soon spawned civilian suburbs laid out as straight as troops on parade. In A.D. 106, the outpost became the capital of the Roman province of Lower Pannonia. The importance of Aquincum can be judged by the magnitude and beauty of the Roman vestiges unearthed in widely separated areas of present-day Budapest.

The remains of the centre of the civil city—shrines, public

baths, markets, workshops and villas—run alongside the suburban railway tracks. Every day, coachloads of school-children are led through the maze of surviving walls and restored columns. A mile away, the students of one Budapest school don't have to go anywhere to study ancient Rome. Valuable mosaics have been left exactly where they turned up during the construction of the building: in the basement and next door in what would otherwise have been the school playground.

When the over-stretched Roman empire faltered, tribes as fearsome as the Vandals and Huns moved in for the kill. The Dark Ages enveloped Aquincum early in the 5th century when the city fell to Hun warriors. But the driving force of the conquest, the mighty Attila, died in 453, and other tribes overthrew the Huns. In the age of great migrations, waves of nomads pushed, or were pushed, ever westward. For better or worse, the only period of relative stability came during occupation by the Avars. But they, too, were conquered.

A proud heritage: Óbuda's Roman theatre, Esztergom's religious art.

The Hungarians

The tribes which finally triumphed—the traditional date is 896—had wandered a long way from their home base between the River Volga and the Ural mountains. (Related tribes from the same homeland ended up in Finland. Specialists label both the Finnish and Hungarian peoples, and their strange, mutually incomprehensible languages, as Finno-Ugric.) The first great Hungarian leader, Prince Árpád, founded a dynasty which led Hungary into statehood. Árpád's tribe was known as the Magyars; later, all Hungarians were to call themselves Magyars, and the tribe's name became the name of the country and its language, as well.

On Christmas Day in the memorable year of A.D. 1000, Hungary crowned its first king, Stephen I. Like his father, Prince Géza, King Stephen accepted Christianity and the authority of the pope; he was to attain sainthood.

A landmark of 1222, the Golden Bull—a sort of Magyar Magna Carta—spelled out the rights of the citizens, nobles and freemen alike. But civilization suffered a tragic setback in 1241, when the country was overrun by Mongol hordes. It was the first of

many military and political disasters to afflict Hungary over the centuries, into modern times.

King Béla IV set about reviving the young nation from the wreckage. He granted a new charter for the reawakening city of Pest and, across the Danube, founded the town

17

Challenging Tongue

Hungarian is such a distinctive, intricate language that most foreigners despair of finding their way through the maze of conjugations, suffixes and diacritical marks. Furthering the feeling of foreignness, only a handful of international words carry over into Hungarian. You may recognize *garázs* (garage), *posta* (post office), *trolibusz* (trolleybus) and a few more, but even such universal words as hotel, police and restaurant are different in Hungarian.

On the other hand, several Magyar words have enhanced other languages: czardas (from the music played at the wayside inn called a *csárda*); goulash and paprika; and *coach*—a four-wheeled carriage developed in the 15th century in the Hungarian village of Kocs (pronounced coach)!

of Buda on a plateau which he prudently enclosed within walls.

With the end of the Árpád dynasty in 1301, a series of foreign kings ruled Hungary—a cosmopolitan royal roster drawn from all over Europe. In the middle of the 15th century, a hero emerged to rally not only the Hungarians, but other Christian peoples as well. János Hunyadi, the viceroy of Hungary, led the armies which turned back a long-threatening and seemingly invincible Turkish juggernaut. His 1456 triumph at Nándorfehérvár (now Belgrade) is remembered to this day by Catholics all over the world; and in commemoration, church bells ring and the Hungarian radio even relays the toll of the angelus every noontime.

The son of János Hunyadi, known as Matthias Corvinus, reigned as Hungary's king from 1458 to 1490, a golden age of civic and intellectual development. Buda became an advanced centre of Renaissance culture and Pest flourished in trade and industry. King Matthias employed Italian artists to expand and beautify the Royal Palace on Castle Hill and he commissioned exquisite illuminated volumes to fill its library.

16th-Century Defeats

With the death of Matthias, feuding noblemen squabbled over the succession, reversing the movement towards national progress and security. An army of peasants, led by György Dózsa, rose in rebellion in 1514, but the insurrec-

Gül Baba's tomb: one of the well-preserved relics of Turkish rule.

tion failed and the leaders were tortured to death; harsh laws were enacted to reinstate the ancient deprivations of the serfs.

All the while, the Turks had been massing for war against a weakened Hungary. The fateful battle was fought near Mohács in southern Hungary in 1526. The invaders killed Hungary's King Louis II and much of the army he led. In a slow-motion disaster, the Turks finally occupied Buda in 1541. The nation was demoralized and dismembered: the north and west fell to the Habsburg empire, Transylvania became a so-called independent principality under Turkish auspices, and central Hungary bowed under direct Turkish rule.

Occupation by the Ottomans ushered in an era of **19**

inertia, rather than oppression. During the century and a half of Ottoman rule, little was accomplished apart from the construction of fortifications and public baths. Visitors were appalled to find Buda decaying, and an official who went to the other side of the river despaired: "Alas, poor Pest! Pestilence should be thy name". But the worst was yet to come. Pest and later Buda were subjected to long, devastating sieges before the Turks were finally routed by the armies of allied Christian powers. In 1686 Buda, "liberated", lay in ruins.

Under the Habsburgs

With the dominion of the pashas at an end, Hungary found itself under the stern administration of the Habsburgs. Dissatisfaction festered, and in 1703 Hungarians went to war for independence. The leader was a Transylvanian prince with a handlebar moustache, Ferenc Rákóczi II. Outnumbered and betrayed, the Hungarians lost the struggle in 1711.

But the Vienna connection meant more than just political subjugation. The country took great economic strides in the 18th century as a Habsburg province. Factories, theatres and newspapers were opened; Pest expanded its role in international trade and Buda was restored to its position as Hungary's administrative centre. And the two cities were linked by a new pontoon bridge wide enough for two lanes of carts and two files of pedestrians.

In the middle of the 19th century, Hungarians fought a new war for independence from the Habsburgs. The initial rebellion of 1848 was led by the poet Sándor Petőfi, but he was cut down in battle at the age of 26. To crush the insurrection, Emperor Franz Joseph I summoned help from the Czar of Russia. The combined Austrian and Russian armies finally triumphed in August 1849. The revolutionary statesman Lajos Kossuth, who had headed a provisional government, and other leaders of the independence struggle fled the country.

Defeat was followed by political repression, but economic advancement gradually resumed. Soon after peace returned to Hungary, the prodigious Chain Bridge inaugurated uninterrupted year-round traffic across the Danube; a railway was opened between Pest and Vienna; and trading began on the Pest stock exchange. In 1873 the cities of Pest, Buda and Óbuda—with a combined population approaching 300,000—merged into the metropolis of Budapest, big and strong enough to be the nation's undisputed capital.

A new political framework had been created in 1867. Under a compromise designed to curtail home-rule agitation, the Austro-Hungarian empire was established. Hungary was granted its own government, but key ministries were shared with the Austrians. The Dual Monarchy, as it was called, oversaw the development of modern Budapest with its proud boulevards and buildings. It also set the stage for the 20th century's jolting political changes.

Into War and Revolution

Hungary fought World War I on the losing side. As part of the Austro-Hungarian empire, the country was obliged to aid its German allies. Hundreds of thousands of Hungarian troops died on two fronts, and at home the hardships multiplied.

In October 1918, the monarchy was toppled by what is now referred to as the Bourgeois Democratic Revolution. King Charles IV of Austria-Hungary, crowned Hungarian king in Buda's Matthias Church less than two years earlier, was deposed to make way for the Hungarian Republic.

This was soon displaced by a short-lived Hungarian Soviet Republic. Among the leaders were Hungarians who had participated in the Bolshevik revolution and army veterans who had become communists while prisoners of war in Russia. The proclamation of a Hungarian dictatorship of the proletariat was vigorously opposed in many circles. It was overthrown after only 133 days in power.

The new right-wing regime, headed by Admiral Miklós Horthy, initiated a purge. Meanwhile, reprisals of another sort were laid out in the Treaty of Trianon (1920), which punished Hungary for its role in World War I. About two-thirds of Hungary's territory was handed over to its neighbours. Shrunken in size and spirit, torn by strife and crippled by economic problems, Hungary heard a vengeful voice from across the border: Adolf Hitler was promising a new order.

Hungary slipped into World War II in a series of small, reluctant steps: German troops were allowed to cross Hungarian territory and a Hungarian force was sent to help Hitler fight the Soviet Union. But the Horthy government nimbly avoided total involvement on the Axis side until March 1944 when the Germans occupied Hungary. This precluded a separate peace.

As the Soviets moved closer to Budapest, a Hungarian fascist regime led by Ferenc Szálasi was installed to support the Germans in a fight to the

Museum of Hungarian Working Class features a historic poster display.

Celebrated Magyars

Because of the obscurity of their language, perhaps, Hungarian authors and poets have won little fame abroad. Conversely, when it comes to universal abstractions, the country has produced more than its share of notables.

In science, several Hungarians won fame in the United States: Nobel laureate Albert Szent-Györgyi, atomic pioneers Leo Szilárd and Edward Teller, and cybernetician John von Neumann. Péter Goldmark cut his niche in history by inventing the LP record.

Hungarians have played second fiddle to nobody in the musical world since Franz Liszt opened his academy in his Budapest home. Twentieth-century composers, conductors and soloists from Hungary include Béla Bartók, Zoltán Kodály, Antal Doráti, Eugene Ormándy, Sir George Solti and Joseph Szigeti.

Hungarian artists, too, have achieved international recognition: László Moholy Nagy, famed for his constructions; Marcel Breuer, architect and designer associated with the Bauhaus; and Victor Vasarély, the Op art painter.

One field in which Hungarians have excelled from the beginning is the cinema. Among legendary film-makers, Sir Alexander Korda was born Sándor Korda, and director Michael Curtiz began his career as Mihály Kertész. Some memorable actors with Hungarian roots are Leslie Howard, George Sanders and Béla Lugosi.

---

death. The final siege went on for weeks. When the Red Army finally secured all of Budapest on February 13, 1945, the capital could count only one out of every four buildings intact.

People's Republic

Post-war Hungary was transformed from a republic (1946) into a People's Republic (1949). Radical new economic directions were spelled out in a Three-Year Plan, followed by Five-Year plans. The government and party were led by Mátyás Rákosi, who was dismissed in 1956 for what are described as serious political crimes, personality cult and economic mistakes. It was a year of tumultuous change for Hungary.

"The events of 1956", an uprising which resulted in a heavy toll of life and property, as well as the exodus of more than 200,000 Hungarians to the West, broke out in Budapest on October 23. Within days, an interim coalition was formed. Headed by Imre Nagy, it proclaimed Hungary's neutrality and withdrawal from the Warsaw Pact. On November 4, with Soviet troops in Budapest, a new communist-led government was announced, directed by János Kádár.

When it was all over, the new administration set about improving economic conditions and relaxing the earlier political severities. The new slogan, "He who is not against us is with us", reversed the previous hard-line dictum and meant that average Hungarians could go about their daily lives without harrassment. The standard of living visibly improved. Millions moved into new housing. Hundreds of thousands were able to buy cars and take holidays in the West.

Every year, the number of foreigners visiting Hungary greatly exceeds the country's population. The border they cross is notable for a refreshing effort at de-emphasizing red tape. The scars of wars and revolutions have now all but disappeared. The monuments to past trials and glories, alongside the new accomplishments, are open to inspection.

What to See

Buda and Pest look like pieces from two different jigsaw puzzles which fit quite by chance. Hilly Buda is the last frontier of the Transdanubian mountains; in Pest, across the river, begins the Great Plain, stretching east as flat as Kansas.

The attractions are too varied and widely dispersed to absorb in a quick, easy survey. Though the various coach excursions serve as a useful introduction, the city is most easily approached by degrees—a bit of Buda and a part of Pest, then back across the river again.

For reasons of organization, though, we have split the city into halves along the course of the Danube. We begin in Buda, covering the Castle District, the hills beyond, ancient Óbuda and other riverside precincts on the right bank. Then over to Pest with its boulevards, shops and museums. In between, we cast a glance at Margaret Island, a quiet green isle equidistant from the urban pressures of Buda and Pest.

The best place to start, most would agree, is in the Buda Castle District, with its concentration of history and art... and a view that's not to be missed.

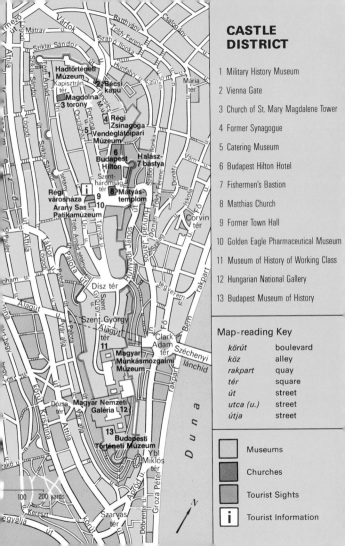

CASTLE DISTRICT

1 Military History Museum

2 Vienna Gate

3 Church of St. Mary Magdalene Tower

4 Former Synagogue

5 Catering Museum

6 Budapest Hilton Hotel

7 Fishermen's Bastion

8 Matthias Church

9 Former Town Hall

10 Golden Eagle Pharmaceutical Museum

11 Museum of History of Working Class

12 Hungarian National Gallery

13 Budapest Museum of History

Map-reading Key

körút	boulevard
köz	alley
rakpart	quay
tér	square
út	street
utca (u.)	street
útja	street

☐ Museums

☐ Churches

☐ Tourist Sights

ℹ Tourist Information

The Castle District

This fascinating zone of cobbled streets, hidden gardens and medieval courtyards hovers above the rest of Budapest on a long, narrow plateau. Dozens of historic and beautiful buildings are concentrated here. Every second house, it seems, bears a plaque identifying it as a *műemlék* (monument). You can walk uphill from the river—or ride the vintage train *(sikló)* that shuttles between a terminus at Clark Adam tér and the Royal Palace.

The southern part of the plateau is occupied by the

palace, but we begin in the larger northern district, where 14th- and 15th-century aristocrats and artisans, civic and church officials resided.

The spire of **Mátyás-templom** (Matthias Church) towers gracefully over the old town. Here the 15th-century King Matthias wed Beatrice of Aragon. Founded by King Béla IV in the 13th century, the parish Church of Our Lady is also known as the coronation church. The Emperor Franz Joseph I was crowned here as king of Hungary in

In the Castle District (left), an orchestra plays in the open air.

1867, to the tune of Liszt's *Coronation Mass*, composed for the occasion. Nowadays a symphony orchestra and chorus perform classical religious works every Sunday at 10 a.m. mass.

During the Turkish occupation, the church was converted into the city's main mosque. Today visiting Hungarians pause reverently at the **Loreto Chapel,** in the south-west corner of the church, to regard a red marble statue of the Virgin. According to legend, the Turks buried the statue inside one of the chapel walls, but the figure made a miraculous reappearance during the siege of 1686. The pasha's troops took this as a signal that their time was up and prepared to surrender Buda.

The church was rebuilt in Baroque style after the return of the Christian forces; in the 19th century it was totally reconstructed along neo-Gothic lines. This is the version which was reassembled during the long restoration programme that made good the destruction of World War II. The unusual abstract designs which decorate the interior and roof of the church date from the 19th-century refurbishing; the motifs are Hungarian, not Turkish.

The **church museum,** on the premises, contains medieval stone carvings, sacred relics, historic vestments and works of religious art. Replicas of the Hungarian royal crown and coronation jewels are displayed, but you can view the genuine articles in Pest (see p. 65). The museum begins in the crypt and rambles up and around the church, offering at one spot an excellent view down onto the nave.

In the centre of Szentháromság tér (Trinity Square), on which the church stands, a votive column crowded with statues of saints and angels recalls a bubonic plague epidemic of the 18th century. The survivors built the monument in gratitude for being spared.

The other buildings facing the square are very much a mixed bag. On the north side, a neo-Gothic structure put up at the beginning of the 20th century now serves as a residence hall for students. On the west side, a modern whitewashed brick building, a latter-day reflection of the surrounding architecture, houses a centre for visiting foreign journalists. Outside stands a contemporary statue of a long-haired man, nude but for his hat, holding a horn with which to broadcast the latest news.

The Baroque two-storey white building with a jutting corner balcony is the former Town Hall. Below the balcony there's a statue of Pallas Athena, who carries a shield emblazoned with the coat of arms of the town of Buda.

A much grander monument rises on the far side of Matthias Church—an equestrian statue of King (and Saint) Stephen I, who made Hungary a Christian country. He wears both a crown and a halo.

Halászbástya (Fishermen's Bastion), on the eastern edge of Castle Hill, could pass as an authentic medieval monument in a remarkable state of repair. Actually, this Disneyesque array of turrets, terraces and arches was built at the beginning of the 20th century, just for fun. From here, the views over the Danube are glorious. The architect even provided arches at every turn, so photographers can hardly avoid artistic framing of their shots of the river, its bridges and the Pest skyline across the way.

Incidentally, you might well wonder why ramparts at this altitude should refer to fishermen. It seems that the area behind the church was the site of a medieval fish market; and in the 18th century, local fishermen were responsible for defending the fortifications.

Turning away from the Danube: the view westward from Fishermen's Bastion focuses on the startling and controversial six-storey reflective-glass façade of the **Budapest Hilton Hotel.** Hungarian architect Béla Pintér took the bold approach in his design for a modern hotel wedged between historic monuments. The hotel's main façade, facing Hess András tér, integrates the remains of a 17th-century Jesuit college formerly on the site. Parts of an adjoining 13th-century abbey have also been incorporated into the building. An ancient milestone uncovered during the excavation of the site is displayed in the lobby; it marked the boundary of the Roman empire.

Hess András tér is named after the man who ran Buda's first printing shop, right here, in the 1470s. (Like the Chinese, the Hungarians put the last name first; we would call the printer András Hess.) The statue in the little square honours Pope Innocent XI for his help in organizing the army which finally routed the Turks from Buda. Notice the amusing bas-relief of a hedgehog on the house at No. 3; in the 18th century, it was an inn called the Red Hedgehog.

29

Historic Streets

The quaint Castle District lends itself to relaxed roaming with no hard and fast itinerary. Only four streets wide at its most expansive, the plateau is easily covered on foot. Here are some of the highlights to look for, starting with the easternmost street and working towards the western ramparts.

Táncsics Mihály utca. No. 7: Beethoven lived for a while (in 1800) in this solid old building. Next door, at No. 9, an 18th-century ammunition dump became a 19th-century prison which held, among others, the statesman Lajos Kossuth and the writer Mihály Táncsics, after whom the street is now named. No. 16: note the 18th-century religious mural between the bow windows upstairs. No. 26: just inside the doorway ancient Jewish tombstones are displayed. This house served as a synagogue *(Régi Zsinagóga)* from the end of the 14th century and now contains an exhibition of architectural and artistic remains.

At the northern end of the

Reflected in the glass façade of the Budapest Hilton, the fanciful towers of Fishermen's Bastion look even more surreal.

street, **Bécsi kapu** (Vienna Gate) provides a reminder of the walled city of yore, although the actual gate is a reconstruction. A couple of appealing, intricately decorated 18th-century houses add to the charm of the square. Thomas Mann lived at No. 7 from 1935 to 1936.

Fortuna utca. The house at No. 4, a hotel in the 18th and 19th centuries, has been given over to the **Hungarian Museum of Commerce and Catering** *(Magyar Kereskedelmi és Vendéglátóipari Múzeum).* The furnishings of historic hotel rooms, restaurants and coffee houses are assembled here, along with original menus, table settings and waiters' uniforms.

Like the rest of the district, this street has had to be rebuilt after every war, siege and invasion. Following the expulsion of the Turks, the medieval ruins were used as building blocks for new Baroque houses. After the devastation of World War II, many minor but attractive details of the architecture were lovingly restored.

Tárnok utca. This southerly extension of Fortuna utca contains a number of fine Baroque buildings. At No. 14, now an "espresso" restaurant, **31**

the upper storey juts out, as it did in the Middle Ages. The geometric frescoes on the front walls date from the 16th century. Up the street, at No. 18, an 18th-century chemist's shop called the **Golden Eagle** *(Arany Sas)* now serves as a museum. The exhibits cover the development of pharmaceutical science from ancient times, both in Hungary and around the world. Some of the architectural elements of the shop itself, begun in the 15th century, are also of interest.

Országház utca, which means Houses of Parliament Street, is not, as you might think, on the wrong side of the river. Parliamentary sessions took place in the building at No. 28 at the turn of the 19th century. It now belongs to the Academy of Sciences. At No. 2 Országház utca, a restaurant occupies what was once a grand 15th-century mansion; the courtyard, reminiscent of a medieval cloister, is noteworthy. Several other buildings on this street incorporate picturesque medieval features, sometimes just beyond the doorway; don't be shy about peering into courtyards, just in case.

Úri utca. This street is a treasure-trove of medieval vestiges. In the entryways of Nos. 31, 32, 35, 36, 38 and 40, among other houses, you'll find groups of sediles—built-in seats. The 14th-century dwelling at No. 31 retains the original stone window frames. Whatever their ages, virtually all of the buildings in the area maintain the same roof-line, but differing colour schemes and embellishments make each one distinctive.

At the top end of Úri utca stands a rather bleak but venerable tower *(Magdolna-torony),* all that remains of the Church of St. Mary Magdalene. There has been a church on this spot since the 13th century. During the Turkish occupation, it was the only one left in Christian hands; the Catholics and Protestants shared the premises. The church suffered particularly grave damage in the last days of World War II, when the German army high command was holding out in the district. Miraculously, the Gothic tower escaped destruction.

Tóth Árpád sétány. This promenade along the western ramparts of the Castle District offers panoramas of the Buda Hills, rather than any outstanding monuments. And in the valley below you can see some metropolitan aspects of Buda, including the white im-

Many charming buildings in the Castle District date back to medieval times.

mensity of Southern Railway Station *(Déli pályaudvar)* and the cylindrical glass tower of the Budapest Hotel.

The northern end of the walk is cluttered with cannon—historic cast-iron guns laid out on display. The building at No. 40, much bigger than it looks, houses the **Museum of Military History** *(Hadtörténeti Múzeum)*. The exhibits range from pikes, swords and crossbows to a self-propelled missile launcher and a Mig-21 (parked in the courtyard). Selected documents and relics illustrate Hungary's efforts at self-defence over the centuries.

♠ The Royal Palace

Returned to its former splendour, the Royal Palace *(Budavári Palota)* monopolizes the southern skyline of the plateau. Construction began rather modestly under Béla IV in the 13th century, but succeeding monarchs were intent on impressing their countrymen.

Under the Ottoman empire the palace fell into disrepair and the remains were destroyed in the siege of 1686. During the 18th and 19th centuries reconstruction, renovation and expansion turned the building into approximately the neo-Baroque monument of today. But it had to be rebuilt from the ground up after the siege of 1945, when the palace served as command post for the German occupation forces. Earlier it had been the headquarters and residence of the reviled Admiral Horthy. But in spite of this chequered recent history, the palace has been restored with every care. And in fact it's probably better than ever, for out of the ruins came revelations of past glories.

To reach the palace, its fortifications and museums, you can either descend on foot from Dísz tér, in the southern part of the Castle District, or take a long walk up through the nicely landscaped grounds

from Szarvas tér, near the complex road system on the west side of Elizabeth Bridge. A special bus (marked "V") shuttles between the museums and Clark Adam tér, at the Buda end of the Chain Bridge.

The solid stone walls of the restored fortifications guarding the southern approaches to the palace are now curtained with ivy. You can climb the spiral stairs to the ramparts for delightful Danube views. Within the palace complex are the national library and three museums.

The **Budapest Museum of History** *(Budapesti Történeti Múzeum)* occupies the Baroque south wing. This exhibition throws light on 2,000 years of the city's history. Displays include Roman statues, early Magyar saddles and weapons, Turkish utensils and 19th- and 20th-century Hungarian documents and photographs. During the most recent reconstruction programme, forgotten floors of the palace were discovered beneath the parts known before the war. The restored medieval passageways, fortifications and gardens now form part of the museum. Important sculptures

View from the top: Buda's Royal Palace surveys Pest, across the way.

from the 14th and 15th centuries also were uncovered, and they are on view in the Gothic Knights' Hall and the Royal Chapel. The sound of Gregorian chants coming from loudspeakers hidden in the chapel underlines the medieval aura.

The **Hungarian National Gallery** (*Magyar Nemzeti Galéria*) is installed in the central area of the palace, under the dome; the entrance faces the Danube. Within the bare historic walls, an impressive modern museum was created. Hungarian painters and sculptors from the Middle Ages onwards are represented. The artist best known abroad is the 19th-century painter Mihály Munkácsy, celebrated for his vast output of family scenes, portraits, landscapes and melancholy historical compositions. Note, too, the Impressionist Pál Szinyei Merse.

In the north wing, the **Museum of the History of the Hungarian Working Class** (*Magyar Munkásmozgalmi Múzeum*) proves popular with comradely delegations from abroad. Exhibits deal with exploitation under capitalism, the struggles of early Hungarian communists and recent triumphs. Ideology aside, art lovers will not want to miss the big collection of posters.

Vantage Points

Gellért-hegy (Gellért Hill) rises only 770 feet above sea level, but it looms right alongside the Danube, providing a perfect vantage point. The **panorama** of Pest and Buda, the bridges and river traffic suggest the short answer to the mystery of Budapest's universal appeal: the city is simply beautiful.

The hill and the district are named after the Italian missionary, St. Gerard (in Hungarian, Gellért), who converted the Hungarians to Christianity. His success was mostly posthumous, for his efforts were cut short when militant heathens threw him off the hillside into the Danube. A statue of the saint stands on the eastern slope at the approximate spot from which his martyrdom was launched.

At the summit of Gellért Hill sprawls a fortress with a deceptively ancient look about it. The **Citadella** (Citadel) was built in the middle of the last century. In the final struggle of World War II, the occupying German army held out here. In recent years, the renovation of the citadel has been earnestly pursued. The once-menacing walls, nearly 10 feet thick, now encircle a restaurant, café and hotel.

The conspicuous modern addition to the hilltop, a gargantuan Liberation Monument, can be seen from many parts of the city. It is dedicated "To the heroic Soviet liberators from the grateful Hungarian people" for ousting the German occupiers. On the reverse side of the monument are engraved the names of Red Army soldiers who died in the struggle.

On the slopes below the Citadel lies a modern park, Jubileumi-park, dedicated on the 20th anniversary of the liberation. It is a focus for patriotic occasions, as well as everyday recreation.

The Buda Hills

Now for some alternatives to city sightseeing for visitors who need a break from historic monuments. Excursions to the chain of wooded hills rising west of the Danube make a pleasant change from metropolitan hubbub.

A cog railway *(fogaskerekű-vasút)* chugs to **Szabadság-hegy** (Liberty Hill) from a terminal across the road from the Hotel Budapest. Comfortable modern trains built in Austria ascend through suburban greenery, past admirable villas and gardens, into open spaces —ski country in season.

Near the last stop of the cog railway, the **Pioneer Railway** *(Úttörővasút)*, run by youngsters, begins its 7½-mile route. The narrow-gauge line traverses what would seem to be unexplored forest—but for the well-marked hiking trails all along the way. School-children in smart uniforms work as station-masters, switchmen, ticket-sellers and conductors; only the engine-drivers are adults.

Summer sightseers take over the ski-lift *(libegő)* for a "flight" of about a mile. The lower terminus is at 93 Zugligeti út, and the trip ends near the top of János-hegy (János Hill), altitude 1,735 feet. A look-out tower on the hilltop surveys a radius of more than 45 miles—but misty skies often blur that far horizon.

North of János-hegy and nearly as high (1,630 feet), Hármashatár-hegy provides another good look-out point for views of Budapest and the Danube. No funicular or other exotic means of transport goes to the top, but some interesting vehicles leave the hill in the opposite direction. The wind currents here make Hármashatár Hill an effective starting point for hang-gliders.

Sas-hegyi Természetvédelmi Terület (Eagle Hill Nature

Reserve), surrounded on all sides by the city, is described as a living outdoor museum. Nature lovers can try to identify the rare species of flowers, butterflies, birds... even snakes amid unusual rock formations. This hilltop sanctuary opens week-ends only; the rest of the time the flora and fauna have Sas-hegy all to themselves.

Admire the view from the Citadel. Or go for a ride on the Pioneer Railway. A school girl serves as conductor... but adults drive the trains.

Riverside Buda

After the aerial perspectives, the view from the river bank becomes more meaningful. People on the Pest quays never tire of gazing across the Danube to the skyline of Citadel and castle. Less obviously, from the Buda side the view of sophisticated though dead-level Pest has its share of curiosities and delights. And from either side, the bridges themselves, always in sight, add to the allure, stitching together the disparate halves of Budapest.

The area of prime interest to tourists extends north

from Szabadság híd (Liberty Bridge), opened in 1896 as the Franz Joseph Bridge. On the Buda side, the bridgehead is Szent Gellért tér (St. Gellért Square). The ponderous old Gellért Hotel, inaugurated in 1918, was badly damaged in the war but dutifully restored to its original Eclectic design. By no accident, the hotel was built alongside ancient hot springs and it remains a leading centre of medicinal baths. The swimming pool makes artificial waves.

The steep hillside comes right down to the river road as it runs north from the Gellért, finally retreating at the approaches to Elizabeth Bridge. This leaves room for another thermal bath between hill and river. **Rudas fürdő** (Rudas Baths) has been in business for 400 years. Though the building has been destroyed, rebuilt, enlarged and much tampered with over the centuries, a graceful Turkish dome still rises over one octagonal pool, creating a wonder of geometric contrasts as sunlight filters through openings in the cupola. The radioactive water here is also said to make a therapeutic drink.

Of all Budapest's bridges, the lightest on its feet is Erzsébet híd (Elizabeth Bridge), a

1960s successor to a turn-of-the-century span demolished at the end of the last war. It's a suspension bridge in the manner of the Golden Gate of San Francisco. Crossing this bridge towards Buda, the head-on view takes in the St. Gellért monument high on the hillside, above a garden and manmade waterfall. The Buda-bound traffic disgorges onto a complicated system of viaducts and underpasses. In the parkland interspersed among all these engineering projects you may notice another Turkish bath, Rácz fürdő, across the road from the north edge of Gellért Hill. A dome from the Turkish era still covers one bathing pool.

This is the old Tabán district of Buda, where the ferrymen and other noted characters used to live. Only a few houses are left. One of them, a restored Louis XVI mansion at 1–3 Apród utca, was the birthplace of Professor Ignác Semmelweis (1818–65). He discovered the cause of puerperal fever, greatly improving world life-expectancy tables. The upper floor of the building now shelters the **Semmelweis Museum of the History of Medicine** (*Semmelweis Orvostörténeti Múzeum*). Multilingual guides in white smocks

BUDAPEST AND THE HILLS

2 Hercules Villa
3 Roman Camp Museum
4 Military Amphitheatre
5 Ski-lift
6 Pioneer Railway
7 Cog Railway
8 Sas-hegy Nature Reserve

point out gruesome ancient surgical instruments and anatomical models, and there are enlightening exhibits illustrating the path of medicine from witch doctors' amulets to modern times.

Northward from the museum, the riverside area has a character of its own. The hillside facing the Danube, leading up to the Royal Palace, is adorned with arcades, terraces, ceremonial staircases and neo-Classical statues. The architect of this scheme, Miklós Ybl (1814–91), who also designed the Basilica, the Opera House and other monumental buildings, is himself the subject of a monument near the river.

The often-clogged traffic roundabout at the Buda end of the Chain Bridge occupies Clark Adam tér, a square named, in back-to-front Hungarian style, in memory of a Scottish engineer called Adam Clark. He oversaw construction of the bridge, a wonder of

19th-century technology. The man who designed it, William Tierney Clark, an English engineer, was no kin to Adam Clark. The **Széchenyi lánchíd** (Chain Bridge), the first across the Danube, was opened to traffic in 1849, blown up by German sappers towards the end of the last war, but soon rebuilt.

Straight ahead of the bridge, Adam Clark constructed a tunnel beneath the Castle District plateau. Because of the juxtaposition of bridge and tunnel, a standard little joke in Budapest claims the bridge is pulled into the tunnel when it rains, so the chains don't rust. Left of the tunnel is the terminus of the vintage train that runs uphill to the Castle District.

The street north from Clark Adam tér, Fő utca (meaning Main Street), follows the original Roman route linking the Danube military outposts. About half a mile north of the Chain Bridge, at **Batthyányi tér,** the metro, bus and tram systems meet the suburban railway; there's a boat station at this important junction, too. This is the best place in town for an all-encompassing view of the Hungarian Houses of Parliament, directly across the river. The effect is rather like a mutation of London's parliament building, with the Danube substituted for the Thames.

The terminal of the Vienna stagecoach used to be right around the corner and, on the west side of Batthyányi tér, an 18th-century hostelry was famous. The emperor and many dignitaries stayed at the White

The towers of Inner City Parish Church, begun in the 12th-century, rise alongside Elizabeth Bridge. **43**

Cross Inn, a venue for carnival balls and festivities of the district, called Víziváros (Watertown). The palatial two-storey **Rococo building** has been preserved, but its role has changed a bit; now it's a nightclub.

Szent Anna templom (St. Anne's Church), on the south side of the square, reveals Italian influences on Hungarian architecture of the mid-18th century. Tall twin towers top the Baroque façade, embellished with statues. The oval-domed interior contains more 18th-century statues and frescoes.

Farther north along Fő utca, a crescent surmounts the dome of a Turkish bath established in the 16th century. **Király fürdő** (Király Baths), a rambling green stone building, expanded over the centuries as Baroque and neo-Classical additions were made. The authentic Turkish section has survived, with an octagonal bathing pool under the largest of the domes. After the expulsion of the Turks the royal treasurer took possession of the baths, but in the 19th century they were owned by a family called König. The name means "king" in German, which is *király* in Hungarian, hence the modern title.

An offbeat attraction of this district, at 20 Bem József utca, is a 19th-century iron foundry, now operated as a museum *(Öntödei Múzeum)*. A statue honours the originator of the enterprise, a Swiss industrialist named Abraham Ganz. The factory maintained production from 1845 all the way to 1964 and was noted for its tramwheels. Museum exhibits follow the evolution of technology from the Iron Age to the 20th century and include some handsome examples of the founder's art—iron stoves, statues, ships' propellers and bells.

The main street of this area, Mártírok útja, curves gradually towards the Danube and finally leads its tram, bus and car traffic across Margit híd (Margaret Bridge). This connects with the southern tip of Margaret Island, then deflects from the conventional arrow-straight trajectory. Thus from certain angles the bridge appears to end in mid-air. But it really does reach Pest. The big white post-war building at the bridgehead, in an architectural style reminiscent of government offices in Washington, D.C., is the Socialist Worker's Party headquarters. In Budapest slang the building is called the White House.

Back in Buda, hilly streets zigzag north-westward from the bridge approaches up to the **Gül Baba türbéje** (tomb). This meticulously preserved relic of the Turkish era stands at 14 Mecset utca. The mausoleum was built in the middle of the 16th century by order of the pasha of Buda. It covered the grave of Gül Baba, a well-known dervish whose funeral the sultan himself attended. After the expulsion of the Turks, the octagonal building was used for a time as a Jesuit chapel. Restoration in recent years has been enhanced by a gift of art works from the Turkish government.

Another reminder of the Ottoman occupation may be found farther north along the embankment, at the **Császár uszoda.** A rheumatological hospital has grown around the original Turkish bath, built about 1570 as Veli Bey's Bath. A hemispherical cupola covers an octagonal bathing pool, surrounded by four rectangular chambers. The water is rich in calcium and sulphur.

Óbuda

Heavy traffic rumbles along Korvin Ottó utca, the principal artery leading out of Budapest to the north. At its intersection with Nagyszombat utca, the road travels alongside the almost flattened but instantly identifiable remains of a Roman amphitheatre, one of the biggest outside Italy. This is part of Aquincum, capital of the Roman province of Lower Pannonia, later called Óbuda (Old Buda).

The **Military Amphitheatre** *(Katonai Amfiteátrum)* as it is known to distinguish it from a smaller one a couple of miles to the north, dates from the 2nd century. Here, gladiators performed for the amusement of the Roman legionaries who guarded this far frontier. Up to 16,000 spectators could be packed in when the contest drew a full house. The events took place on an elliptical arena more than 140 yards long. After the fall of the empire, a fortress was built on the site, and in later centuries houses took over the floor of the all-but-forgotten stadium. The ruins were excavated and very partially restored starting in the 1930s.

At 63 Korvin Ottó utca, workmen building an apartment block came upon the remains of public buildings from the Roman era. They constructed the new house around the "digs" which now form part of the basement. The prize discovery was a **45**

Two thousand years on, a Roman fresco decorates a wall in Óbuda.

hunting mural of an archer on horseback, a work of considerable grace. Details of the comprehensive heating and plumbing system can also be seen, and some artefacts found on the spot are displayed in this historic hideaway, known as the **Roman Camp Museum** *(Római Tábor Múzeum)*.

Elsewhere in Óbuda, the ruins of a large bathing installation built for the Roman legion have been uncovered and protected in what is now the basement of a house at 3 Flórián tér. (The museum entrance is around the corner in Kórház utca.) The complexities of the baths, central heating system and all, intrigue visitors. Archaeologists of the distant future may be fascinated by the area on the northwest side of Flórián tér, the site of Budapest's first major multistorey shopping centre.

The remains of a grand Roman residence known as **Hercules Villa** lie in and around a modern school at 21 Meggyfa utca. The villa contained the finest mosaic floors found in all Pannonia. The central panel of the most famous scene, said to portray

Hercules and his wife Deianira, was created out of small squares of marble and basalt in the early 3rd century.

The most extensive of the Roman achievements to come to light in Budapest, the civil town of **Aquincum,** accommodated the artisans, merchants, priests and other non-military personel attached to the legion. All the elements of a civilized town are here, from running water to central heating. The foundations of villas, workshops and markets have been uncovered. Clumps of poplars enliven the expanse of walls, knee-high to chest-high, and a few columns have been reconstructed to help the imagination. More has yet to be unearthed.

The site extends just east of Szentendrei út, the highway which, as route 11, continues on to the town of Szentendre. If you're travelling on the suburban railway *(HÉV)*, get off at the Aquincum stop and cross the highway, then go under the railway bridge. An ordinary tram ticket suffices.

At the entrance to the excavations, you can buy an inexpensive leaflet including a map of the civil town pointing out such sights as the Sanctuary of the Goddess Fortuna Augusta and the baths with their cold-, tepid- and hot-water pools. Even with a map you could lose your way in the far-flung ruins.

An imitation Roman building on the site houses a **museum** of the statues, pots, glassware, coins, tools and objects of everyday Roman life found in the ground here. Surrounding the museum on three sides, the **lapidarium** overflows with sarcophagi, columns and stone-carvings. The original inscriptions, of course, are all in Latin, posing yet another linguistic challenge to the foreign visitor.

Black and Blue

The Danube, blue in song only, originates in the Black Forest and empties into the Black Sea. At 1,776 miles from source to mouth, the Danube is Europe's second-longest river (after the Volga). It's longer than the Orinoco, the Irawaddy or the Rhine. Flowing through eight countries, the Danube goes under six different names; the Hungarians call it the Duna.

Inside Budapest the river, between 300 and 500 yards wide, is spanned by eight bridges. During the great flood of 1838 it rose 31.7 feet. Plaques in churches and elsewhere show the high-water mark—well above your head.

Margaret Island

The Roman empire's élite escaped the cares of the day on this island halfway between Aquincum and Pest. In later eras, princes and plutocrats took refuge in the peace and quiet of mid-Danube. Margaret Island still serves as a sanctuary, but for more than a century the ordinary citizens of Budapest have been allowed to enjoy it. Within sight of the busiest parts of town, the feather-shaped, forested island is insulated from all the noise and bustle. You couldn't dream of a happier project.

Margaret Island is 1½ miles long and a few hundred yards wide at the middle. With its ageless woods, vivid flower-beds and varied recreational facilities, it's a favourite spot for sports, amusements or just meditating. The island has been kept virtually free of motor traffic. Except for summer Sundays, the birds often have the place to themselves.

The southern end of the island is joined to "mainland" Buda and Pest by Margaret Bridge, a modern replacement for the original 19th-century span. It was destroyed in 1944, with needless loss of life, when German demolition charges went off prematurely.

Near the southern tip of the island, a tall bronze monument—shaped like a Hungarian version of yin and yang—commemorates the centenary of the unification of Buda and Pest. Margaret Island, equidistant between the two, is the obvious place for it.

The sports establishments on the island include Pioneers' Stadium *(Úttörőstadion)*, the National Sports Swimming Complex *(Hajós Alfréd-uszoda)* and the huge Palatinus Outdoor Public Swimming Complex *(Palatinus strand)*. The Palatinus installation, with cold- and warm-water pools, can hold 20,000 swimmers and sunbathers. There's even an artificial wave-maker.

Alongside the turn-of-the-century water tower, an open-air theatre *(Szabadtéri Színpad)* presents concerts, opera and ballet performances in the summer. The theatre's immense stage is conducive to lavish sets and productions. The park has a separate open-air cinema.

Near the outdoor theatre, you can wander through the ruins of a **Dominican Convent** *(Domonkos kolostor romjai)* founded by the 13th-century Hungarian King Béla IV. He

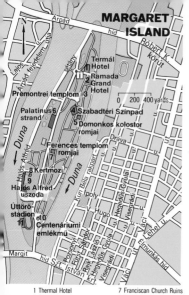

1 Thermal Hotel
2 Grand Hotel
3 Premonstratensian Chapel Ruins
4 Open-air Theatre
5 Dominican Convent Ruins
6 Palatinus Swimming Complex
7 Franciscan Church Ruins
8 Open-air Cinema
9 National Sports Swimming Complex
10 Centennial Monument
11 Pioneers' Stadium
ⓘ Tourist Information

stratensian Chapel *(Premontrei templom)*, a 20th-century reconstruction of a 12th-century church. The bell in the tower is said to be the oldest in Hungary; it survived the Turkish demolition of the church because it was buried nearby. The history of the reconstituted St. Michael's Church is spelled out on signs on the front of the building—in Latin, English, German, French, Polish, Russian and Hungarian.

The woods near the chapel are thickly populated with statues and busts of Hungary's foremost writers and artists.

In 1866 deep drilling operations on Margaret Island hit a gusher—scalding hot mineral water. Soon the island became well-known as a therapeutic spa for sufferers from an ample range of ailments, from rheumatism to nervous disorders. Two large spa hotels have been set up at the north end of the island, accessible via Árpád Bridge. Taking advantage of the water and the prize location are the century-old Grand Hotel and, under the same management (Ramada), the even bigger modern Thermal Hotel. People taking the cure are tempted by all manner of distractions on the premises—restaurants, cafés, bars and a nightclub.

enrolled his daughter in the convent when she was 11 years old, and she never left. Her burial place is marked by a marble plaque. She was called Princess (later Saint) Margaret; the island is named after her.

Another archaeological site on the island reveals the remains of a 13th-century Franciscan church *(Ferences templom romjai)* and monastery.

50 And then there is the **Premon-**

Pest

The bulk of modern Budapest lies to the east of the Danube in what, until little more than a century ago, was the autonomous city of Pest. The government buildings, big stores, museums and nightlife are concentrated in Pest. There are no hills to climb on this side of the river, but plenty of worthwhile sights to see along busy streets and imposing boulevards.

From the viewpoint of a Roman general defending Buda and western civilization, the Pest side of the river meant nothing but trouble. He could only stare out at the flatlands—badlands—and wonder when the barbarians would try to ford the Danube. In A.D. 294, to make it harder for any invaders to launch an amphibious attack, the Romans established an outpost on the left bank. They called it Contra-Aquincum, and it forms the very core of innermost Pest.

The medieval town grew around the Roman beachhead, evolving into a long, narrow strip, with the Danube to the west and defensive walls on the other sides. The Kiskörút, or inner boulevard of Pest (see p. 65), follows the contours of those city walls—fragments of which are still to be seen. The enclosed area—District V of modern Budapest—contains a stimulating sample of what's best in Pest: historic monuments, riverside hotels and promenades, and shopping the locals claim is the nearest thing to Paris.

The oldest church—indeed, the oldest surviving structure—in all of Pest is **Belvárosi templom** (Inner City Parish Church). It's hemmed in alongside the elevated approach road to Elizabeth Bridge. Viewed from the front it appears to be contemporary with several other nearby churches. The twin Baroque towers and the façade, with nicely balanced windows, date from the early 18th century and were restored twice thereafter. But the church was founded in the 12th century. Parts of the original Romanesque construction can be discerned, but these elements blend into the Gothic with little more than a ripple in the walls and roof. The Turks who occupied Budapest in the 16th century turned the church into a mosque and carved a *mihrab* (prayer niche) on the Mecca side of the chancel wall.

The plaza alongside the church, Március 15. tér, takes **51**

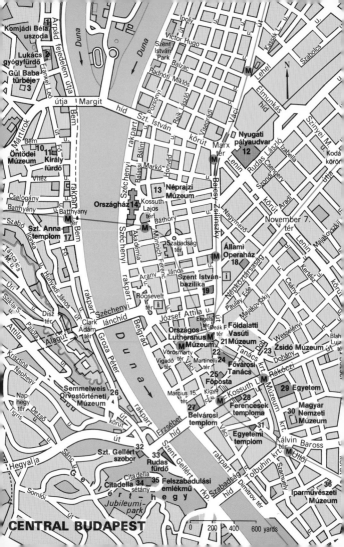

CENTRAL BUDAPEST

Komjádi Béla
uszoda

Lukács
gyógyfürdő 2

Gül Baba
türbéje 3

Öntödei
Múzeum 10

Királyi
fürdő 11

Szt. Anna
templom 17

Nyugati
pályaudvar 12

Néprajzi
Múzeum 13

Országház 14

Állami
Operaház 18

Szent István-
bazilika 19

Zsidó Múzeum 23

Országos
Lutheranus
Múzeum 20

Földalatti
Vasúti
Múzeum 21

Fővárosi
Tanács 24

Főposta 25

Egyetem 29

Magyar
Nemzeti
Múzeum 30

Semmelweis
Orvostörténeti
Múzeum 26

Belvárosi
templom 27

Ferencesek
temploma 28

Egyetemi
templom 31

Szt. Gellért
szobor 32

Rudas
fürdő 33

Felszabadulási
emlékmű 35

Citadella 34

Iparművészeti
Múzeum 36

0   200 400   600 yards

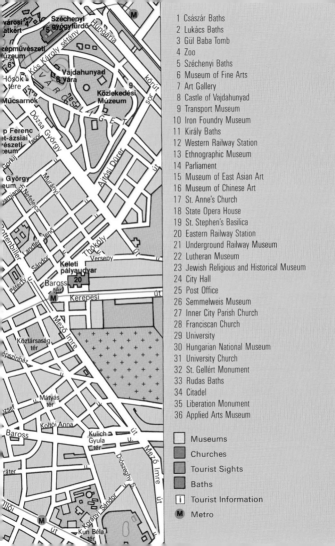

1 Császár Baths
2 Lukács Baths
3 Gül Baba Tomb
4 Zoo
5 Széchenyi Baths
6 Museum of Fine Arts
7 Art Gallery
8 Castle of Vajdahunyad
9 Transport Museum
10 Iron Foundry Museum
11 Király Baths
12 Western Railway Station
13 Ethnographic Museum
14 Parliament
15 Museum of East Asian Art
16 Museum of Chinese Art
17 St. Anne's Church
18 State Opera House
19 St. Stephen's Basilica
20 Eastern Railway Station
21 Underground Railway Museum
22 Lutheran Museum
23 Jewish Religious and Historical Museum
24 City Hall
25 Post Office
26 Semmelweis Museum
27 Inner City Parish Church
28 Franciscan Church
29 University
30 Hungarian National Museum
31 University Church
32 St. Gellért Monument
33 Rudas Baths
34 Citadel
35 Liberation Monument
36 Applied Arts Museum

Museums

Churches

Tourist Sights

Baths

i   Tourist Information

M   Metro

its name from the day in March 1848 when the revolution for Hungarian independence broke out in Pest. A sunken park created around the excavations of **Contra-Aquincum** catches the spring sunshine and excludes winter winds. Here children play amid the much-restored rockpile representing the 3rd-century Roman outpost. Above stands a modern fountain with statues symbolizing Roman legionaries in action.

An ornate two-storey structure, termed the only surviving Baroque mansion in Pest, lies just up the street in Pesti Barnabás utca. Notice the marker next to the doorway—a sculpted finger pointing to the level the Danube attained during the flood of 1838. A restaurant has operated in this building for 150 years.

Cobbled centrepiece of an expansive pedestrian zone, **Váci utca** is the Bond Street of Budapest. The narrow street

empts shoppers with the last word in Hungarian fashions, s well as art works, cosmetics, furnishings, jewellery and handicrafts. Several large bookstores along Váci utca sell Hungarian-published books in foreign languages. Also in the street are the offices of the major airlines and the high-rise premises of the International Trade Centre and Central European International Bank. With a variety of cafés, clubs and restaurants, the Taverna Hotel and entertainment complex is a new Váci utca attraction.

Lift your eyes above shop-window level and study some of the turn-of-the-century buildings on this street. They include intriguing experiments in modern architecture, notable for their unusual angles, window shapes and sculptural additions. An illuminated sign reading Pesti Színház (Pest Theatre) hangs over the street. In the entrance of the theatre **55** a plaque observes that Franz Liszt made his Pest debut as a pianist here at age 12.

Váci utca runs into the busy yet relaxed square named after Mihály Vörösmarty, a nationalistic poet and dramatist of the 19th century. (Cars are now banned here.) Not many pastry shops become national monuments, but the establishment on the north side of the square, the Gerbeaud, certainly qualifies. It used to be owned by the Gerbeaud family of Swiss confectioners; enthusiasts say the quality of the cakes and strudel hasn't deviated since the old days. The sumptuous interior with its high-ceilinged halls has been preserved, and in pleasant weather the terrace is a favourite spot for people-watching calorie-collectors.

A concert hall has stood on the site of the newly refurbished **Vigadó** since 1832, but not without a couple of long, involuntary intermissions. The first hall was destroyed in the shelling of the 1848 revolution, the second in the closing stage of World War II. In 1980 an acoustically perfect auditorium was opened; it's concealed behind the restored façade of mid-19th-century Hungarian-Oriental-Moorish style. The list of conductors and per-

formers who appeared in the old Vigadó sums up the history of 150 years of European music: Liszt, Brahms, Wagner, Bartók, Prokofiev, Rubinstein, Heifetz, Casals, Gigli, Björling, von Karajan....

Cruise boats for Budapest sightseeing tours and trips to the Danube Bend leave from the embarkation point at Vigadó tér. In the square between the river and the concert hall stands a marble obelisk engraved simply "1945" and, in Russian and Hungarian, "Glory to the Soviet hero-liberators".

Inland again, **Martinelli tér**, the site of an outdoor market in the 18th century, offers room enough to step back and admire the architecture. The seven-storey building at No. 5 is considered one of Europe's best examples of pre-modern design. Ceramic tiles ranged in horizontal bands decorate the upper floors in a scheme that was considered revolutionary when the house was completed in 1912. An Art Nouveau building two doors down also catches the eye. It's notable for the mosaic fantasy at roofline, a patriotic and religious scene surrounded by "3-D" embellishments. The former Servite Church on the square was built in Baroque style in the early 18th century. Martinelli tér also boasts an eastern-bloc rarity: a high-rise parking garage with room for 300 cars.

Just off the square, Budapest's **City Hall** *(Fővárosi Tanács)* fills an entire street in Városház utca. The imposing Baroque building served as a home for Hungarian veterans disabled in the fighting against the Turks. The 19th-century neo-Classical Pest County Hall *(Pest megyei Tanács)* lies just beyond a bend in the same street.

If you're caught in the rain in this part of town, you can duck into the **Paris Arcade** *(Párizsi udvar)* for some indoor window-shopping. This early 20th-century project sports a high vaulted ceiling and some indescribably quaint architectural touches. Even the jumbo telephone kiosks were specially designed.

A pedestrians-only shopping street, **Kígyó utca,** runs between Váci utca and the heavy traffic of Felszabadulás tér (Liberation Square). Across all the lanes of cars and buses (but accessible only by pedestrian subway), you can see the refined Baroque lines of a Franciscan church topped by an unexpected neo-Gothic spire. On this site stood a 13th-century church which became a mosque under Turkish rule. Set into the wall of the church, on the Kossuth Lajos utca elevation, is another reminder of the 1838 flood: a sculptural tribute to Baron Miklós Wesselényi, shown standing in a rowboat rescuing people from their rooftops.

A large shop next door to the church, in Károlyi Mihály utca, specializes in religious vestments, candles, statues and icons.

Károlyi Mihály utca contains some distinguished institutions: the Library of the Eötvös Loránd University of Arts and Sciences, the Petőfi Literary Museum, and the university faculties of political science and law (on Egyetem tér). Take a look, too, at **University Church** *(Egyetemi templom)* just off the square in Eötvös Loránd utca. It was built in the 18th century by the Order of St. Paul, the only monastic body of Hungarian origin. The monks themselves fashioned some of the richest wood-carvings inside the church—the stalls, the choir and the Baroque organ, which delights the eyes as much as the ears. The church, bigger within than seems likely from the street, has two graceful towers with bulbous spires in the Budapest style.

In this part of Pest, near the inner boulevard, you stand the best chance of coming upon traces of the medieval city wall. In many cases houses have been built around parts of the wall, so you have to peer into courtyards to find the high crenellated form of Pest's first defences. Some addresses for the archaeological sightseer: 21 Múzeum körút, 28 Magyar utca, 13 Királyi Pál utca, 17 and 19 Bástya utca and 16 Tolbuhin körút.

This façade in Martinelli tér is one of Budapest's outstanding examples of Art Nouveau design.

From Engels Square

An attractive fountain graces Engels tér, one of the busiest squares of Budapest. The fountain, called the Danubius, is crowned by a bearded man symbolizing the Danube. Three female figures below represent tributaries of the mighty river, the Tisza, the

Dráva and the Száva. After the war a sprawling inter-city coach terminal was built on the square, bringing bustle and diesel fumes to the area.

Deák tér, only a few steps away, straddles all three metro lines. No more apt place could have been chosen for an **Underground Railway Museum** *(Földalatti Vasúti Múzeum);* it is even situated below ground. (The museum entrance is in the pedestrian underpass beneath Tanács Körút.) On view are antiquated and modern metro cars and equipment. Budapest's original underground line, inaugurated in 1896, was the first in continental Europe. It's still in operation, from Vörösmarty tér to Mexikói út, beyond City Park.

Above ground, a new museum adjoins the neo-Classical Evangelical Church building in Deák tér. The National Lutheran Museum *(Evangélikus Országos Múzeum)* contains a valuable collection of old bibles and chalices, plus documents concerning distinguished Protestant statesmen who strongly influenced the history of predominantly Catholic Hungary. The gigantic statue of Martin Luther in the courtyard next door perpetuates the memory of the Reformation leader.

Anker Palace, an overpowering building topped by two domes and a heavy pyramidal roof, dominates the far side of Deák tér. This one-time insurance company headquarters, adorned with a jumble of classical elements, was one of the few stuctures in Budapest to be left unscathed by the bombs and shells of World War II.

The main avenue leading north, Bajcsy-Zsilinszky út, named after a wartime resistance leader executed in 1944, continues the inner boulevard system. Many of the houses along here are proud examples of the novelties introduced into Budapest architecture at the turn of the century.

The biggest church in Budapest backs onto the boulevard. Construction of the **Basilica** dragged on from 1851 to 1905, long enough to employ three different architects, who chose neo-Classical, Eclectic and neo-Renaissance themes. The formal name of the church is St. Stephen's Parish Church *(Szent István templom)*, but everyone calls it the Basilica, even though this is an architecturally inaccurate title. King (St.) Stephen I appears in sculptured form above the main portal and on the altar. The dome, now 315 feet high, collapsed in 1868 and needed re-doing. The Basilica is big enough to hold more than 8,000 worshippers, and often does.

Due west of the Basilica, at the Pest end of the Chain Bridge, **Roosevelt tér** honours the wartime U.S. president. (The plaque, in what might be an attempt at a compromise between Hungarian and American usages, identifies him as Delano Franklin Roosevelt.) The building directly facing the bridge, embellished to the last Art Nouveau detail, is the turn-of-the-century Gresham Palace. On the north side of the square stands the 19th-century neo-Renaissance home of the Hungarian Academy of Sciences. The statue in front depicts Count István Széchenyi (1791–1860), founder of the Academy and the dynamo behind the audacious Chain Bridge project. This first permanent link between the eastern and western halves of Hungary is now called Széchenyi lánchíd, permanently linking the count's name with his brainchild.

Recent construction along the embankment south of

Inside the Parliament building, seen, below, from Szabadság tér.

Roosevelt tér has restored the area to its pre-war position as a centre of luxury hotels. The first of them was the Duna Intercontinental, followed by the Forum Hotel Budapest and the Atrium Hotel. All were built under international agreements. From these hotels, the view across the Danube is priceless: the Citadel, the sprawling palace, the Fishermen's Bastion and the high-flying spire of Matthias Church.

Szabadság tér (Freedom Square), a vast expanse of shade trees and lawns, has its share of monuments, too, including another obelisk dedicated to Soviet soldiers. Official buildings, most of them ostentatious, surround the square. The former Stock Exchange, a showy Eclectic

Kálvin tér preserves a memento of Budapest's medieval city wall.

structure, now belongs to Hungarian Television; the Hungarian National Bank headquarters opposite is the work of the same architect.

The **Houses of Parliament** (*Országház*) were built to symbolize the grandeur of the Austro-Hungarian empire. In its day the building was called the biggest in the world. The architect, Imre Steindl (1839–1902), may have had the British parliament on his mind; in any case, the neo-Gothic arches and turrets of Hungary's riverside legislature inevitably remind one of the Westminster style. Out of character, however, is the great dome. At 315 feet, it's the same height as that of the Basilica, putting church and state on an equal plane.

Individual tourists are not admitted to the building, but group excursions are run by the various tour agencies when parliament is not in session. Guides point out the many works of art, the grandiose central stairway where the red carpet is always rolled out, and just off the former Chamber of Deputies, the Victorian brass cigar-park with numbered perches for the convenience of caucusing lawmakers who might have wanted to nip inside just long enough to vote.

Tourists are escorted into the Assembly Chamber and seated at the desks of members (the left and right sides of the semi-circular layout no longer have political significance) to be lectured on how the National Assembly is elected and does its work.

Across Kossuth Lajos tér **63**

from the Parliament building, the **Ethnographic Museum** (*Néprajzi Múzeum*) occupies an 1890s building originally meant to be the seat of the Supreme Court (hence the statue of Justice on the façade). The main hall, with its vaulted, frescoed ceiling, is vast enough to serve as a railway station and pompous enough for a royal palace. On permanent display are examples of old-time Hungarian peasant art and culture: textiles, clothing, implements, ceramics and religious icons. As in many Budapest museums, all signs and explanations are printed in Hungarian only.

Naive painting celebrates life in the Hungarian countryside.

Beyond the Inner City

Breaking out from the inner city, there are no more ancient monuments—indeed, few buildings more than 150 years old. But the charm of the Pest which expanded so confidently in the 19th and early 20th centuries is hard to resist. Here are the majestic boulevards, the ingeniously decorated apartment blocks, the grand public buildings, the theatres and cafés.

The Little Boulevard *(Kiskörút)* follows the path of the medieval city wall. The first section starts at the Pest end of Liberty Bridge; it's called Tolbuhin körút (after a Soviet marshal). The road may seem too hectic and businesslike to hold any appeal for sightseers, but the building at No. 1–3 is full of surprises. It's a vast, old-fashioned **covered market**, with a ceiling six stories above the floor, brimming with local colour and exotic smells. This used to be Budapest's central market; now it's an overgrown food bazaar for ordinary shoppers. Don't miss the paprika stalls with their garlands of peppers.

At Kálvin tér the boulevard veers northward along the trajectory of the city wall. The unaffected lines of an early 19th-century Calvinist church stand out, a reminder of the days when this was a quiet, almost rural, crossroads. Kálvin tér has since evolved into one of Budapest's biggest and busiest traffic intersections.

From here the boulevard is called Múzeum körút. It's dominated by the neo-Classical bulk of the **Hungarian National Museum** *(Magyar Nemzeti Múzeum)*. This impressive building, with Corinthian columns and richly sculptured tympanum, stands back in its own sizable garden. Inside, amid monumental architectural and ornamental details, the whole story of Hungary unfolds. On display are prehistoric remains and ancient jewels and tools, longbows, locks and keys. From the Turkish era a 17th-century tent is all decked out with carpets on the floor and walls. The 19th-century exhibits range from army uniforms to a piano owned by Liszt, and by Beethoven before him.

For Hungarian visitors, though, there's no argument about which exhibit is the stellar attraction: the Hungarian **royal regalia.** They were returned to Budapest in 1978 after more than three decades in custody in the United States as spoils of war (including a spell in Fort Knox). The crown, attributed to St. Stephen, the great 11th-century king, has more meaning than most. In Hungary it is a powerful symbol of national pride. Also on show are the 11th-century coronation robes, the oriental-style sceptre, the 14th-century gilded orb, and a 16th-century replacement for a ceremonial sword. All are cherished as a supreme national treasure, even more so because of their post-war odyssey. **65**

Beyond the university buildings, the boulevard crosses busy Rákóczi út (named after an 18th-century prince). This is the main east-west avenue of Budapest, and a major shopping street for goods ranging from shoes and antiques to TV sets. Rákóczi út runs straight towards the Eastern Railway Station *(Keleti pályaudvar)* but swerves at the last moment to create a modern plaza with a sunken promenade. The design of the station has been described as Eclectic in style. Statues of James Watt, inventor of the steam engine, and George Stephenson, of the steam locomotive, stand in niches of honour on the façade.

A final curiosity just off the inner boulevard at 2–8 Dohány utca: a mid-19th-century synagogue built in a striking Byzantine-Moorish style. This is the biggest of about 30 synagogues still operating in Budapest. Next door, the **Jewish Religious and Historical Collection** *(Zsidó Múzeum)* contains relics and works of art reflecting many centuries of Jewish life and death in Hungary. Among the exhibits: a 3rd-century gravestone, exquisite medieval prayerbooks and chilling documents on the fate of the Budapest ghetto in World War II.

The Nagykörút

The Great Boulevard *(Nagykörút)* makes a leisurely semi-circle about four miles long, embracing all of Pest from Margaret Bridge to Petőfi Bridge. It comprises Szent István körút, Lenin körút, József körút and Ferenc körút. Though it changes names four times, the boulevard has a rather consistent character—not exceptionally elegant, but full of enthusiasm. Enterprising city planners pushed the project to completion for the thousandth anniversary of the Hungarian nation in 1896. With its wide roadway and ornate architectural monuments, the boulevard remains a good idea. And they don't build domes and towers like those any more.

Just off Ferenc körút at 33–37 Üllői út, a building pulsating with architectural shocks houses the **Museum of Applied Arts** *(Iparművészeti Múzeum)*. The style of the brick-and-ceramic-tile palace can only be described as Fantasy Hungarian with strong eastern influences. Designed by Ödön Lechner and Gyula Pártos, it was opened in 1896. As for the exhibits, they tell a terse history of ceramics in China, Europe and, in particular, Hungary. Also on show

The Eastern Railway Station is a showy relic of the Steam Age.

are furniture, textiles, oriental rugs, metalwork, clocks and curios made by extremely talented Hungarian and foreign hands.

A museum of more specialized interest, just beyond the ring of Lenin körút, is the Philatelic Museum *(Bélyegmúzeum)* at 47 Hársfa utca.

All the stamps ever issued by Hungary can be viewed here, so there are gripping historical and human-interest themes.

The long segment of the boulevard now known as Lenin körút has been a traditional centre of Budapest's cultural as well as commercial life. Along here are theatres, cinemas and, less obviously, publishing houses and the haunts of literary and artistic characters. At the boulevard's intersection with Dohány utca, **67** the **Hungária Café** (formerly known as the New York) looks just as it did when the 20th century was new. The café's astonishing neo-Baroque-Eclectic-Art Nouveau interior has been restored to its original gaudy glory. And once again it's a popular meeting place of actors, writers and nostalgia buffs.

Lenin körút finally runs out at Marx tér, site of the Western Railway Station *(Nyugati pályaudvar)*. With its high-flying steel framework and cast-iron pillars, this was an architectural sensation of the 1870s. The French firm that built it went on to even greater heights with a daring project in Paris, which became known as the Eiffel Tower.

Most Stately Avenue

You may never learn how to pronounce the name of **Népköztársaság útja,** but you'll surely admire its harmonious style. Budapest's most attractive avenue, modelled after the Champs-Elysées in Paris, was a bold stroke of the 1870s. The city planners pushed it straight out from the Inner Boulevard to City Park, gradually widening the avenue along the way and pausing for breath only at a couple of spacious squares.

Népköztársaság útja, meaning People's Republic Avenue, originally was called Sugár út (Radial Avenue). Later it was known as Andrássy út, and for some years it bore Stalin's name. Under whatever title, the avenue has a roomy, patrician feeling. The buildings that line it blend nicely, yet almost every one has unique features—a fountain or statue in the courtyard, a mosaic or frieze on the façade, columns or arches....

The **Postal Museum** *(Postamúzeum)* is tucked away in a large, formerly aristocratic edifice near the beginning of the avenue at 3 Népköztársaság útja. Even if you can't understand the explanations, written in Hungarian only, you will appreciate the rarity of the ancient telephone switchboards, telegraph keys, postboxes, and the telephone of Franz Joseph I. On view is the prototype of a revolutionary telegraph transmitter, with the letters of the alphabet assigned to the keys of a piano; but the idea was ahead of its time and won little acclaim.

The **State Opera House** *(Állami Operaház),* designed by Miklós Ybl, is the most admired piece of architecture on the avenue. Its Italianate style and restrained proportions fit in beautifully with the surroundings. Statues of 16 great opera composers stand high above the entrance; alongside the portico in positions of honour are sculptures of Franz Liszt and his less celebrated contemporary, Ferenc Erkel, composer of the Hungarian national anthem and director of the opera house when it opened in 1884.

The interior design, noted for its pleasing proportions, evinces a general air of great luxury within the bounds of taste. The auditorium, with its splendid four-tiered gallery, provides excellent acoustics. Opera is so popular in Budapest that a second, larger opera house, the Erkel Theatre, was built to ease the pressure for tickets.

Across the avenue from the opera house, in a late 19th-century palace, Hungary's best dancers study at the State Ballet Institute.

An area two or three streets away has suffered the nickname of **Budapest's Broadway.** With the highest concentration of theatres of any single neighbourhood in the capital, as well as the Moulin Rouge nightclub, it's a lively part of town.

The first of the avenue's main intersections, the crossing of Lenin körút, is a bustling place called November 7 tér, commemorating the date of the Bolshevik revolution. Farther from the centre of town the avenue takes another break at Kodály körönd (circle), named after the composer and educator Zoltán Kodály (1882–1967), who lived here. The curving façades of the buildings ranged around this square are embellished with classical figures and inlaid designs of endless variety.

As the avenue heads out of town, posh villas and mansions in garden settings predominate. Most are now embassies or government offices, but the house at 103 Népköztársaság útja holds the **Museum of East Asian Art** *(Hopp Ferenc Keletázsiai Múzeum)*. Ferenc Hopp was an art collector who died in 1919, bequeathing his villa and his hoard of Asian art works to the state. Since then, other collections have been added, bringing the inventory to some 20,000 items. A related institution, the **Museum of Chinese Art** *(Kína Múzeum)*, occupies another enviable villa in the same district, at 12 Gorkij fasor. It specializes in ancient Chinese sculpture, ceramics and handicrafts.

Népköztársaság útja ends in an outburst of pomp at **69**

Heroes' Square *(Hősök tere)*, a wide-open space generously endowed with winter winds. Here stand the statues of patriotic import that form the **Millenary Monument,** begun on the thousandth anniversary of the Magyar conquest. At the heart of the ensemble rises a 118-foot column supporting a winged figure. Around the pedestal, statues show seven tribal chiefs riding horses. The carved likenesses of historical figures starting with King Stephen I stand in a semicircular colonnade, and there are all the requisite allegorical works as well. In front of this, the stone tablet of the Hun-garian War Memorial commemorates the heroes who died for national freedom and independence.

Facing each other across the expanse of Heroes' Square, two neo-Classical structures seem at first glance to be reflections of one another, and indeed they were designed by the same architect. The considerably larger building on the left (north) side is the **Museum of Fine Arts** *(Szépművészeti Múzeum),* an institution of international significance.

On view from ancient times are Egyptian statues and mummy cases, Greek and Roman sculpture and vases. (A note

about the Hungarian legends: I.E. 3–1 SZ. = 3rd–1st century B.C.; I.SZ. 3. SZ = 3rd century A.D.)

The museum's holdings of Old Masters, of which about 600 can be seen at any time, include many sublime works of the Italian Renaissance. An area of unexpected strength is the Spanish school, with seven El Grecos and an ample selection of works by Velázquez, Murillo, Zurbarán and Goya. Many other masters are represented, from Hans Memling and Bruegel the Elder to Frans Hals, Rembrandt and Vermeer. Another surprise is the trove of French Impressionists and Post-Impressionists: Monet, Pissarro, Renoir, Cezanne, Gauguin and others.

It's really something of a miracle that these treasures hang here at all. The museum was shot up during the war, and in 1944 the paintings were tossed into railway freight wagons for hasty evacuation to Germany. Yet, very soon after the end of hostilities, the whole precious cargo, with only a few minor losses, was returned.

Temporary exhibitions of Hungarian and foreign paint-

Nightlife runs the gamut from opera to spectacular floor-shows.

ing and sculpture are held in the Art Gallery *(Műcsarnok)* on the far side of the square. This high-roofed one-storey building was designed in the form of a Greek temple.

Not far from the gallery, Dózsa György út widens to form Procession Square *(Felvonulási tér)*. If you like a parade, with plenty of red flags, this is the place to be on Liberation Day (4 April) or May Day. The statue of Lenin is by Pál Pátzay.

The City Park
(Városliget)

Beyond the Millenary Monument and all the exaggerated formality sprawls a park where Hungarians can relax, stroll in the woods, spoil their children with ice-cream and cheap plastic toys, hire a rowing boat, even visit another museum.

The City Park, about 250 acres in area, began to evolve in the early 19th century. Most of the present amenities, such

One wing of the castle holds the Hungarian Agricultural Museum *(Magyar Mezőgazdasági Múzeum)*, which deals with the history of hunting, fishing and farming. There's also a simulated wine cellar displaying old wine presses and bottles; oddly, the place is heated even in summer to protect the exhibits.

In the palace courtyard stands a unique statue of a 13th-century personage known only as Anonymous. He was the royal scribe who wrote the first Hungarian chronicles. A suitably anonymous face peers from deep inside a monk's cowl.

Outside the palace area, another statue shows the American president George Washington looking over a little lake—so far from the Delaware River and the Potomac. It was erected in 1906 by Hungarian émigrés living in the United States.

Sculpted elephants stand guard at the elaborately decorated entrance to the **Zoo** *(Fővárosi Állatkert)*. Inside, some 4,000 live animals stand by to entertain visitors. Most of them are kept in traditional

as the artificial lake which reflects the turrets of a make-believe castle, were added during preparations for the Thousand-Year festivities of 1896.

The **Castle of Vajdahunyad** *(Vajdahunyad vára)* reproduces aspects of the fabulous castle of the Hunyadi family in Transylvania (in an area which became part of Romania). It was built as a prop for the Millenary Exhibition but proved so popular that it was reconstructed in permanent form.

73

cages, but there are some refreshing exceptions, such as a monkey island in a lake. A hot-house on the zoo grounds displays tropical flora along with some appropriate but unlovely fauna—serpents and crocodiles.

The zoo adjoins **Vidám Park** (Amusement Park), a standard roller-coaster and dodgem establishment. For the foreign tourist, its principal attraction is the chance to watch young Hungarians having fun.

Across the street lies the overblown triple-domed **Széchényi Baths,** considered one of Europe's largest medicinal bath complexes. In a spa city like Budapest, it is probably to be expected that piping-hot spring water should bubble under the city park. The Széchényi installation treats various physical disorders and provides its share of swimming pools.

Near the easternmost point of the park (at 26 Május 1. út), some worthy old trains, planes, cars and motorcycles may be examined in the **Transport Museum** (*Közlekedési Múzeum*). The exhibits skim the history of transport from the days of sail to the space age. In the museum grounds, an antique railway dining car now serves as a restaurant.

Excursions

Danube Bend

North of Budapest, where the Danube changes its mind and abandons its easterly course for a southerly tack, stretches the beautiful region known straightforwardly as Dunakanyar, the Danube Bend. The river is at its most alluring here, the lush countryside delights, and the towns glow with historic charm.

Scarcely 12 miles upstream from Budapest, easily reached by car, bus or suburban railway, is the captivating town of **Szentendre.** Though the area has been inhabited since the Stone Age, the present character of Szentendre remains frozen in the 18th century: tidy, Baroque and painted all the colours of the rainbow.

Marx tér, the cobbled main square, so perfectly embodies the spirit of times past that the whole ensemble has been classified as a national historical monument. (In over 200 years, the only thing about the square that's changed is its name.) The cast-iron Rococo cross in the centre of the square was erected in 1763 by the Serbian businessmen of Szentendre. By then, Serbs fleeing Ottoman rule made up most of the population of the town, to which they brought their religion, art and architecture.

The towers of seven churches dominate the Szentendre skyline. The one on Marx tér, a mid-18th-century Baroque church with some Rococo details on the portal and belfry, is known as the **Greek church;** officially it's the Blagoveštenska Eastern Orthodox Church. Alongside, in what was a schoolhouse in the 18th century, the Ferenczy Museum displays art works of the Hungarian Impressionist Károly Ferenczy and his two children.

Other churches of more than routine interest in the town: the Catholic Parish Church, founded in the Middle Ages, with an ancient sundial on the wall; and the Belgrade Church, an 18th-century Greek Orthodox cathedral noted for a richly sculpted iconostasis. Around the corner is the entrance to the Collection of Serbian Ecclesiastical Art *(Szerb Egyháztörténeti gyűjtemény),* where precious icons, carvings and manuscripts have been gathered together.

Of all the museums in this artists' town, the one dedicated to the 20th-century ceramic artist Margit Kovács draws the biggest crowds. Here you'll see attenuated sculptures of wide-eyed damsels and stooped tragic figures in an instantly recognizable style. Opposite the Catholic Parish Church, a smaller museum vibrates with the happy, warm colours of paintings by Béla Czóbel, a much-travelled Hungarian Impressionist who settled in Szentendre.

About 2 miles north-west of town, typical old houses transplanted from the countryside have been assembled at the **Open Air Village Museum** *(Szabadtéri Néprajzi Múzeum).* With its 18th-century tim-

ber church and whitewashed thatch-roofed cottages—and not a TV antenna in sight—this simulated "village" provides an ideal setting for historical films, as several producers have noticed.

Upriver, where the Danube makes a hairpin bend, historic **Visegrád** is set in surpassingly scenic country, where verdant hills come down almost to the water's edge. The strategic importance of this potential bottleneck on the river has been evident since the 4th century, when the Romans built a fort here.

The most enterprising construction work, in the Middle Ages, transformed Visegrád into a proper regal city. The Angevin kings of Hungary built their **palace** here, each monarch adding new luxury and a few dozen more rooms to the 14th-century nucleus. But the palace fell into ruin during the Turkish occupation and its former splendour was all but forgotten until archaeologists started digging it up in the 1930s. Only part of the main building has been unearthed; to give a better idea of the whole, certain areas have been reconstructed (using obviously new materials to differentiate these sections from the original elements).

Among the most celebrated sights of the five-level structure: the superb **Hercules Fountain** (a rare vestige of Hungarian Renaissance architecture); the vaulted galleries

Ceramics by Margit Kovács reflect Szentendre's quiet beauty.

Itinerant beekeepers set up their hives all through the rolling countryside. Right: Lions' Well in Visegrád.

of the Court of Honour; and the restored Lions' Fountain. Up the hillside, the hexagonal tower popularly called the Tower of Solomon contains a museum displaying fragments and reconstructions of items from the palace. Finally, near the top of the hill are the ruins **78** of the **Citadel,** with spectacular

views of the mountains and the river.

From Budapest, Visegrád may be reached by bus, but an altogether more inviting way to go is by ferryboat or hydrofoil. The boats land right in front of the palace.

Esztergom, cathedral city and medieval capital of all Hungary, is about 30 miles from Budapest by road, but just across the river from Czechoslovakia. In this part of the Danube Bend the river it-

self becomes an international frontier. The ruins of a bridge which, until World War II, linked the two countries make a melancholy sight from the heights of Castle Hill.

The great domed **Basilica of Esztergom** *(Esztergomi Székesegyház),* the biggest church in Hungary, stands on the site of an 11th-century house of worship. In 1823, shortly after construction began, Beethoven offered to conduct his *Missa Solemnis* for the consecration of the church. But the work went too slowly, and when the ceremony finally took place, in 1856, it was Liszt's *Esztergom Mass* that was performed.

The red-marble side chapel called the **Bakócz-kápolna,** a pure example of Italian Renaissance style, was built as a separate church in the early 16th century. It was moved stone by stone to the basilica in the 19th century and reassembled. Note the white marble altar sculpted by a Florentine master. The **treasury** contains Hungary's richest store of religious objects, including a cross of crystal from 9th-century Metz and the 15th-century Calvary of King Matthias.

Alongside the basilica the remains of a medieval **royal palace** have been excavated and, to an extent, restored. Among the highlights: St. Stephen's Hall, the frescoed Hall of Virtues with the signs of the zodiac on the great arch, and the 12th-century royal chapel.

Down at riverside, Esztergom's **Christian Museum** *(Keresztény Múzeum)* is rated the most important provincial collection in Hungary. It definitely comes up to world standards, especially in its supply of superb 14th- and 15th-century Italian paintings. Housed in the former Episcopal Palace, the museum is run by the Catholic Church and subsidized by the state. Elsewhere in the building are photographs of some of the approximately 170 churches built in Hungary since the end of World War II.

Take time to stroll along the restful riverfront promenades nearby. And if you're in no hurry, you can take the boat on its effortless downstream journey back to Budapest.

Lake Balaton

Hungarians may be deprived of a seacoast but they take their solace in Lake Balaton, a freshwater haven surrounded by a little world of varied beauty: fertile plains and abrupt hills, orchards and vineyards, and villages with historic churches and whitewashed thatched cottages. At about 60 miles south-west of Budapest, Balaton lies within daytrip distance by car or coach (the journey can be made by motorway) or by express train.

Balaton is counted as Middle Europe's biggest lake, with an area of nearly 230 square miles. Yet its average depth is less than ten feet. In winter it quickly freezes from end to end. In summer the shallow water is subject to wind-driven waves; when a real storm blows up, the tiny sea gets so rough that even the ferryboats quit.

But for most of the summer the hot sun warms the calm lake nearly to air temperature, luring thousands into the swim. The mildly alkaline water is said to be positively healthful for bathing. The fish certainly thrive in it: about 40 species inhabit the lake. Balaton pike-perch *(fogas)* is often singled out as the tastiest of all.

Fishermen operate from shore, from boats and lounging on platforms protruding from the lake. Ice-fishing has been popular at Balaton since antiquity, when winter was the only season the catch could be preserved for sale in distant parts. Another commercial product comes from the lake—the reeds which grow along much of the shore. They make a good roofing material and have other practical uses.

More conventional agriculture flourishes all along the circumference of Lake Balaton, enhancing the appeal of the countryside with fruit trees, rippling expanses of wheat and vineyards. Some of Hungary's most popular wines originate here, so many, in fact, that a whole holiday could easily be devoted to studying them all.

Now for a brief survey of the points of greatest interest along the lake, taking them counter-clockwise from the eastern (Budapest) end. The only complication is the nomenclature; a couple of dozen of the towns have names beginning "Balaton", badly muddying the waters for new arrivals. BALATONAKARATTYA, for example, is the first town on Highway 71, the north shore road. Then comes BALATON-KENESE, and so forth. Some

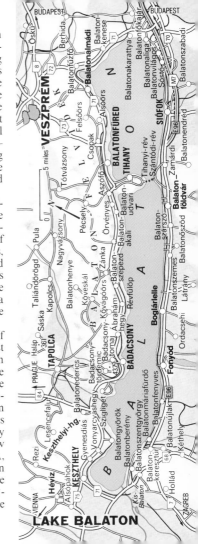

of the names can barely be squeezed onto the road signs.

Balatonalmádi, a fast-growing resort town, claims to have the biggest, most modern beach on the north shore—"capacity 12,000". Parks, hotels and a complete shopping centre round out the picture.

The road leads about 8 miles farther west to **Balatonfüred,** a busy pleasure port with a long history as a spa. The local mineral water, at 1 forint per glass, is dispensed to the public from a pagoda-like well-head in the middle of Gyógy tér (Therapeutic Square). It's cool enough to be refreshing, but the taste—as if it had come out of a rusty pipe—hints at its medicinal properties. Between the square and the lake-front a large park shaded by tall plane and poplar trees is studded with

Visitors to Balaton take a break at an outdoor café with a view.

statues traditional and modern. In addition to its sanitoria and resort hotels, Balatonfüred has a campsite big enough for 3,000 people.

The **Tihany peninsula,** largely given over to a national park, protrudes to within about a mile of the south shore. Life here is a split-level affair—an ancient church stands on a precipice overlooking the port, and at intermediate altitudes there's a village and its independent lake.

Starting at the top: The **Abbey Church** *(Apátság),* an 18th-century Baroque construction, rises above a crypt nearly a thousand years old. Here stands the tomb of King Andrew I, founder of this Benedictine abbey. In a country ravaged by so many invasions, the Romanesque crypt represents a rare survival from the earliest times of the Hungarian nation. King Andrew is also commemorated in a joltingly contemporary sculpture in front of the church—a stone figure wrapped in an aluminium cloak.

The streets and lanes along the upper reaches of **Tihany** town charm visitors. They're lined with thatch-roofed, stone cottages in traditional style.

At an altitude of more than 80 feet above Lake Balaton, the peninsula's Inner Lake (Belső-tó) yields tons of fish every year. Because it is so small—less than half a mile long—the green hills surrounding the little lake look like real mountains. To the south are the domes of defunct geysers.

Beyond Tihany the north coast traffic thins out, so travellers can relax and enjoy the views, vineyards and villages. The region of **Badacsony** produces notable wines on hill-

83

sides of volcanic soil. The volcanic past is evident at first sight of the astonishing conical green hills arrayed here. The black basalt slabs used to pave the back roads provide another clue to the violent birth of this land. The view up to the evocative Badacsony mountains is a high-spot of an excursion to Lake Balaton; so is the panorama from the top, with the vineyards sloping down to the lake in regimented rows. The next step is obvious: sample the local pride. The wine always tastes better when you're beside the vines.

The road moves inland after Badacsony, skirting the ancient village of SZIGLIGET, watched over by the moody remains of a medieval fortress.

At the western end of the lake, the town of **Keszthely** used to be owned lock, stock and barrel by one family—the Festetics. The 101-room **Festetics Palace** is one of Hungary's important Baroque monuments. Count György Festetics founded Europe's first agricultural school, now Keszthely's University of Agricultural Sciences, in 1797. He also amazed townspeople by building the *Phoenix*, the biggest ship seen on Balaton till then, a three-master powered with help from 24 oarsmen.

Keszthely's **Balaton Museum** surveys the lake from many viewpoints—geology, biology, history and ethnology.

The highway continues around the end of the lake to the first town on the south shore. This road and rail junction has a folk museum and the longest name: BALATON-SZENTGYÖRGY. To the west lies KIS-BALATON (Little Balaton), a national reserve noted for its rare birdlife.

When the highway (now route 7) finally comes in sight of the lake, Balaton's endless children's beach begins. All along the south shore the soft, white sandy bottom of the lake goes out seemingly to infinity before the water becomes deep enough to dive into. However, this is no problem for sailing, wind-surfing (board sailing) or simply paddling about. To protect the lake from pollution, motorboats (hence water-skiing) have been banned.

A volcanic hill with twin peaks hangs over **Fonyód**, the centre of a string of south coast resorts. Fonyód's harbour is one of Balaton's major maritime installations. Long after the bathers have packed up, fishermen stake out the unusually long pier and surrounding beaches.

At SZÁNTÓD the great lake

is squeezed to its narrowest; the Tihany peninsula lies just across the way. This has always been a vital ferry station. Until 1928 oarsmen propelled the boats. Modern ferryboats make the crossing in less than ten minutes, but there's plenty of nautical excitement and fresh air. Although ferries and pleasure boats stop at many Balaton ports, the Szántód-to-Tihany route has the only car ferries on the lake.

The largest town on the south coast, **Siófok**, boasts a beach with room for tens of thousands of sunbathers and a harbour big enough to shelter all the ferries and cruise ships on the lake. A shady recreational park stretches east from the port and winds up in an ambitious new development of lake-front hotels. Around the harbour a lively assortment of cafés, bars, restaurants and entertainment facilities stand within easy reach.

In the 3rd century, Roman engineers built the first canal at Siófok to divert excess water from the lake. The Sió canal leads all the way from the harbour to the River Danube, down near the Yugoslavian frontier. The fastest, most direct way to return to Budapest from Siófok is via the M7 motorway.

What to Do

Some visitors come to Hungary with the most serious of intents. They potter about the Roman ruins or go birdwatching or sink into a therapeutic thermal bath. Other single-minded tourists sign up for hunting expeditions or horse-riding excursions. There are even package tours for bald men seeking the panacea of Hungarian hair-tonic and scalp treatment.

Most people, though, have broader horizons, and for them Budapest offers a wide variety of activities: excellent museums, pleasant boat trips, profitable shopping, plenty of sports, music of the highest standard, nightlife and renowned food and drink.

Shopping

Hungarian artisans, who provide the bulk of the best buys, offer some new lines as well as the dependable traditional designs. Other promising goods include low-priced books and records, along with foodstuffs —no big surprise in the land that invented paprika. In Hungarian shops and stores, the price tag tells the whole story. A VAT or sales tax of 25 per cent, included in the price, is added to most goods and services (see p. 112).

In addition to all the normal retail outlets, tourists can find a select range of Hungarian and imported goods in Intertourist and Utastourist shops (many of them in hotels), which accept hard currency only. Prices are usually listed in U.S. dollars, but almost all convertible currencies and credit cards are accepted. Two special shops in Budapest sell art, antiques and coins for foreign currency only. Keep your receipts in case of any questions at customs—on leaving Hungary or returning home.

Budapest's Best Buys

Antiques. Paintings, furniture, vases, jewellery, coins, leatherbound books, knick-knacks. The items for sale in hard-currency shops are suitable for export; in other shops, be sure to ask whether it's permitted to take the goods out of Hungary. (Precious art works may not leave.)

Books. Hungarian publishers produce very inexpensive picture books, travel guides and literary works written in or translated into English, French, German, Italian and **86** Spanish.

Carpets and rugs. Warm colours, rugged fabrics and harmonious designs distinguish Hungarian carpets and rugs of all sizes. They're advantageously priced—even the homespun, hand-knotted originals.

Ceramics. The best-known of the Hungarian factories, at Herend, near Lake Balaton, has been turning out porcelain plates, cups and vases since 1839. Other firms operate at Kalocsa and Pécs. Most of the designs available in Budapest shops are floral, but you'll even see imitation Chinese vases. Porcelain figurines of typical Hungarian characters are also popular.

Copper and brass. Plates, bowls, vases, ashtrays—and Turkish-style coffee sets.

Elixir. Some foreigners fly to Hungary just to buy bottles of the much-publicized tonic and suspected cure-all called Béres Csepp. Sold only at shops of the Herbaria enterprise; no prescription necessary.

Food products. Some items can be hand-carried out of the country: paprika in sachets or the ready-made sauce in tubes; strudel or cakes packed in sturdy boxes by the better confectioners' shops; and salami—the highest-quality Hungarian

At Tihany, Hungarian artisan produces distinctive hand-turned pottery.

spicy sausage, full-size or in more portable dimensions. (For export restrictions, see pp. 111–112.)

Furs. Small private workshops transform Hungarian and imported pelts into stylish winter hats and coats at very competitive prices.

Hair lotion. Thinning hair is said to be arrested by the use of Bánfi capillary lotion, another of Hungary's alleged miracle cures from the Herbaria shops, and at ordinary perfumeries as well. (If it works, forget the fur hat.)

Kitsch. If you're in the mood, buy a model of a Portuguese caravel with "Budapest" inscribed on the sail, or a simple air thermometer enshrined in a Rococo setting worthy of a reliquary—also marked "Budapest" as an afterthought.

Leather goods. Cowboy's whip and matching wine-bottle... from the Hungarian *puszta*. If time permits, you can have a pair of shoes made to fit and to last. Other interesting buys include leather gloves and wallets.

Linens. Embroidered table-cloths, napkins, doilies; each region, and virtually every village, has its own traditional designs.

Liqueurs and wine. The local apricot, cherry or plum brandy makes an inexpensive souvenir. Or take home a bottle of the best Tokay wine (some types come in gift packs).

Records and tapes. Aside from Liszt and Bartók, works galore. Hungarian performers have recorded many classic and modern pieces; also folk music, gypsy violins, Hungarian pop—all at low prices.

Rubik's cube. Budapest Professor Ernő Rubik invented this addictive little puzzle, which can be solved in less than a minute—or weeks or never, depending on your three-dimensional imagination.

Shirts and blouses. Embroidered in primary colours, peasant-style blouses are a long-lasting reminder of Hungary. Men's shirts, off the rack or made to measure, include some bargains.

Silver. The workmanship of trays, pitchers, candelabra and smaller items is highly regarded, and the prices are considered extremely favourable.

Woodwork. Look for peasant-carved boxes big and small, bowls, walking sticks and chess sets.

Sports

For spectators or participants, Hungary offers a busy little world of sports. The strongest points involve horses and ball games. Aside from scuba divers and deep-sea fishermen, the only sportsmen likely to be disappointed are visiting golfers, who are completely out in the cold in Hungary.

Soccer, known by its Magyar name, *labdarúgás* (literally, kick-ball), draws the largest crowds. The big matches take place in Népstadion, the much-admired People's Stadium,

Lake Balaton anglers covet the fogas, or giant pike-perch.

with its graceful dimensions and full range of equipment. If you can't get a ticket, there are more than 3,200 other soccer grounds in the country.

Basketball, water-polo and **athletics**—fields in which Hungary often does well internationally—also attract sizable audiences in Budapest.

One of the pleasures of going to the **races** at the local tracks is looking at the spectators: workingmen, universal horse-players in Damon Runyon stripes and little old ladies who seem to be respected handicappers. Flat races *(galopp)* are run Sundays and Thursdays in summer, trotting races, year-round on Wednesdays and Saturdays. (Off-track betting at state lottery offices is also legal.)

Active Sports

To get closer to the horses, you can go for a ride—for an hour or on a week-long trek. Half a dozen stables and **horse riding** schools are within 30 miles of Budapest. In addition, package tours for horse-lovers, featuring friendly, lively Hungarian horses, start at many points in the country and last from five to ten days. IBUSZ issues a brochure, *Riding in Hungary,* with details. If you can't part with your horse, the agency says

Tourist shows recapture the romance of Hungary's puszta

you can buy it and take it home.

Combine sports with sightseeing on a **cycling** tour to sites within a 30-mile radius of Budapest. Or pedal around the Balaton area for a week or more. Excursions by bike are another speciality IBUSZ.

On a hot summer's day, you may seek nothing more strenuous than a swim. Budapest has numerous **swimming** pools, including two elaborate installations on Margaret Island. But in this spa city, be sure to check the water temperature before you dive in!

For **sailing** and **wind-surfing,** the place to go is Lake Balaton or, closer to Budapest, the smaller Lake Velence. **Fishing** in the lakes or the Danube requires a permit from the Hungarian National Fishing Association (MOHOSZ, Budapest V, Október 6. u. 20). Try for bass, carp, catfish, pike and pike-perch.

Tennis is very popular in Hungary, but facilities for visitors are limited. And then there is **mini-golf,** played mostly around Lake Balaton.

For Children

Keeping children amused in Budapest is no big problem. The most obvious places to go are all in a row in the City Park: the zoo, the amusement park (with 50-year-old roller-coaster and modern rides) and the Budapest circus, one of Europe's best. Engrossing marionette shows by talented puppeteers take place in two special theatres, and outdoors in summer. The Pioneer Railway, in the hills of Buda, employs children as station-masters and ticket-collectors. Or try a boat ride on the Danube, or the City Park lake.

An all-day excursion (aimed at adults) goes to the Hungarian *puszta* for, among other things, a show of horses which know some circus-style tricks, and a run-past of free horses, manes flying, on the prairie.

Free of charge, an equestrian spectacle is presented on summer Sunday mornings in front of the Royal Palace: Hussars in flamboyant 19th-century uniforms ride their sensitive, disciplined horses through a close-order drill.

At Lake Balaton resorts, travel agencies organize children's parties, with story-teller, contests, children's songs, snacks and gifts.

Nightlife

Budapest has all the wholesome attractions you'd expect—heavily subsidized theatre, music and folklore—plus a few hedonistic surprises. Evenings are never boring.

Theatrical life is extremely active: on average, several new productions are premièred each week in Hungary. The language poses a problem, of course, but there's no obstacle to sharing the wealth of the musical scene.

Opera, operetta, concerts, ballet and recitals follow a year-round rhythm. When the opera houses and concert halls

Opera is at its grandest on Margaret Island's open-air stage. Right: Dancers from various regions keep Hungarian folk traditions alive.

close for the summer, outdoor venues take over: grand opera in the Margaret Island open-air theatre, chamber music in the courtyard of a Baroque mansion, broad comic opera in the remains of an ancient monastery within a modern hotel. Though the performances are impeccable by any standards, and the costumes resplendent, tickets remain relatively affordable compared with the prices in many western capitals.

To quicken the pace of cultural life, there are annual festivals and special events. The Budapest Spring Festival in March shows off the best in Hungarian music, dancing and art. In late September and October, Budapest Art Weeks provide the framework for special concerts and theatrical programmes featuring famous foreign artists.

Folklore also goes outdoors in summer, but most nights one or another company of

Hungarian dancers—amateur or professional—can be seen on stage at the Municipal Folklore Centre, Fehérvári út 47 in the southern part of Buda (XI). The dancers, in brilliant costumes, are full of spirit and enthusiasm—just like the music. They can even sing while they whirl and stomp their boots. The accompaniment may be provided by a large orchestra including a cymbalom, an instrument related to the dulcimer with a tone resembling at times a banjo, harp or harpsichord; it's a thrill to hear when a master performs at hair-raising speed. The repertoire runs from the *csárdás* to boot-slapping Lads' Dances, wedding dances and dances devised in the 18th century to lure country bumpkins to army recruiting officers.

The schedules of operas, concerts, folklore performances and other attractions of interest to foreign tourists are published in *Programme in Hungary,* issued free every month with parallel texts in German, English and French. It also lists major jazz and pop concerts, as well as rock concerts approved for young people which take place in summer at the Buda Youth Park, near the foot of Buda Castle Hill. For other popular doings,

look for announcements on walls, light posts or pillars.

Hungarians, who all have to study film appreciation in school, are keen film-goers. But the tourist is out of luck, because nearly all the foreign movies shown in Budapest are dubbed into Hungarian.

Turning to the racier side of Budapest nightlife, establishments with names as exotic as the Moulin Rouge and Maxim's present international floor-shows with big production numbers, including glamorous, minimally dressed dancers. But strip-tease is ruled out. The nightclubs open at 10 p.m. and keep going, noisily and expensively, until 4 or 5 a.m. Elsewhere in town, mostly in and near the major hotels, are nightspots with dancing but no show. You'll also notice scores of discotheques and inviting, dimly-lit bars, which keep late hours.

For visitors who prefer the excitements of the gambling casino, the Budapest Hilton provides roulette, baccarat, blackjack and slot machines, while the Lido offers roulette and slot machines. All transactions are in deutsche marks, and most of the conversation is in German, except for the obligatory *"Faites vos jeux, messieurs"*.

Wining and Dining

Hungarians savour life's pleasures more than most people, perhaps because their long history has seen so many defeats and deprivations. When it comes to eating and drinking, they don't miss a chance to reaffirm the joy of living. The most modest restaurant posts a 50- or 60-item menu every day, and the food is as good as it is abundant. The wines maintain a 2,000-year record of excellence. And the service is quick and attentive. In addition, when the waiter adds up the bill, there's no need for foreboding. By the standards of western Europe, it's all a bargain.

Because paprika has been associated with Hungarian cooking for several hundred years, many foreigners imagine that Magyars wake up to goulash and gulp hot peppers the rest of the day. On the contrary, the use of condiments tends to be subtle, with inspired combinations.

Choosing a Restaurant

Hungary's 18,000 or so eating places are divided into a dozen or more categories, none of them, unfortunately, called a "restaurant". If you see the sign "restaurant", it normally means foreign tourists are catered for. Such establishments may even have a menu in English and French in addition to the usual German and Hungarian.

An *étterem* serves a wide range of food and drinks, the prices pegged to the classification bestowed on it—luxury, first, second or third class. A *vendéglő* also provides food and drinks; the decor is often rustic and prices are moderate. Gypsy musicians usually lurk in both types of restaurant at dinner time.

Among the other types of eating places: a *bisztró* is small and reasonably priced; a *büfé* serves hot and cold snacks; a *csárda* is a country inn, often complete with regional atmosphere and romantic music; an *önkiszolgáló* is a self-service snack-bar; and a *snackbar* is an *önkiszolgáló* with pretensions.

Recently the government has franchised many eating places (with less than a dozen employees) to private operators. The profit motive has upgraded them, while the competition has encouraged the standard state-run establishments to do better.

By law, all eating places must offer at least two set

Gypsy violins are an inevitable part of a night out in Budapest.

vided for the benefit of foreign clients.

The *à la carte* menu is long and complicated, in keeping with the Hungarian enthusiasm for fine food. Even if you find a menu translated into a language you understand, a certain amount of confusion is inevitable. The lists are organized with categories where Hungarians expect to find them. Thus, desserts are normally printed on the first, not the last page. Drinks often appear on a separate list and may be served by a different waiter.

When to Eat

Breakfast *(reggeli)* is served between 7 and 10 a.m. Most establishments provide a "continental" version—bread and rolls, butter and jam, coffee or tea. However, some hotels routinely add eggs, cold meats, cheese and yoghurt.

Lunch *(ebéd)* is eaten between noon and 2 or 3 p.m. It's the main meal of the day for most people. This means soup, a main course and dessert, with beer or wine or soft drinks, followed by coffee.

At dinner *(vacsora)*, from 7 to 10 or 11 p.m., people usually skip the soup and may forego the meat course for a cold plate. Wine is the most popu-

menus *(napi menü)* every day. These low-priced "package deals" usually include soup, a main course and dessert.

Translations are rarely proar accompaniment, and while lunchers often stretch it with mineral water, the dinner wine is drunk undiluted.

Hungarian Cuisine

The first Magyars cooked their food in a pot over an open fire. New seasonings and nuances came from France, Italy and Turkey. Paprika was introduced from America in the 17th century, developing over the years into the characteristic piquant, red condiment. The spice is available in "hot" and mild varieties, and although it's the keystone of Hungarian cuisine, many dishes contain no paprika at all. Most food is cooked in lard or rendered fat rather than oil or butter, which sometimes taxes delicate stomachs unaccustomed to the Hungarian method.

Some specialities worth looking for:

Appetizers *(előételek)*. For starters try *libamáj-pástétom,* a flaky pastry shell filled with goose-liver paté mixed with butter and béchamel sauce, spices and brandy. *Hortobágyi húsos palacsinta* (pancakes Hortobágy style)—thin pancakes filled with minced meat and dressed with sour cream—make a delicious beginning to a meal. A vegetarian speciality, *paprika-szeletek körözöttel*

töltve, combines sliced green peppers, ewe's cheese, spices and a dash of beer.

Soup *(levesek)*. *Gulyásleves* (goulash soup) is the real thing: chunks of beef, potatoes, onion, tomatoes and peppers, with paprika, caraway seeds and garlic for added flavour. (Note that what is called goulash abroad is a Hungarian meat stew actually named *pörkölt.*) *Szegedi halászlé* (Szeged fisherman's soup) is a sort of paprika-crazed freshwater bouillabaisse: pieces of giant pike-perch and carp boiled in a stock lengthily concocted from fish heads, tails and bones, with onions and, of course, paprika. On a hot summer day, sample *hideg almaleves* (cold apple soup): creamy and refreshing with a dash of cinnamon.

Fish *(halételek)*. *Paprikás ponty* (carp in paprika sauce) and *pisztráng tejszín-mártásban* (trout baked in cream) show the extemes to which the Hungarians go to glamourize their lake and river fish. *Balatoni fogas* (pike-perch from Lake Balaton) is considered a prime delicacy. (Note that some of the fish are equipped with an infinity of tiny bones, slowing the eating.)

Meat *(húsételek)*. *Fatányéros* (mixed grill) combines over- **97**

sized chunks of pork, beef, veal and perhaps goose liver, roasted over a spit and served on a wooden platter. *Csikós tokány*, called a cowboy dish, consists of strips of beef braised in a mixture of diced bacon, onions, sliced pepper and tomatoes, served with *galuska* (miniature dumplings). Finally, what could be more Hungarian than *töltött paprika* (stuffed pepper)? Green peppers are filled with minced pork, rice, onions, garlic and then blanketed in tomato sauce.

Game and fowl *(vadak, szárnyasok)*. The Hungarian treatment enhances tastes as rich as *vaddisznó* (wild boar) and *őz* (venison). As for poultry, you'll surely be offered *csirke-paprikás* (chicken paprika), with the two main ingredients of the title—plus onion, green peppers, tomato and sour cream.

Sweets *(tészták)*. Do strive to save some strength for the last course, for the Hungarians excel at desserts. The microscopically thin pastry of *rétes* or strudel ought to be framed in the bakers' hall of fame. The adjectives (and fillings) to look for: *almás* (apple), *mákos* (poppy-seed), *meggyes* (sour cherry) and *túrós* (cottage cheese). Or you could go the

whole hog with *Gundel pala csinta*, named after a famed restaurant owner: pancake filled with a nut-and-raisin paste, drenched in a creamy chocolate and rum sauce and then flambéed. For simple tastes there are ice-cream *(fagylalt)*, cheese *(sajt)* or frui *(gyümölcs)*.

Hungarian Wines

Most of the wine made in Hungary is white, the mos famous and inimitable being Tokay *(Tokaji* on the bottle) The volcanic soil of the Tokay region, in north-east Hungary has produced a wine fit for kings since the Middle Ages. I was a favourite of Catherine the Great and Louis XIV, and inspired poetry from Voltaire and song from Schubert. Some prosaic specifications: *Tokaji furmint* is dry; *Tokaji szamo rodni*, medium-sweet; and the full-bodied *Tokaji aszú*, very sweet. The quality is graded from 3 to 5 *puttonyos* (points)

Less celebrated but perfectly satisfying white wines come from the Lake Balaton region Look for the prefixes "Bada csonyi", "Balatonfüredi" and "Csopaki". The Roman em perors liked Balaton wines so much they had them shipped to Rome.

The best known Hungarian

red, *Egri bikavér* (Bull's Blood of Eger), is a full-bodied hearty wine. More subtle are the *pinot noir* from the same town of Eger and a splendid *Villányi burgundi.*

Budapest waiters are most helpful about wines, so don't hesitate to ask for a recommendation when you order your meal.

Budapest's stately coffee houses serve memorable strudel snacks.

Other Drinks

Hungarian beers go well with heavy, spicy food. Or you have the choice of brews from Czechoslovakia, Austria and perhaps Germany. Well-known international soft drinks are bottled in Hungary, competing with local fizzy products and fruit juices.

Espresso coffee—strong, black, hot and usually sweet —is consumed day and night. There's no alternative except for tea, made to undemanding

standards with familiar brands of imported tea-bags. (The closest you can get to white coffee in most Budapest bars is a tiny cup of espresso with a mini-pitcher of milk or cream on the side.)

As an aperitif you may be offered a "puszta cocktail", menacingly blending apricot brandy, digestive bitters and Tokay sweet wine. After dinner, you may want to compare some of Hungary's extraordinarily good fruit brandies *pálinka).* Look for *alma* (apple), *barack* (apricot), *cseresznye* (cherry), *körte* (pear) and *szilva* (plum). And now you know what all those beautiful orchards are for.

Tipping

Tipping is very much a fact of life in the People's Republic. If you have been served well, which is most probable in almost any Budapest restaurant, it's customary to tip the waiter 10 to 15 per cent. The waiter who brings the bill and takes your money is probably not the one who served you, but don't worry; all the gratuities are pooled.

To Help You Order...

Could we have a table?
The bill, please.
Keep the change.

I'd like...

beer	**sört**
bread	**kenyeret**
butter	**vajat**
cheese	**sajtot**
coffee	**kávét**
fish	**halat**
fruit juice	**gyümölcslét**
lemonade	**limonádét**
meat	**húst**
milk	**tejet**
mineral water	**ásványvizet**
mustard	**mustárt**

Lenne szabad asztaluk?
Kérem a számlát.
A többi a magáé.

Kérnék...

noodles	**metéltet**
potatoes	**burgonyát**
rice	**rizst**
salad	**salátát**
salt	**sót**
sandwich	**szendvicset**
soup	**levest**
sugar	**cukrot**
tea	**teát**
vegetables	**főzeléket**
water	**vizet**
wine	**bort**

...and Read the Menu

alma	apple	kacsa	duck
aranygaluska	sweet dumpling	káposzta	cabbage
ananas	pineapple	kappan	capon
bableves	bean soup	kapucineres	coffee
bakonyi betyárleves	"outlaw" soup	felfújt	soufflé
		kolbászfélék	sausages
bárányhús	lamb	liba	goose
békacomb	frog's legs	málna	raspberries
borda	chop	marhahús	beef
borjúhús	veal	meggy	sour cherries
burgonya	potatoes	narancs	orange
citrom	lemon	nyelvhal	sole
cseresznye	cherries	nyúl	rabbit
csirke	chicken	őszibarack	peach
csuka	pike	palacsinta	pancakes
dinsztelve	braised	paradiscom	tomatoes
dió	nuts	ponty	carp
diszóhús	pork	pörkölt	stew
édeskömény	caraway seeds	pulyka	turkey
eper	strawberries	ráksaláta	crab salad
erőleves	consommé	ribizli	red currants
húsgombóccal	with meat dumplings	rántva	breaded
		rostélyos	stewed steak
fasírozott	meatballs	saláta	lettuce
fogas	pike-perch	sárgabarack	apricot
fokhagyma	garlic	sárgarépa	carrots
főve	broiled	sonka	ham
galuska	dumplings	sülve	roasted
gesztenye	chestnuts	sültkrumpli	chips (French fries)
gomba	mushrooms		
görögdinnye	watermelon	sütve	fried
gulyásleves	goulash (soup)	töltött	stuffed
		uborka	cucumber
hagyma	onions	vegyesfőzelék	mixed vegetables
halsaláta	fish salad		
húsleves	meat soup	zeller	celery
italok	drinks	zöldborsó	peas

BLUEPRINT for a Perfect Trip

How to Get There

Although the fares and conditions described below have all been care-fully checked, it is advisable to consult a travel agent for the latest information.

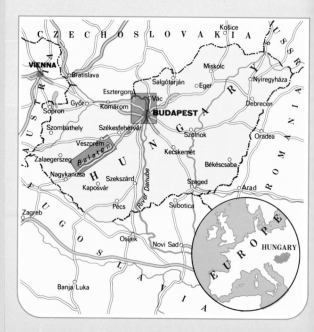

BY AIR

Scheduled Flights

Scheduled service departs daily from London to Budapest. You can ly direct, or via Rome or Frankfurt, but there may be an extra charge or flights routed through Vienna.

Daily connecting flights link the larger American and Canadian ities to Budapest, while many other Canadian and American cities offer connections on specified days.

Charter Flights and Package Tours

From the United Kingdom: Several British companies organize packages to Budapest. These holidays usually last for seven nights and include bed, breakfast and the cost of a visa, perhaps even a half-day ightseeing tour. Weekend trips are also available.

From North America: Package tours to Bucharest or Transylvania, or o Warsaw, Vienna and Prague, make stops in Budapest. These combined tours last for two weeks and include round-trip air fares and hotels, plus meals and services as specified in each itinerary.

BY RAIL

Trains leave from London's Victoria station every morning, arriving at Budapest the following afternoon. The most direct route is via Dover to Ostend and Vienna. Otherwise you can change stations in Paris and continue on the legendary Orient Express by way of Strasbourg, Stuttgart, Munich, Salzburg and Vienna. Bookings should be made several months in advance for this popular train, and even on he Ostend route you must reserve your seat.

An Interrail card available to travellers under 26 and valid for a month of unlimited travel in most European countries costs little more than the fare to Budapest. The Rail Europ Senior Card (obtainable before departure only) entitles senior citizens to purchase rail tickets for European destinations at a discount.

BY HYDROFOIL

From May through to mid-September a hydrofoil service operates daily on the River Danube from Vienna, with departures three times a week in April and until the end of October. Travel time to Budapest averages 4½ hours.

When to Go

Hungary crows about its 2,000 hours of sunshine per year, higher than the average for Central Europe. The best time to catch some of that sunshine is in the summer, when both temperatures and tourism are at a peak. July and August tend to be the most warm and sunny months, but mild temperatures usually hold from early May to the end of October.

Hotel rates are reduced during the off-season, but no other special advantages await tourists in winter. All the attractions of Budapest continue year-round. Even the theatrical and operatic season keep going in the summer at open-air locations.

Average monthly temperatures in Budapest:

	J	F	M	A	M	J	J	A	S	O	N	
°F	27	34	43	54	63	68	72	72	64	52	43	3
°C		− 3	1	6	12	17	20	22	22	18	11	6

Planning Your Budget

To give you an idea of what to expect, here's a list of some average prices in Hungarian forints—Ft. (except in those cases where prices are normally quoted in U.S. dollars). They can only be regarded as *approximate,* however, as inflation pushes the cost of living ever higher.

Airport transfer. Taxi to central Budapest Ft. 230–260, airline bus Ft. 20.

Camping. Daily rate per person with car and tent or caravan (trailer) Ft. 100–200.

Car hire. $22–55 per day plus $0.25–0.50 per kilometre.

Cigarettes (per packet of 20). Hungarian Ft. 20–40, Western (made in Hungary under licence) Ft. 40–60, Western (imported) Ft. 80–90.

Entertainment. Theatre and opera tickets from Ft. 400, discotheque Ft. 70–100, nightclub (minimum) Ft. 500 per person.

Excursions. Half-day $10, full-day up to $40.

Hairdresser. Woman's haircut from Ft. 150, shampoo and set or blow-dry from Ft. 300, permanent wave from Ft. 300. Man's haircut from Ft. 100.

Hotels (double room with bath and breakfast). ***** $140, *** $60, * $30.

Meals and drinks. Lunch in moderate restaurant approx. Ft. 200, in expensive restaurant approx. Ft. 1,400. Dinner à la carte, moderate approx. Ft. 350, expensive approx. Ft. 1,700. Bottle of wine Ft. 140–550, beer Ft. 40–70, soft drink or mineral water Ft. 18–55.

Museum entry. From Ft. 20.

Supermarket. Bread Ft. 13 per kilo, litre of milk Ft. 15, butter Ft. 28 for 250 grams, cheese Ft. 75–150 per kilo, instant coffee (imported) Ft. 150 for 50 grams, salami Ft. 350 per kilo, eggs Ft. 28–30 per dozen. (Prices vary according to the season.)

Transport. City bus Ft. 3, tram Ft. 2, metro Ft. 2. Sample taxi fares: Castle District to Heroes' Square (Hősök tere) Ft. 75, Vigadó tér to Opera Ft. 45.

An A–Z Summary of Practical Information and Facts

> A star (*) following an entry indicates that relevant prices are to be found on page 105.
> Listed after many entries is the appropriate Hungarian translation, usually in the singular, plus a number of phrases that should help you when seeking assistance.

A **ACCOMMODATION.** See also CAMPING. It's prudent to book accommodation well in advance, for rooms are often in short supply. The tightest season is the summer, but crowds also descend for trade fairs, exhibitions and major international conferences when you might not expect them. If you arrive without a reservation, though, all is not lost. Tourist information or travel agency offices at the airport, railway stations and border-crossing points can usually arrange for accommodation—in a private home if all else fails.

Hotels* *(szálloda)* are graded by the star system: a five-star hotel is truly luxurious, and a one-star budget hotel has few amenities. Except for the very top international hotels in Budapest, don't expect air conditioning, swimming pools or saunas. Most hotels in the three-to-five star class have their own shopping arcades, tourist agency and airline offices and a variety of sightseeing programmes. Hotel rates drop by as much as 30% outside the summer tourist season.

Accommodation in **private homes**—a room with or without breakfast, or a self-contained **flat**—can be booked through travel agencies in Budapest and other towns. The rates in Budapest are about the same as those of moderate hotels, but lower in the country.

The equivalent of English "Bed and Breakfast" establishments are found along major roads and in holiday centres. Often the sign *Szoba kiadó* is supplemented by its German equivalent, *Fremdenzimmer*. You don't need a travel agency or reservation; just knock on the door.

I'd like a single room/ double room.	**Egyágyas/Kétágyas szobát kérek.**
with bath/with shower	**fürdőszobával/zuhanyozóval**
What's the daily rate?	**Mibe kerül naponta?**

AIRPORT* *(repülőtér)*. All international flights operate from Buda- **A** pest's Ferihegy Airport, the country's only commercial airfield; there are no domestic flights at all. Among the facilities at Ferihegy: porters, baggage trolleys, currency exchange desks, accommodation and car hire desks, a news-stand, a buffet and restaurant, a post office with international telegraph service and a duty-free shop. Terminal 1 serves foreign airlines, while Terminal 2 is reserved for the use of MALÉV, the Hungarian national airline.

It takes half an hour to travel from the airport to the centre of Budapest. MALÉV operates an airport bus service between Ferihegy (on the south-east outskirts of Budapest) and the Engels tér bus terminal (platform 1):

Ferihegy–Budapest centre, every half hour from 6 a.m. to 10.30 p.m.
Budapest centre–Ferihegy, every half hour from 5 a.m. to 10 p.m.

Where do I get the bus to the city centre/to the airport?	**Hol a buszmegálló a városközpont felé/a repülőtér felé?**

BABY-SITTERS. Except for the luxury hotels, which can usually **B** arrange for baby-sitters and provide cots, highchairs, etc., this could be a problem, since no organized sitter service exists in Hungary. It may come to mobilizing one of the hotel maids or a friend of the desk clerk, and there may well be a language problem.

Can you get me/us a baby-sitter for tonight?	**Tudna nekem/nekünk biztosítani ma estére egy baby-sittert?**

CAMPING* *(kemping)*. Budapest has two large camping grounds, but **C** the country's biggest concentration of sites is around Lake Balaton. All told there are more than 200 campsites in Hungary. They are generally open between May 1 and the end of September. Each site is graded according to international standards. The top (three-star) sites have more facilities, a larger area for each family, and tents and cabins for hire.

A list of the major campsites and their facilities—from supermarkets and currency exchange offices to beaches and night-clubs—along with a detailed map is issued by the Hungarian Camping and Caravanning Club *(Magyar Camping és Caravanning Club—MCCC)*:

Üllői út 6, H-1088 Budapest VIII.; tel. 336-536

CAR HIRE*. See also DRIVING. Hiring a car in Hungary involves no special problems; arrangements and conditions are similar to those encountered elsewhere. The minimum age requirement is 21, and the driver should be in possession of a valid licence, held for at least one **107**

C year. A deposit has to be paid, though this is normally waived for holders of accepted credit cards. Bills must be settled in hard currency. All cars are insured, but supplementary coverage is available at an extra charge. By advance arrangement the car may be dropped off at another Hungarian town or in another country for an extra fee.

Although international car hire firms do not operate directly in Hungary, both Hertz and Avis have arrangements with Hungarian state agencies like Cooptourist and Volántourist. Cars, with or without drivers, may be booked either directly through these agencies or through travel bureaux in hotels, at the airport, etc.

I'd like to hire a car.	**Egy kocsit szeretnék bérelni.**
large/small	**nagy/kis**

CIGARETTES, CIGARS, TOBACCO* *(cigaretta, szivar, dohány).* Shops called *Dohánybolt* or *Trafik* stock tobacco products, as do most hotels and supermarkets. A wide range of cigarettes from Hungary and neighbouring countries are available at relatively low prices. Intertourist shops sell hard-to-get foreign brands for hard currency.

Restrictions on smoking cover most public places, including all cinemas, theatres and concert halls. Smoking is banned on public transport, including the ticket and waiting-room areas of railway stations. But long-distance trains have some smoking carriages.

I'd like a packet of cigarettes.	**Kérek egy csomag cigarettát.**
filter-tipped	**filteres**
without filter	**filter nélküli**
A box of matches, please.	**Egy doboz gyufát kérek.**

CLIMATE and CLOTHING. Hungary's vaunted temperate climate is subject to fluctuation. While the average July temperature may look flawless at 20°C (68°F), the mercury can lurch into tropical swelter or down to a very brisk chill with little warning. So summer visitors should pack for all eventualities. Raincoats may also be useful some summer nights. In winter, be prepared for snow and bracing cold.

As for formality, a certain Middle European seriousness persists, though there are no definite rules. Evening gowns and dark suits are standard at the Opera House, but jeans are also acceptable. On warm summer days, jackets and ties are abandoned in most areas of life. Headwaiters don't discriminate against informally dressed clients. For official or business meetings, suits are appropriate but by no means
108 essential.

Post offices *(postahivatal)*. Local post offices are usually open from 8 a.m. to 5 p.m., Monday to Friday, and until noon or 1 p.m. on Saturdays. Main post offices operate from 7 p.m. until 8 p.m., Monday to Saturday.

Post offices handle mail, telephone, telegraph and telex services, but not international money transfers. Stamps *(bélyeg)* can also be bought at tobacconists or where postcards are sold. Postboxes are painted red and usually decorated with a hunting horn.

The use of poste-restante (general-delivery) service is not widespread in Hungary. It's better to have letters addressed to your hotel or, if your exact plans are uncertain, to your embassy.

Telephone *(telefon)*, **telegrams** *(távirat)* **and telex.** Call boxes (telephone booths) for local calls are usually green-and-yellow or white, while those for international calls are red. Illustrated, self-explanatory instructions are posted. Long-distance and international calls are best made through your hotel switchboard or at a post office.

A modern international telecommunications centre with all telephone, telegraph and telex services operates at the corner of Petőfi Sándor utca and Martinelli tér (Budapest V.) from 7 a.m. to 8 p.m., Monday to Friday, and until 7 p.m. on Saturdays, with limited service on Sunday mornings and public holidays.

Directory enquiries in foreign languages, tel. 172-200

express (special delivery)	**expressz küldemény**
registered	**ajánlott**
airmail	**légiposta**
I'd like a stamp for this letter/ this postcard, please.	**Kérek egy bélyeget erre a levélre/ a képeslapra.**
I'd like to send a telegram.	**Táviratot szeretnék feladni.**

COMPLAINTS. Every establishment in Hungary has a "complaint book" *(vásárlók könyve)* on the premises, but problems are resolved slowly through such channels. It's much wiser to try to sort out any difficulties face-to-face with the manager. Above all, relax and keep your temper in check. Threats will get you nowhere, while patient good humour is always a good policy.

C

CONVERTER CHARTS. For fluid and distance measures, see pp. 113/114. Hungary uses the metric system. The only slight variation from standard European practice is that most products in food markets are sold and labelled in dekagrams rather than grams (10 dekagrams = 100 grams = $3^1/_2$ ounces).

Temperature

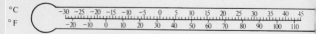

Length

Weight

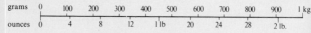

CRIME and THEFT. Though violent crime is rare in Hungary, visitors ought to take elementary precautions to protect their property. This means locking car doors and hotel rooms. When you park your car, place valuables out of sight or lock them in the luggage compartment. Don't leave jewellery, money or documents in your hotel room; use the hotel's safe instead.

CUSTOMS *(vám)* **and ENTRY REGULATIONS.** See also DRIVING. Everyone needs a valid passport to visit Hungary. In addition (except for citizens of Finland, Austria and the socialist countries), everyone needs a visa. This may be obtained through travel agents or direct from any Hungarian diplomatic mission—it usually takes less than 48 hours. If you haven't the time or inclination, you can arrive without a visa and be issued one at the frontier or airport (but train passengers must have visas in advance). Visas are generally valid for a maximum 30-day visit, which can be extended.

Green and red customs channels are provided at the airport. If you have nothing to declare, use the green lane (spot checks do take place). Here are the main items you may take into Hungary duty-free and, upon your return home, into your own country:

Into:	Cigarettes		Cigars		Tobacco	Spirits		Wine
Hungary	250	or	50	or	250 g.	1 l.	and	2 l.
Australia	200	or	250 g	or	250 g.	1 l.	or	1 l.
Canada	200	and	50	and	900 g.	1.1 l.	or	1.1 l.
Eire	200	or	50	or	250 g.	1 l.	and	2 l.
N. Zealand	200	or	50	or	250 g.	1 l.	and	4.5 l.
S. Africa	400	and	50	and	250 g.	1 l.	and	2 l.
U.K.	200	or	50	or	250 g.	1 l.	and	2 l.
U.S.A.	200	and	100	and	*	1 l.	or	1 l.

* a reasonable quantity.

Among the items forbidden: narcotics, explosives, weapons, and materials deemed obscene or ideologically subversive.

Currency restrictions. Visitors may be required to report the currencies they're carrying, though there is no limit on the foreign funds permitted. As for Hungarian currency, it is forbidden to arrive with or to take out more than 100 forints. Note that there is a restriction on the amount of forints that may be re-exchanged when leaving the country.

Registration. If you're staying at a hotel, campsite or officially recognized guest accommodation, registration will be done automatically. (You'll have to leave your passport at the hotel desk overnight.) But if you stay in unofficial private accommodation, your host is responsible for having you registered within 48 hours.

Leaving Hungary. The customs officer may ask what you're taking out of the country in the way of commodities and currencies (see also VAT below). Keep handy all sales slips and currency exchange receipts. Aside from museum-worthy antiques and works of art, which require special permits for export, the only customs problem which might surprise you concerns food: you can take out of Hungary only enough food to be used during your travels, for a maximum of three days, including no more than 500 grams of any one kind of food. Salami hoarders beware! For full details on the ins and outs of customs regulations, see the leaflets available at travel agencies and hotels.

C **VAT.** VAT (sales tax) of 25% is included in the purchase price of most goods in Hungary. Foreign tourists buying a minimum 25,000-forint worth of goods in one shop at one time can demand a VAT certificate, have it stamped at the border customs and claim back the VAT amount in hard currency—providing they can prove with exchange receipts that they have changed their hard currency to forint in excess of their purchases.

I have nothing to declare. **Nincs elvámolni valóm.**

D **DRIVING IN HUNGARY**

To take your car into Hungary you need: passport and visa; valid driving licence; car registration papers; adequate insurance.

Cars from most European countries are automatically considered to be fully insured, with these exceptions: vehicles from France, Italy, Portugal, Spain, Greece, Turkey and Iceland, which must carry proof of insurance ("green card").

Driving regulations. Cars must be fitted with a nationality plate or sticker and rubber mudguards. You are required to carry a set of spare bulbs, a first-aid kit and a red warning triangle for display in case of an accident or breakdown. The driver and front-seat passenger must use seat belts; children under six are prohibited from travelling in the front seat. Drivers and passengers of motorcycles and scooters have to wear crash helmets. It is not permitted to lend a foreign-registered car to anyone, be it a Hungarian resident or another tourist.

Drive on the right and pass on the left. Hungary's accident rate is one of Europe's highest. Drive with special vigilance until you've had time to take the measure of the local drivers. At road crossings where signs indicate no priorities, the vehicle on the right has the right of way. Pedestrians have the right of way at pedestrian crossings, marked with white stripes. (If you're a pedestrian, don't count on it!) In built-up areas, blowing the horn is forbidden except, of course, if it helps prevent an accident. At night and when visibility is poor, headlights should be dipped. On any road except a motorway (expressway), be alert for unexpected obstacles—livestock, horse-drawn wagons and bicycles, for instance. These can pose a real danger.

Hungary's expanding motorway system is well maintained and toll-free. Yellow emergency telephones, for use in case of breakdown or accident, are spaced every 2 kilometres (1¼ miles) along the **112** Budapest–Balaton expressway.

Speed limits. Limits are 100–120 kilometres per hour (60–75 mph) on motorways, 80 kph (50 mph) on country roads and 60 kph (37 mph) within residential areas. Limits are lower for buses, heavy lorries, cars towing caravans (trailers) and motorcycles.

The police are strict about speeding. You could be fined 300 forints on the spot for exceeding the limit, with considerably higher penalties for what's considered dangerous speeding.

Alcohol. In Hungary, drinking and driving are totally, dangerously incompatible. The permissible limit for blood alcohol content is zero; even a glass of beer rings the bell. The law is especially severe on anyone causing an accident while under the influence of alcohol, and on hit-and-run drivers. Foreigners receive no leniency in these cases. Otherwise, the traffic police are very helpful and considerate to foreign tourists.

Fuel and oil *(benzin; olaj)*. Filling stations are distributed along the motorways and main roads at intervals of 10 to 30 kilometres. On minor roads, they are up to 50 kilometres apart. Stations are usually open from 6 a.m. to 10 p.m. All-night service is available at all Shell and at some major ÁFOR stations. Fuel generally comes in three octane ratings—98, 92, 86—and unleaded (rare). Brands available are ÁFOR, AGIP, BP and Shell. Most service stations will change your oil or wash your car, but they are rarely equipped for handling repairs.

Fluid measures

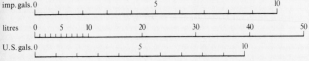

Parking. The use of meters is widespread in central Budapest. Most allow parking at will, but in the area of greatest congestion, bright red 60-minute meters have been installed. Elsewhere in urban areas, there are automatic parking-ticket vending-machines, or you may be approached by parking attendants who collect a fee and issue official receipts. If you leave your car in a prohibited zone so as to impede traffic, it will quickly be towed away by the police.

Road signs and signposts. Standard international pictographs relate information and warnings on all Hungarian roads. Motorways are indicated by green signs, all other main roads by dark blue.

D **Distances.** Here are some approximate road distances in kilometres between Budapest and some regional centres and border-crossing points of interest to users of this guide:

Balatonfüred	130	Rábafüzes	250
Esztergom	60	Siófok	105
Hegyeshalom	170	Sopron	210
Keszthely	155	Visegrád	45

To convert kilometres to miles:

km	0	1	2	3	4	5	6	8	10	12	14	16
miles	0	½	1	1½	2	3	4	5	6	7	8	9	10

Breakdowns/Accidents. Remember to put out the red warning triangle 50 yards behind your car. Accidents must be reported—to the police in case of personal injury. The "yellow angels" of the Hungarian Automobile Club *(Magyar Autóklub)* come to the rescue of any driver in distress on any major road. They do on-the-spot repairs—free for members of affiliated auto clubs. But finding spare parts for Western-made cars can be a problem of availability as well as of price. The Automobile Club also offers a wide range of services—information, insurance, reservations, guided tours, legal advice. The Club's headquarters is at:

Budapest II., Rómer Flóris u. 4/a; tel. 152-040

For breakdown service in Budapest, telephone 260-668

Full tank, please.	**Kérem, töltse tele a tankot.**
Check the oil/the tires/	**Ellenőrizze az olajat/a**
the battery, please.	**gumikat/az akkumulátort.**
I've had a breakdown.	**Meghibásodott a kocsim.**
There's been an accident.	**Baleset történt.**
Can I park here?	**Szabad itt parkolnom?**

E **ELECTRIC CURRENT.** Throughout Hungary the current is 220-volt, 50-cycle A.C. Plugs are the standard continental type, for which British and North American appliances need an adaptor.

EMBASSIES and CONSULATES *(nagykövetség; konzulátus)*

Canada	Budapest II., Budakeszi út 32; tel. 767-711
Great Britain	Budapest V., Harmincad u. 6; tel. 182-888
U.S.A.	Budapest V., Szabadság tér 12; tel. 124-224

EMERGENCIES. See also EMBASSIES AND CONSULATES, HEALTH AND MEDICAL CARE, POLICE, etc.

Emergency telephone numbers throughout Hungary:

Ambulance	04
Fire	05
Police	07

GUIDES and INTERPRETERS *(idegenvezető; tolmács)*. Guides/ interpreters can be hired by the day or half-day through travel agencies in Budapest. These guides, however, may not be qualified to handle the more difficult linguistic problems that arise in certain business or technical discussions. State organizations dealing with foreigners usually provide staff interpreters for such occasions.

We'd like an English-/French-/ German-speaking guide.

Egy angolul/franciául/németül beszélő idegenvezetőt kérünk.

HAIRDRESSERS and BARBERS* *(fodrász; borbély)*. Even in small neighbourhood shops the service is expert and accommodating... and very cheap by Western standards. "First-class" establishments in the luxury hotels charge only slightly higher prices. Tipping is customary; give about 15%.

haircut	**hajvágás**
shampoo and set	**mosás és berakás**
shampoo and blow-dry	**mosás és szárítás**
permanent wave	**tartós hullám**
colour rinse	**festés**
manicure	**kézápolás**
Not too short.	**Ne nagyon rövidre.**
A little more off (here).	**(Itt) Egy kicsit többet kérek levágni.**

HEALTH and MEDICAL CARE. Many visitors come to Budapest from abroad to regain their health at the therapeutic baths which make this one of the leading European spa cities. But if an accident or sudden illness should interfere with your holiday, the Hungarian National Health Service (abbreviated *Sz.T.K.*) and the emergency squad *(Mentők)* are well equipped to handle any unexpected problems. Most Hungarian doctors and dentists also have private practices.

H To find one, ask at your hotel desk or at your consulate, which will have a list of local doctors who speak your language.

It is perfectly safe to drink tap water *(csapvíz)* in Budapest.

Pharmacies. Look for the sign *gyógyszertár* or *patika*. In Hungary these shops sell only pharmaceutical and related products—not the wide assortment of goods available in their British or American counterparts. (For toiletries and cosmetics, go to an *illatszerbolt;* for photo supplies, to a *fotószaküzlet.*)

Several Budapest pharmacies stay open round the clock. Their addresses are always displayed on an illuminated sign in the window of every other pharmacy.

Where's the nearest pharmacy?	**Hol a legközelebbi patika?**
I need a doctor/dentist.	**Orvosra/Fogorvosra van szükségem.**
I have a pain here.	**Itt érzek fájdalmat.**
headache	**fejfájás**
stomach ache	**gyomorfájás**
a fever	**láz**
a cold	**megfázás**

HITCH-HIKING *(autóstop).* Public transport in Hungary is good and cheap so there's not much cause for hitch-hiking. It is not illegal, but not encouraged, either.

HOURS. See also COMMUNICATIONS and MONEY MATTERS. Most shops are open from 10 a.m. (some food shops from 6 or 7 a.m.) to 6 p.m., Monday to Friday, and until 2 p.m. on Saturdays. Only a few establishments—mostly tobacconists, florists and pastry shops—stay open on Sundays. Department stores operate from 9 a.m. to 7 p.m., Monday to Friday, and until 2 p.m. on Saturdays. Many local stores are open until 7 p.m. on Thursdays.

Hairdressers work from as early as 6 or 7 a.m. to as late as 9 p.m., Monday to Friday, until 4 p.m. on Saturdays.

Museums generally are open from 10 a.m. to 6 p.m., daily except Mondays and certain holidays (admission free on Saturdays). Some small museums operate fewer hours, so it's best to check before you go.

L **LANGUAGE.** Hungarian, which is totally unrelated to the languages of surrounding countries, is the mother tongue of more than 95% of the population. The people speak very clearly, without slurs or swallowed sounds; since every word is stressed on the first syllable, a sort of monotone often ensues.

By far the most widely known foreign language is German. A minority of Hungarians (mostly the younger generation) know English, and even fewer know some French. All Hungarians study Russian for four years in secondary school.

The Berlitz phrase book HUNGARIAN FOR TRAVELLERS covers most of the situations you are likely to encounter in Hungary.

To get you started, here are the most commonly noted signs you'll see:

bejárat	entrance
eladó	for sale
húzni	pull
kijárat	exit
műemlék	monument
nyitva	open
tilos	prohibited
tólni	push
zárva	closed

And a phrase or two:

Do you speak English/French/German?	**Beszél Ön angolul/franciául/németül?**
Good morning	**Jó reggelt**
Good afternoon	**Jó napot**
Good evening	**Jó estét**
Good night	**Jó éjszakát**
Thank you	**Köszönöm**

LAUNDRY and DRY-CLEANING *(mosoda; vegytisztító).* Hotels usually take care of laundry and cleaning problems with dispatch. If you're staying elsewhere, look for the sign *Patyolat,* which indicates an establishment handling both laundry and dry-cleaning. The larger shops may offer express service.

When will it be ready?	**Mikor lesz kész?**
I must have this for tomorrow morning.	**Erre holnap reggelre van szükségem.**

LOST PROPERTY. A central bureau, Talált Tárgyak Központi Hivatala, deals with lost-and-found problems:

Budapest V., Engels tér 5; tel. 174-961

L A separate office handles property found on vehicles of the Budapest public-transport system:

Budapest VII., Akácfa utca 18; tel. 226-613

| I've lost my wallet/my handbag/ my passport. | **Elvesztettem az irattárcámat/ a kézitáskámat/az útlevelemet.** |

M **MAPS.** Travel bureaux give out free maps of Hungary and Budapest. Maps with much more detail, including bus and tram routes, the locations of all theatres, restaurants and public buildings, are sold a news-stands and bookstores. The maps in this book were prepared by Cartographia of Budapest.

| I'd like a street map. | **Egy várostérképet kérnék.** |
| I'd like a road map of this region. | **Egy erre a vidékre vonatkozó térképet kérnék.** |

MEETING PEOPLE. Hungarians are open and friendly. They are so helpful to foreigners that, if you unfold a map on the street, they may give you directions whether you're lost or not. Because their language is so outlandish, they are genuinely delighted when a foreigner attempts to say a few words in Hungarian.

As for formalities, there is a lot of hand-shaking and kissing on the cheek, and men are still seen to kiss the hand of a lady.

MONEY MATTERS

Currency. The Hungarian *forint* (abbreviated *Ft.*) is divided into 100 *fillér (f)*.

Coins: 10, 20 and 50 f and Ft. 1, 2, 5, 10 and 20.
Banknotes: Ft. 10, 20, 50, 100, 500 and 1,000.

For details of restrictions on import of Hungarian currency, see CUSTOMS AND ENTRY REGULATIONS.

Banks and currency exchange. Official foreign-exchange facilities are found in most banks, hotels and motels, at larger campsites, at travel agencies and in some department stores. The currency-exchange office of the Central European International Bank is situated in Aranykéz utca, in the passage, facing the bank proper.

Banking hours are generally from 9 a.m. to 5 p.m., Monday to Friday, and 9 a.m. to 2 p.m. on Saturdays.

Remember to take your passport with you, and be sure to keep all eceipts. To reconvert forints into foreign currency when you leave Hungary, you must show the relevant receipt. For VAT regulations, ee p. 112.

It is illegal to sell foreign currency to private citizens; don't be empted by generous offers in the street—you risk being cheated.

Credit cards and traveller's cheques. Many tourist-oriented establishments—hotels, restaurants, shops, travel agencies—are geared to accept international credit cards; you'll see the signs on the door. Traveller's cheques and Eurocheques are also easy to cash. Some shops, such as Intertourist branches, deal *only* in foreign currency transactions, accepting cash, traveller's cheques and credit cards.

I want to change some pounds/dollars.	**Fontot/Dollárt szeretnék beváltani.**
Do you accept traveller's cheques?	**Traveller's csekket elfogadnak?**
Can I pay with this credit card?	**Ezzel a hitelkártyával fizethetek?**

NEWSPAPERS and MAGAZINES *(újság; folyóirat).* The Hungarian news agency MTI publishes a daily (except Sunday and Monday) bilingual English-German paper, *Daily News/Neueste Nachrichten,* displayed at most hotels and on almost every news-stand in Budapest. Widely available, as well, are the newspapers of foreign communist parties.

Kiosks in the capital sell a selection of Western newspapers and magazines, including the *Times* of London, the *International Herald Tribune* (edited in Paris), and the weeklies *Time* and *Newsweek.* Newspapers from the West arrive with one day's delay.

A free monthly magazine, *Programme in Hungary,* has parallel texts in German, English and French.

The journal *New Hungarian Quarterly,* published in English, offers profound insights into Hungarian life, culture and politics.

Have you any English-language newspapers?	**Van angolnyelvű újságjuk?**

PHOTOGRAPHY. Hungarian shops sell international brands of film but by no means always what you need in size or type. To be sure you don't run out of your preferred brand, it's wise to carry an adequate supply from home. Film can be processed in Budapest but not very rapidly, so it's usually better to take your exposed film home for development.

The Hungarians are easy about being photographed, but use sense concerning what, who, when and where. All military installations and

P other sensitive places are advertised by "no photography" warning signs.

Some airport security machines use X-rays which can ruin you film. Ask that it be checked separately, or enclose it in a lead-lined bag.

I'd like some film for this camera.	**Ehhez a géphez kérnék filmet.**
black-and-white film	**fekete fehér film**
colour prints	**színes kópiák**
colour slides	**színes diák**
35-mm	**harmincöt milliméter**
super-8	**szuper nyolcas**
How long will it take to develop this film?	**Meddig tart előhívni ezt a filmet?**
May I take a picture?	**Lefényképezhetem?**

POLICE *(rendőrség)*. See also EMERGENCIES. Police wear blue and-grey uniforms. Traffic police and highway patrols dress similarl, but with white caps and white leather accessories to make them more visible. Police cars are blue and white. There is no special police uni detailed to deal with tourist enquiries but the police in general are helpful to foreigners.

Where is the nearest police station?	**Hol a legközelebbi rendőrség?**

PUBLIC HOLIDAYS *(hivatalos ünnep)*

January 1	*Újév*	New Year's Day
April 4	*A felszabadulás ünnepe*	Liberation Day
May 1	*A munka ünnepe*	Labour Day
August 20	*Az alkotmány napja*	Constitution Day
November 7	*A forradalom ünnepe*	Revolution Day
December 25	*Karácsony első napja*	Christmas Day
December 26	*Karácsony második napja*	Boxing Day
Movable date:	*Húsvét hétfő*	Easter Monday

Are you open tomorrow?	**Holnap nyitva tartanak?**

R **RADIO and TV.** Very brief news bulletins for foreigners are broad cast, in summer only, on Budapest Radio and on TV.

Hungarian television broadcasts in colour on two channels, daily except most Mondays. On Channel 2 some imported programmes are transmitted in the original language or, for instance, a Shakespearean play in Hungarian might also have English subtitles. Both radio and television carry bundles of commercials from time to time.

To catch up with the news, you'll need a transistor radio powerful enough to pick up European stations on medium wave at night, or the short-wave transmissions of Voice of America, the BBC, Radio Canada International, etc.

RELIGIOUS SERVICES *(istentisztelet)*. The great majority of Hungarians are Roman Catholics. Other religions are also represented, most notably Protestant, Eastern Orthodox and Jewish. While most churches are open to the public, there are no services expressly for foreigners. If you visit a historic church for sightseeing purposes while a service is in progress, stay in the rear of the building so as not to disturb the worshippers.

TIME DIFFERENCES. Hungary follows Central European Time, GMT + 1. In summer, the clock is put one hour ahead (GMT + 2).

Summer chart:

New York	London	**Budapest**	Jo'burg	Sydney	Auckland
6 a.m.	11 a.m.	**noon**	noon	8 p.m.	10 p.m.

What time is it, please?   **Hány óra?**

TIPPING. Have no fear of giving offence if you offer a tip: the old custom survives in Hungary, and gratuities are expected by a wide assortment of service personnel, as well as taxi drivers and gypsy violinists. There are no iron-clad formulae for the appropriate amount to give, but waiters and taxi drivers normally get 10%, barbers and women's hairdressers 15%. Here are some further suggestions to save the embarrassment of under- or over-tipping:

Porter, per bag	Ft. 25
Bellboy, errand	Ft. 20
Maid, per week	Ft. 100
Doorman, hails cab	Ft. 20

T

Hat-check	Ft. 20
Lavatory attendant	Ft. 10
Gypsy violinist, for personal attention	Ft. 100
Tourist guide (half-day)	Ft. 200
Theatre usher	add Ft. 5–10 to programme for sale
Filling station attendant	round up amount on pump (+ Ft. 10 for checking air and oil, Ft. 5 for cleaning windscreen)

Keep the change.　　　　　　　　　**A többi a magáé.**

TOILETS. Budapest is well supplied with public conveniences—in metro stations, parks and squares, museums and, of course, in hotels, restaurants and cafés. The sign may point to *mosdó* or *W.C.* (pronounced *vay*-tsay), and if pictures don't indicate which room is which, you'll have to remember that *férfi* means "men" and *női* means "women".

Where are the toilets?　　　　　　　**Hol a W.C.?**

TOURIST INFORMATION OFFICES *(turista információs iroda).* The Hungarian travel company IBUSZ has offices in some 15 foreign cities, providing information, tour bookings, etc. Among them:

Great Britain　Danube Travel Ltd., General Agent IBUSZ-Hungary, 6, Conduit Street, London W1R 9TG; tel. (01) 493-0263

U.S.A.　IBUSZ Hungarian Travel Ltd., Suite 500, 630 Fifth Avenue, Rockefeller Center, New York, NY 10020; tel. (212) 582-7412

In Budapest and in all tourist areas, IBUSZ and competing travel agencies such as Budapest Tourist, Cooptourist, Siótour and Volántourist, as well as all regional travel agencies, run networks of offices handling money exchange, housing problems, excursions and general information. They are found in and near hotels, railway stations, busy shopping areas and at the airport. Many are open during normal office hours, but in summer the more important units stay open until 8 or even 10 p.m.

Tourinform. The Hungarian Tourinform service, situated at Sütő utca 2 in central Budapest, provides information on accommodation, entertainment and other tourist information in English, French, German, Russian and Spanish. You can also call 179–800 in Budapest to obtain answers to your questions. If you prefer to write, contact Tourinform, P.O.B. 185, 1364 Budapest.

The Tourinform service operates from 7 a.m. to 9 p.m., Monday to Friday, to 8 p.m. on Saturdays and from 8 a.m. to 1 p.m. on Sundays.

Where's there a tourist office?   **Hol találok turista irodát?**

TRANSPORT*. The Budapest Transport Company *(Budapesti Közlekedési Vállalat—BKV)* operates a comprehensive public transport service which commuters of almost any city might envy: fast, clean and stunningly cheap. No place in Budapest is more than 500 metres from a bus, tram, trolley bus or metro stop. Maps of all the lines, both surface and underground, are sold at major stations.

Buses *(busz).* Blue Ikarus buses, made in Hungary, cover some 450 miles on more than 200 routes in Budapest. A bus stop is marked by a blue-bordered rectangular sign with the silhouette of a bus and the letter "M"—for *megálló*. At most stops a sketch map of the route, a list of the stops, the hours of operation and even the minimum and maximum number of minutes between buses are posted. You must have a blue ticket *before* you board a bus. Automatic dispensers sell them at major bus stops and pedestrian subways, or you can buy them at metro change booths, travel bureaux and tobacco shops. Inside the bus, validate your ticket in one of the red punching devices near the doors; keep the serial number facing up. Then hold onto your ticket in case an inspector should ask for it. Though you'll see very few passengers punching tickets, it doesn't mean they're dishonest; the majority buy cheap monthly passes allowing unlimited travel. Signal at the door when you want to get off.

Trolley buses *(trolibusz).* To save fuel, these lines are being expanded. But they still constitute only a tiny proportion of the whole municipal system. Use a yellow tram ticket.

Trams *(villamos).* Yellow trams or streetcars, usually in trains of three or four, cover a 120-mile network. Ten of the 50 tram lines run all night. You need a yellow tram ticket which you must validate on board. The same tickets also serve on the suburban railway within the city limits, and the original Millenary underground (subway) line, now called metro No. 1.

T **Underground** (*földalatti* or *metró*). Underground (subway) line No. 1, the Millenary line, was opened in 1896—the first in continental Europe. It operates modern tram-like cars and requires a yellow tram ticket. The new metro lines, 2 and 3, use Soviet wide-gauge trains. Some of the stations are quite spacious and splendid. All three lines converge at Deák tér, but there is no free transfer.

Trains (*vonat*). There are three suburban commuter lines *(HÉV)*, of which the Batthyányi tér to Szentendre route is of interest to tourists. When you want to get off one of these trains you have to slide the door open by hand. It closes again automatically.

Inter-city trains run by Hungarian State Railways *(Magyar Állam-vasutak—MÁV)* operate from three Budapest stations—the historic Keleti (East) and Nyugati (West) stations and the spacious modern Déli (South) terminal. First- and second-class tickets are sold, as well as rail passes good for seven or ten days of unlimited travel within Hungary. (Train compartments are marked 1 and 2.)

Taxis. Metered vehicles both state-owned and private serve Budapest, mostly from taxi ranks near the big hotels, metro and train stations. They can also be hailed on the street when the roof sign saying "Taxi" is lit. Taxis can also be summoned by phone: 222-222 or 666-666. Private taxis are usually cleaner and the drivers, more polite.

If you're going beyond the city limits you'll be charged the return fare to the boundary line. Tips are customary.

Boats. Motor launches ply the Budapest section of the Danube from about 9 a.m. to 8 p.m. daily during the tourist season. Bus tickets are used. Among the principal stations are Gellért tér, Batthyányi tér and Petőfi tér, and there are several stops on Margaret Island. Sightseeing excursion boats operate from Vigadó tér, from where boats and hydrofoils leave for Visegrád and Esztergom,

I want a ticket to …	**Kérek egy jegyet … -ba/-be/-ra/ -re*.**
single (one-way)	**egy útra**
return (round-trip)	**oda-vissza**
first/second class	**első/másod osztály**
Will you tell me when to get off?	**Megmondaná, hol szálljak ki?**

---

* In Hungarian, prepositions are replaced by suffixes. Choose one that sounds harmonious with the place name.

SOME USEFUL EXPRESSIONS

yes/no	**igen/nem**
please/thank you	**kérem/köszönöm**
excuse me	**bocsásson meg**
where/when/how	**hol/mikor/hogy**
yesterday/today/tomorrow	**tegnap/ma/holnap**
day/week/month/year	**nap/hét/hónap/év**
left/right	**bal/jobb**
big/small	**nagy/kicsi**
cheap/expensive	**olcsó/drága**
hot/cold	**meleg/hideg**
open/closed	**nyitva/zárva**
free (vacant)/occupied	**szabad/foglalt**
Does anyone here speak English/French/German?	**Van itt valaki aki angolul/franciául/németül beszél?**
I don't understand.	**Nem értem.**
Please write it down.	**Kérem, írja ezt le.**
Waiter!/Waitress!	**Pincér!/Pincérnő!**
I'd like ...	**Kérnék ...**
Just a minute.	**Egy pillanat.**
Help me, please.	**Segítsen kérem.**

NUMBERS

0	**nulla**	13	**tizenhárom**	40	**negyven**
1	**egy**	14	**tizennégy**	50	**ötven**
2	**kettő**	15	**tizenöt**	60	**hatvan**
3	**három**	16	**tizenhat**	70	**hetven**
4	**négy**	17	**tizenhét**	80	**nyolcvan**
5	**öt**	18	**tizennyolc**	90	**kilencven**
6	**hat**	19	**tizenkilenc**	100	**egyszáz**
7	**hét**	20	**húsz**	101	**százegy**
8	**nyolc**	21	**huszonegy**	200	**kettőszáz**
9	**kilenc**	22	**huszonkettő**	300	**háromszáz**
10	**tíz**	23	**huszonhárom**	500	**ötszáz**
11	**tizenegy**	30	**harminc**	1,000	**egyezer**
12	**tizenkettő**	31	**harmincegy**	2,000	**kétezer**

Index

An asterisk (*) next to a page number indicates a map reference.

INDEX

126

Selection of Budapest Hotels and Restaurants

Where do you start? Choosing a hotel or restaurant in
place you're not familiar with can be daunting. To help you fin
your way amid the bewildering variety, we have made
selection of the best options in Budapest and the Lake Balato
area.

Our own Berlitz criteria have been price and location. In th
hotel section, for a double room with bath without breakfas
higher-priced means above Fts. 6,000.00; medium-priced Ft
2,900.00 to Fts. 6,000.00; lower-priced about Fts. 2,500.00 t
Fts. 2,900.00. Special features where applicable, plus regula
business hours are also given. No extra service charges ar
added to the bills, as a rule.

Tipping: about 10 per cent to be added to the bill. Hot
reservations: through the usual channels and services.

HOTELS

HIGHER-PRICED
(above Fts. 6,000.00)

Atrium Hyatt
Budapest V.,
Roosevelt-tér 2.
Tel. 1/383-000
Tlx. 22-5485
Fax 188-659
*Indoor gardens. Three restaurants.
Conference centre.*

Duna Intercontinental
Budapest V.,
Apáczai Csere János-u. 4.
Tel. 1/175-122
Tlx. 22-5277
Fax 184-973
*On the Danube. Superb views of
Buda Castle.*

Hilton
Budapest I.,
Hess András-tér 1/3.
Tel. 1/751-000
Tlx. 22-5984
Fax 751-000/extn. 320
Beautiful setting and views.

Thermal
Budapest XIII., Margitsziget
Tel. 1/321-100
Tlx. 22-5463
Spa hotel on Danube island.

MEDIUM-PRICED
(Fts. 2,900.00–Fts. 6,000.00)

Béke
Budapest VI.,
Lenin-krt. 97.
Tel. 1/323-300
Tlx. 22-5748
Fax 533-380
Downtown. First class amenities.

Buda Penta
Budapest I.,
Krisztina-körút 41/43.
Tel. 1/566-333
Tlx. 22-5495
Fax 556-964
Near castle and park.

Flamenco
Budapest XI.,
Tas Vezér-u. 7.
Tel. 1/252-250
Tlx. 22-4647
Spanish food, music and style.

Fórum
Budapest V.,
Apáczai Csere János-u. 12/14.
Tel. 1/178-088
Tlx. 22-4178
Fax 179-808
Modern. Roof swimming pool.

Gellért
Budapest XI.,
Szt. Gellért-tér 1.
Tel. 1/852-200
Tlx. 22-4363
Fax 666-631
Excellent spa facilities.

Grand Hotel Hungária
Budapest VII.,
Rákóczi-út 90.
Tel. 1/229-050
Tlx. 22-4987
Ideal transit hotel.

Nemzeti
Budapest VIII.,
József-körút 4.
Tel. 1/339-160
Tlx. 22-7710
*Downtown. Nineteenth-century
dining traditions.*

Novotel
Budapest XII.,
Alkotás-u. 63-67.
Tel. 1/869-588
Tlx. 22-5496
Fax 665-636
Superb cuisine.

Olympia
Budapest XII.,
Eötvös-út 40.
Tel. 1/568-011
Tlx. 22-6368
*Swimming and tennis in forest
setting.*

Ramada Grand Hotel
Budapest XIII., Margitsziget
Tel. 1/111-000
Tlx. 22-6682
Fax 533-029
*Mediaeval setting on Margaret
Island.*

Royal
Budapest VII.,
Lenin-körút 47/49
Tel. 533-133
Tlx. 22-4463
Traditional hotel in heart of town.

LOWER-PRICED
*(about Fts. 2,500.00 –
Fts. 2,900.00)*

Aero
Budapest IX.,
Ferde-u. 1/3.
Tel. 1/274-690
Tlx. 22-4238
Near airport.

3

Astoria
Budapest V.,
Kossuth Lajos-u. 19.
Tel. 1/173-411
Tlx. 22-4205
Traditional hotel. Downtown.

Budapest
Budapest II.,
Szilágyi Erzsébet fasor 47.
Tel. 1/153-230
Tlx. 22-5125
Superb views on all sides.

Emke
Budapest VII.,
Akácfa-u. 1/3.
Tel. 1/229-230
Tlx. 22-5789
In lively city centre.

Erzsébet
Budapest V.,
Károlyi Mihály-u. 11.
Tel. 1/382-111
Tlx. 22-7494
Hungarian cuisine.

Európa
Budapest II.,
Hárshegyi-út 5/7.
Tel. 1/767-122
Tlx. 22-5113
Excellent recreational facilities.

Expo
Budapest X.,
Dobi István-u. 10.
Tel. 1/842-130
Tlx. 22-6300
*On Budapest International
Fairground.*

Ifjúság
Budapest II.,
Zivatar-u. 1/3.

Tel. 1/353-331
Tlx. 22-5102
Economically priced.

Metropol
Budapest VII.,
Rákóczi-út 58.
Tel. 1/421-175
Tlx. 22-6209
Lively setting.

Palace
Budapest VIII.,
Rákóczi-út 43.
Tel. 1/136-000
Tlx. 22-4217
Hungarian food, gypsy music.

Rege
Budapest II.,
Pálos-út 2.
Tel. 1/767-311
Tlx. 22-5660
Recreation centre. Entertainment.

Stadion
Budapest XIV.,
Ifjúság-u. 1/3.
Tel. 1/631-830
Tlx. 22-5685
Near People's Stadium.

Taverna
Budapest V.,
Váci-utca 20.
Tel. 1/348-999
Tlx. 22-7707
In centre of business district.

Volga
Budapest XIII.,
Dózsa György-út 65.
Tel. 1/290-200
Tlx. 22-5120
New catering centre.

LAKE BALATON AREA
(Lower- and medium-priced)

Annabella
Balatonfüred
Beloiannisz-u. 25.
Tel. 86/42-222
Tlx. 32-282
Cozy recreational complex.

Auróra
Balatonalmádi,
Bajcsy-Zsilinszky-út 14.
Tel. 86/38-811
Tlx. 32-347
Near the lake. Country food.

Balaton
Siófok
Petöfi-sétány 9.
Tel. 84/10-655
Tlx. 22-4108
Excellent food and wines.

Európa
Siófok
Petöfi-sétány 15.
Tel. 84/13-411
Tlx. 22-4108
Near lake. Regional cuisine.

Hungária
Siófok
Petöfi-sétány 13.
Tel. 84/10-677
Tlx. 22-4108
On lake shore, beautiful views.

Lidó
Siófok
Petöfi-sétány 11.
Tel. 84/10-633
Tlx. 22-4108
Hungarian cuisine and clientele.

Margaréta
Balatonfüred
Széchenyi-u. 29.
Tel. 86/43-824
Tlx. 32-662
Local food and wine.

Marina
Balatonfüred
Széchenyi-u. 26.
Tel. 86/43-644
Tlx. 32-241
Private beach. Wine tasting.

Neptun
Balatonföldvár
Tel. 84/40-388
Tlx. 22-4918
Peaceful setting. Excellent local wine.

RESTAURANTS
(H = high-priced
M = medium-priced
L = lower-priced)

HUNGARIAN RESTAURANTS

Astoria -M-
Budapest V.,
Kossuth Lajos-u. 19.
Tel. 1/173-411
7 a.m.–12 midnight
Wide choice.

Borkatakomba -M-
Budapest XXII.,
Nagytétényi-út 67.
Tel. 1/464-859
5 p.m.–12 midnight
Best Hungarian wines.

Busuló Juhász -L-
Budapest XI.,
Kelenhegyi-út 58.
Tel. 1/451-146
12 noon–12 midnight
Local sweets and beverages.

Csárda (in Hotel Duna Intercontinental) -M-
Budapest V.,
Apáczai Csere János-u. 4.
Tel. 1/175-122
12–4 p.m. and 6–12 midnight
Moderately priced national dishes.

Emke Kalocsa Csárda -L-
Budapest VII.,
Lenin-körút 2.
Tel. 1/220-001
12 noon–1 a.m.
Southern Hungarian specialities.

Margitkert -M-
Budapest II.,
Margit-ú. 15.
Tel. 1/354-791
12 noon–12 midnight
Individually prepared local dishes.

Mátyás Pince -H-
Budapest V.,
Március 15-e tér 8.
Tel. 1/181-650
12 noon–1 a.m.
Hungarian cuisine, gypsy music.

Tokaj (in Hotel Atrium Hyatt) -M-
Budapest V.,
Roosevelt-tér 2.
Tel. 1/383-000
7 p.m.–1 a.m.
Good selection, local wine.

6

NATIONAL SPECIALITIES

Bajkál -L-
Budapest V.,
Semmelweis-u. 3.
Tel. 1/176-839
10 a.m.–10 p.m.
Russian cuisine and drinks.

Berlin -L-
Budapest V.,
Szt. István-körút 13.
Tel. 1/310-314
12 noon–12 midnight
German specialities and music.

La Bodega (in Hotel Flamenco) -H-
Budapest XI.,
Tas Vezér-u. 7.
Tel. 1/252-250
7 p.m.–2 a.m.
Spanish cuisine and setting.

Etoile -H-
Budapest XIII.,
Pozsonyi-u. 4.
Tel. 1/122-242
12 noon–12 midnight
Elegant French restaurant.

Habana -L-
Budapest VI.,
Bajcsy-Zsilinszky-út 21.
Tel. 1/121-039
12 noon–12 midnight
Latin-American food and music.

Japanese Restaurant -M-
Budapest VIII.,
Luther-u. 4/6.
Tel. 1/143-427
6 p.m.–2 a.m.
Oriental specialities and music.

Napoletana -M-
Budapest V.,
Petőfi-tér 3.
Tel. 1/185-714
10 a.m.–12 midnight
Italian cuisine.

Szecsuán -H-
Budapest V.,
Roosevelt-tér 5.
Tel. 1/172-407
12 noon–12 midnight
Traditional Chinese food.

Vörös Sárkány -H-
Budapest VI.,
Népköztársaság-út ja 80.
Tel. 1/318-757
12–3 p.m. and 6 p.m.–1 a.m.
Cantonese restaurant.

**INTERNATIONAL
RESTAURANTS**

**Atrium Terrace (in Hotel Atrium-
Hyatt) -H-**
Budapest V.,
Roosevelt-tér 2.
Tel. 1/383-000
7 a.m.–11 p.m.
Wide variety of dishes.

Belvárosi Kávéház Lidó -M-
Budapest V.,
Szabadsajtó-út 5.
Tel. 1/182-404
10 a.m.–4 a.m.
Continental cuisine.

**Bellevue (in Hotel Duna Interconti-
nental) -H-**
Budapest V.,
Apáczai Csere János u. 4.
Tel. 1/175-122
7 p.m.–2 a.m.
Elegant. Serves dinner until late.

Budavár (in Hotel Buda Penta) -M-
Budapest I.,
Krisztina-körút 41/43.
Tel. 1/566-333
7–10 a.m., 12–3 p.m., 7 p.m.–
12 midnight
Cosy setting. Music.

Gundel -H-
Budapest XIV.,
Állatkerti-út 2.
Tel. 1/221-002
12–4 p.m., 7 p.m.–12 midnight
Traditional cuisine.

Karolina (in Hotel Novotel) -M-
Budapest XII.,
Alkotás-u. 63/67.
Tel. 1/869-588
6.30–10 a.m., 12–3 p.m., 7–11 p.m.
Excellent selection of dishes.

Kárpátia -M-
Budapest V.,
Károlyi Mihály-u. 4–8.
Tel. 1/173-596
12 noon–3 p.m., 6–11 p.m.
Lively atmosphere.

Old Timer (in Atrium-Hyatt) -H-
Budapest V.,
Roosevelt-tér 2.
Tel. 1/383-000
12 noon–3 p.m., 7–11 p.m.
Superb dishes and wine.

Olympia Evergreen (in Hotel Olympia) -L-
Budapest XII.,
Eötvös-u. 40.
Tel. 1/568-011
7 a.m.–11 p.m.
Good food at moderate prices.

Régi Országház -L-
Budapest I.,
Országház-u. 17.
Tel. 1/750-650
11 a.m.–12 midnight
Intimate atmosphere. Good music.

Shakespeare (in Hotel Béke) -M-
Budapest VI.,
Lenin-körút 97
Tel. 1/323-300
7–10 a.m., 12–3 p.m.
Elegant setting.

Százéves -M-
Budapest V.,
Pesti Barnabás-u. 2.
Tel. 1/183-608
11.30 a.m.–12 midnight
Traditional cuisine.

Széchenyi (in Ramada Grand Hotel) -M-
Budapest XIII., Margitsziget
Tel. 1/321-100
12 noon–3 p.m., 7 p.m.–12 midnight
Local specialities.

SPECIALIZED RESTAURANTS

B.B. Weinkeller (in Ramada Grand Hotel) -M-
Budapest XIII., Margitsziget
Tel. 1/321-100
6 p.m.–2 a.m.
Wide choice of food and wine.

Bowling (in Hotel Novotel) -L-
Budapest XII.,
Alkotás-u. 63/67.
Tel. 1/869-588
12 noon–12 midnight
Sports amenities along with good food.

Capri Pizzeria (in Hotel Buda Penta) -L-
Budapest I.,
Krisztina-körút 41/43.
Tel. 1/566-333
11 a.m.–11 p.m.
Italian specialities for a change of pace.

Clark (in Hotel Atrium-Hyatt) -M-
Budapest V., Roosevelt-tér 2.
Tel. 1/383-000
11 a.m.–11 p.m.
Delicacies à la carte.

Gösser Bierstube (in Ramada Grand Hotel) -M-
Budapest XIII., Margitsziget
Tel. 1/321-100
10 a.m.–10 p.m.
Excellent food. Famous Gösser beer.

Piccolino Pizzeria (in Hotel Novotel) -L-
Budapest XII.,
Alkotás-u. 63/67.
Tel. 1/869-588
10 a.m.–10 p.m.
Italian restaurant.

Platán (in Hotel Thermal) -M-
Budapest XIII., Margitsziget
Tel. 1/111-000
7–10 a.m., 12–3 p.m., 7 p.m.–12 midnight
Wide selection.

Tourist information

Phone the *Tourinform Service* in Budapest (tel.: 179–800) for details of excursions, events, accommodation—in fact virtually any advice or help you may need during your visit. Staff speak English, French, German, Russian and Spanish.

The service operates Monday—Friday from 7 a.m. to 9 p.m., Saturday from 7 a.m. to 8 p.m. and Sunday from 8 a.m. to 1 p.m. year-round.

Tipping recommendations

Have no fear of giving offence if you offer a tip: the old custom survives in Hungary, and gratuities are expected by a wide assortment of service personnel, as well as taxi drivers and gypsy violonists. Some suggestions:

HOTEL	
Service charge, bill	generally included
Porter, per bag	Ft. 25
Bellboy, errand	Ft. 20
Maid, per week	Ft. 100
Doorman, hails cab	Ft. 20
RESTAURANT	
Service charge, bill	generally included
Waiter	10%
Hat check	Ft. 20
Lavatory attendant	Ft. 10
Taxi driver	10% (but not less than Ft. 10)
Barber/Women's hairdresser	15% (but not less than Ft. 10)
Gypsy violinist	Ft. 100 (for personal attention)
Tourist guide (half-day)	Ft. 200
Theatre usher	add Ft. 5–10 to programme for sale
Filling station attendant	round off (Ft. 10 for checking air and oil) (Ft. 5 for cleaning windscreen)

BERLITZ PHRASE BOOKS

World's bestselling phrase books feature not only expressions and vocabulary you'll need, but also travel tips, useful facts and pronunciation throughout. The handiest and most readable conversation aid available.

Arabic	French	Polish
Chinese	German	Portuguese
Danish	Greek	Russian
Dutch	Hebrew	Serbo-Croatian
European (14 languages)	Hungarian	Spanish
	Italian	Lat.-Am. Spanish
European Menu Reader	Japanese	Swahili
	Korean	Swedish
Finnish	Norwegian	Turkish

BERLITZ CASSETTEPAKS

The above-mentioned titles are also available combined with a cassette to help you improve your accent. A helpful miniscript is included containing the complete text of the dual language hi-fi recording.

BERLITZ

HUNGARIAN
FOR TRAVELLERS

By the staff of Berlitz Guides

Preface

You are about to visit Hungary. Our aim has been to produce a practical phrase book to help you on your trip.

In preparing this book we took into account a wealth of suggestions from phrase book users around the world. The accent is on helping the traveller in practical, every-day situations.

The contents are logically arranged so you can find the right phrase at the moment you need it.

Hungarian for Travellers features:

● all the phrases and supplementary vocabulary you'll need on your trip

● complete phonetic transcription throughout, enabling you to pronounce every word correctly

● special panels showing replies your listener might like to give you: just hand him the book and let him point to the appropriate phrase. This is particularly useful in certain difficult situations (trouble with the car, at the doctor's, etc.)

● a wide range of travel facts, hints and useful practical information, providing valuable insight into life in Hungary

● a tipping chart (see inside back-cover) and a reference section in the back of the book

● an introduction to some basics of Hungarian grammar

Certain sections will be particularly appreciated by travellers: the extensive "Eating Out" chapter which explains what's on the menu, in the soup and under the sauce, with

6

translations, and the complete "Shopping Guide" which enables you to be almost as specific and selective as you would be at home. Trouble with the car? Turn to the mechanic's manual with its dual-language terms. Feeling ill? Our medical section provides the most rapid communication possible between you and the doctor.

To make the most of *Hungarian for Travellers,* we suggest that you start with the "Guide to Pronunciation". Then go on to "Some Basic Expressions". This not only gives you a minimum vocabulary, it also helps you get used to pronouncing the language.

We are particularly grateful to Mr. David Pulman and Mr Norbert Urban for their help in the preparation of this book, and to Dr. T.J.A. Bennett who devised the phonetic transcription system. We also wish to extend special thanks to Vue Touristique I.P.V., Budapest, and to Prof. Joseph J Hollos for their decisive roles in guiding this project to fruition.

We shall be very pleased to receive any comments, criticisms and suggestions that you think may help us in preparing future editions.

Have a good trip.

Throughout this book the symbols illustrated here indicate sections containing phrases your listener might like to say to *you.* If you don't understand him, just give him the book and let him point to the phrase in his language. The English translation is just beside.

A very basic grammar

Hungarian is a unique, intricate, subtle language belonging to the Finno-Ugric family.* It's completely unrelated to Slavonic, Germanic or any other Indo-European tongue.

Hungarian words are highly derivative, various ideas and nuances being expressed by a root-word modified in different ways. Instead of prepositions ("to", "from", "in", etc.), Hungarian uses a variety of suffixes (tags added to the ends of words) to achieve the same effect. Special endings are also added to verbs, pronouns and other parts of speech. The choice of suffix is partly governed by a complicated set of rules of vowel harmony. What this means is that the vowels in the root-word determine which alternative of the required suffix must be added.

Take a stab at the suffix

In some phrases in this book we have had no alternative but to leave the choice of suffix open, since it depends on the word you wish to insert in front of it. It's impossible for us to give here a watertight summary of the technicalities of vowel harmony. However, if you follow the rules of thumb given below you'll considerably shorten the odds on picking the correct suffix.

● If the basic word is dominated by "open" vowels (e, é, i, í, ö, ő, ü, ű), add that suffix which also contains an "open" vowel.

● If the basic word is dominated by "closed" vowels (a, á, o, ó, u, ú), add that suffix which also contains a "closed" vowel.

Don't worry about making a mistake, you'll be understood—and most likely complimented for trying hard!

Its closest, yet still extremely distant, relative is Finnish.

Articles

1. Definite article (the):

The word for *the* is **a** before a word beginning with a conso
nant, and **az** before a vowel, in both singular and plural
It is indeclinable.

	singular		plural
a vonat	the train	**a vonatok**	the trains
az asztal	the table	**az asztalok**	the tables

2. Indefinite article (a/an):

The indefinite article is always **egy** (the same as the word fo
"one"). It is indeclinable.

egy vonat	a train	**egy asztal**	a table

Nouns

As in English, there is no grammatical gender. However
nouns take various endings depending on their case.

Here is a general model of the declension of nouns based or
the word **könyv** (book), showing the endings to be added
Note, however, that endings are often subject to change
according to the rules of vowel harmony.

case	singular	plural	usage
subject	**könyv**	**könyvek**	the book(s) (is/are ...)
dir. obj.	**könyveket**	**könyveket**	(I read) the book(s)
possess.	**könyvnek a**	**könyveknek a**	of the book(s)
ind. obj.	**könyvnek**	**könyveknek**	to the book(s)
place	**könyvben**	**könyvekben**	in the book(s)
"from"	**könyvről**	**könyvekről**	from the book(s)

Adjectives

1. The adjective precedes the noun, with no endings.

a piros autó   the red car   **a piros autók**   the red cars

2. The comparative of an adjective is formed by adding the endings **-bb**, **-abb**, **-ebb** or **-obb** to its simple form.

3. In the superlative, the adjective takes the same endings but is also preceded by **leg**. Here are some useful examples.

simple	comparative	superlative
jó good	**jobb** better	**legjobb** best
magas tall	**magasabb** taller	**legmagasabb** tallest
szép beautiful	**szebb** more beautiful	**legszebb** most beautiful
nagy big	**nagyobb** bigger	**legnagyobb** biggest

Personal pronouns

subject		direct object (me, etc.)	indirect object (to me, etc.)
I	**én**	**engem**	**nekem**
you	**maga***	**magát***	**magának***
you	**te**	**téged**	**neked**
he / she / it	**ő**	**őt**	**neki**
we	**mi**	**minket**	**nekünk**
you	**maguk***	**magukat***	**maguknak***
you	**ti**	**titeket**	**nektek**
they	**ők**	**őket**	**nekik**

* Polite form for "you".

GRAMMAR

Demonstratives

| this | ez | these | ezek | that | az | | those | azok |

Possessives

To form the possessive case, take the definite article + the personal pronoun + the noun. The noun takes endings (again, governed by a complicated set of rules).

my book	az én könyvem	our book	a mi könyvünk
your book	a maga könyve*	your book	a maguk könyve*
your book	a te könyved	your book	a ti könyvetek
his/her book	az ő könyve	their book	az ő könyvük

Verbs

Because of the complexity of Hungarian verbs we have restricted ourselves to showing how to form the present and future tenses of verbs, including the special cases of the verbs "to be" and "to have".

1. Present tense of the verbs "to be" and "to have":

to be (**lenni**)			
I am	**én vagyok**	we are	**mi vagyunk**
you are	**maga van***	you are	**maguk vannak***
you are	**te vagy**	you are	**ti vagytok**
he/she/it is	**ő van**	they are	**ők vannak**

to have (**vanéki**)			
I have	**nekem van**	we have	**nekünk van**
you have	**magának van***	you have	**maguknak van***
you have	**neked van**	you have	**nektek van**
he/she/it has	**neki van**	they have	**nekik van**

---

* Polite form for "you", "your".

GRAMMAR

2. Present tense of other verbs:

The present tense may be formed in various ways. Here is a common pattern for transitive verbs (i.e. those which can take a direct object) based on the infinitive **olvasni** (to read).

I read	én olvasom	we read	mi olvassuk
you read	maga olvassa*	you read	maguk olvassák*
you read	te olvasod	you read	ti olvassátok
he/she reads	ő olvassa	they read	ők olvassák

Questions: **olvassa ő?** = does he/she read? etc.

3. Future

A simple method of forming the future tense is to use the personal pronoun + the word corresponding to "shall" or "will" (**fogok/fogsz**, etc.) + the infinitive. Here we take the verb **vásárolni** (to shop) as an example (I shall shop/go shopping, etc.).

I ...	én fogok vásárolni	we ...	mi fogunk vásárolni
you ...	maga fog vásárolni*	you ...	maguk fognak vásárolni*
you ...	te fogsz vásárolni	you ...	ti fogtok vásárolni
he/she ...	ő fog vásárolni	they ...	ők fognak vásárolni

Negatives

In a sentence, the word **nem** is usually placed after the subject. There is also a change of word order (inversion).

I am here	**én itt vagyok**
I am not here	**én nem vagyok itt**

---

* Polite form for "you".

Guide to pronunciation

This and the following chapter are intended to make you familiar with the phonetic transcription we devised and to help you get used to the sounds of Hungarian.

As a minimum vocabulary for your trip, we've selected a number of basic words and phrases under the title "Some Basic Expressions" (pages 16–21).

An outline of the spelling and sounds of Hungarian

You'll find the pronunciation of the Hungarian letters and sounds explained below, as well as the symbols we use for them in the transcription. Note that Hungarian has some diacritical signs—special markings over certain letters—which we don't use in English.

The imitated pronunciation should be read as if it were English except for any special rules set out below. It is based on Standard British pronunciation, though we have tried to take into account General American pronunciation as well. Of course, the sounds of any two languages are never exactly the same; but if you follow carefully the indications supplied here, you'll have no difficulty in reading our transcription in such a way as to make yourself understood.

Letters written in **bold** type should be stressed (pronounced louder).

Consonants

Letter	Approximate pronunciation	Symbol	Example	
b, d, f, h, m, n, v, x, z	as in English			
c	like **ts** in nets	ts	arc	orts

s	like **ch** in **ch**ap	ch	**kocsi**	**kaw**chee
	always as in **go**, never as in **gin**	g/gh	**gáz** **régi**	gaaz **ray**ghee
y	like **di** in me**di**um, said fairly quickly	d^y	**ágy**	aad^y
	like **y** in **y**es	y/^{y}	**jég**	yayg
k	always as in si**ck**, never as in **k**ill	k	**kör**	kurr
	always as in **l**eap, never as in ba**ll**	l	**ital**	eetol
y	like **y** in **y**es	y/^{y}	**Károly**	**kaa**raw^y
ny	quite like **ni** in o**ni**on	n^y	**hány**	haan^y
p	always as in si**p**, never as in **p**ill	p	**posta**	**paw**shto
r	pronounced with the tip of the tongue, like Scottish **r**	r	**ír**	$\overline{\text{ee}}$r
s	like **sh** in **sh**oot	sh	**saláta**	**sh**o**ll**aato
sz	like **s** in **s**o	s/ss	**szó** **ész**	s**aw** ayss
t	always as in si**t**, never as in **t**ill	t	**túra**	t$\overline{\text{oo}}$ro
ty	quite like **tti** in pre**tti**er, said quickly	t^y	**atya**	ot^{y}o
zs	like **s** in plea**s**ure	zh	**zsír**	zh$\overline{\text{ee}}$r

Vowels

a	quite like **o** in n**o**t (British pronunciation)	o	**hat**	hot
á	like **a** in c**a**r, but without any r-sound	aa	**rág**	raag
e	quite like **e** in y**e**s, but with the mouth a little more open, i.e. a sound between **e** in y**e**s and **a** in h**a**t	æ	**te**	tæ
é	like **ay** in s**ay**, but a pure vowel, not a diphthong, i.e. neither the tongue nor the lips move during the pronunciation of it	ay	**mér**	mayr

i	like **ee** in feet (short)	ee	**hideg**	**hee**dæg
í	like **ee** in see (long)	e̅e̅	**míg**	**me̅e̅**g
o	quite like **aw** in s**aw** (British pronunciation), but shorter	aw	**bot**	**baw**t
ó	like **aw** in s**aw**, but with the tongue higher in the mouth	a̅w̅	**fotó**	**faw**ta̅w̅
ö	like **ur** in f**ur**, but short, without any **r**-sound, and with rounded lips	ur	**örök**	**ur**rurk
ő	like **ur** in f**ur**, but without any **r**-sound, and with the lips tightly rounded	u̅r̅	**lő**	**lu̅r̅**
u	as in the British pronunciation of p**u**ll	oo	**kulcs**	**koo**lch
ú	like **oo** in f**oo**d	o̅o̅	**kút**	**ko̅o̅**t
ü	a "rounded **ee**"; while pronouncing **ee** as in s**ee**, round your lips as if to pronounce **oo** as in s**oo**n; the resulting sound should be as in French **u**ne or German f**ü**nf	ew	**körül**	**ku**rrewl
ű	the same sound as **ü**, but long and with the lips more tightly rounded	e̅w̅	**fűt**	**fe̅w̅**t

PRONUNCIATION (side margin)

N.B. 1) There are no "silent" letters in Hungarian, so all letters must be pronounced. This means that double consonants are pronounced long, e.g. **tt** in **kettő** (**kæt-tu̅r̅**) sounds rather like **t-t** in a fast pronunciation of part-time. (But a double consonant appearing at the end of a word is pronounced short). It also means that vowels standing next to each other are pronounced separately and do not combine to produce diphthongs.

2) When two or more consonants stand next to each other, the last one can influence the pronunciation of the others. If it is "voiceless", it will make a preceding "voiced" consonant into a "voiceless" one, and vice versa, e.g. *végtelen* is

pronounced as if it were written *véktelen*. The "voiceless" consonants are **c**, **f**, **k**, **p**, **s**, **sz**, **t**, **ty**, and the corresponding "voiced" ones are **dz**, **v**, **g**, **b**, **zs**, **z**, **d**, **gy**.

3) Every word, when pronounced alone, has a strong stress on its first syllable. When words are combined in sentences, the stress on the less important words weakens.

4) The "double" forms of **cs**, **gy**, **ly**, **ny**, **sz**, **ty**, **zs** are **ccs**, **ggy**, **lly**, **nny**, **ssz**, **tty**, **zzs**. If the "double" form is divided at the end of a line, then the single form is written twice, e.g. **cs-cs** instead of **c-cs**.

5) In Hungarian, the letter **j** can combine with a preceding vowel to produce diphthongs, e.g. *új* (pronounced $\overline{oo}$y), *fej* (pronounced fæy), *sajt* (pronounced soyt). In all these cases, the y should be pronounced only fleetingly, as in boy.

Pronunciation of the Hungarian alphabet					
A	o	**GY**	d^{y}e	**NY**	æn^y	**T**	te
Á	aa	**H**	haa	**O**	aw	**TY**	t^{y}e
B	be*	**I**	ee	**Ó**	$\overline{aw}$	**U**	oo
C	tse	**Í**	$\overline{ee}$	**Ö**	ur	**Ú**	$\overline{oo}$
CS	tche	**J**	ye	**Ő**	$\overline{ur}$	**Ü**	ew
D	de	**K**	kaa	**P**	pe	**Ű**	$\overline{ew}$
E	æ	**L**	æl	**Q**	kew	**V**	ve
É	e	**LY**	æl **eep**seelon	**R**	ær	**W**	**doop**lovvay
F	ayf	**M**	æm	**S**	æsh	**Z**	ze
G	ghe	**N**	æn	**SZ**	æs	**ZS**	zhe

PRONUNCIATION

---

*e doesn't appear in the transcriptions, but has more or less the same value as **a** in late.

Some basic expressions

Yes.	Igen.	eegæn
No.	Nem.	næm
Please.	Kérem.	kayræm
Yes, please.	Igen, kérem.	eegæn kayræm
Thank you.	Köszönöm.	kursurnurm
No, thank you.	Nem, köszönöm.	næm kursurnurm
Thank you very much.	Köszönöm szépen.	kursurnurm saypæn
You're welcome.	Szívesen.	sēēvæshæn
Sorry. ·	Sajnálom.	shoynaalawm

Greetings

Good morning.	Jó reggelt.	yāw ræg-gælt
Good afternoon.	Jó napot.	yāw noppawt
Good evening.	Jó estét.	yāw æshtayt
Good night.	Jó éjszakát.	yāw ayᵛsokkaat
Goodbye.	Viszontlátásra.	veesawntlaataashro
See you later.	Viszlát.	veeslaat
This is Mr. ...	Szeretném bemutatni... urat.	særætnaym bæmoototnee ... oorot
This is Mrs. ...	Szeretném bemutatni... urnőt.	særætnaym bæmoototnee ... oornűrt
This is Miss...	Szeretném bemutatni... kisasszonyt.	særætnaym bæmoototnee ... keeshoss-sawnᵛt
I'm pleased to meet you.	Örülök, hogy megismerhetem.	urrewlurk hawdᵛ mægeeshmærhætæm
How are you?	Hogy van?	hawdᵛ von
Very well, thank you. And you?	Köszönöm, nagyon jól. És Ön?	kursurnurm nodᵛawn yāwl. aysh urn

uestions

here?	**Hol?**	hawl
here is ...?	**Hol van ...?**	hawl von
here are ...?	**Hol vannak ...?**	hawl **von**-nok
ow?	**Hogy?**	hawd^y
ow much?	**Mennyi/Mennyit?**	mæn^{y}ee/mæn^{y}eet
ow many?	**Hány?**	haan^y
hen?	**Mikor?**	meekawr
hy?	**Miért?**	meeayrt
ho?	**Ki?**	kee
hich?	**Melyik?**	mæ^{y}eek
hat?	**Mi?**	mee
hat do you call is/that?	**Mi a neve ennek/ annak?**	mee o nævæ æn-næk/ on-nok
hat does this/ at mean?	**Ez/Az mit jelent?**	æz/oz meet yælænt

o you speak ...?

o you speak English/ ench/German?	**Beszél angolul/ franciául/németül?**	bæsayl ongawlool/front-seeaaool/naymætewl
oes anyone here eak English?	**Van itt valaki aki angolul beszél?**	von eet vollokkee okkee ongawlool bæsayl
on't speak uch Hungarian.	**Alig beszélek magyarul.**	olleeg bæsaylæk mod^{y}o-rrool
ow do you say 's in Hungarian?	**Hogy mondják ezt magyarul?**	hawd^y mawnd^{y}aak æst mod^{y}orrool
eg your pardon?	**Bocsánat de nem értem önt.**	bawchaanot dæ næm ayr-tæm urnt
uld you speak ore slowly?	**Elmondaná lassabban?**	ælmawndonnaa losh-shob-bon
uld you repeat it?	**Megismételné?**	mægheeshmaytælnay

Please write it down.	Kérem, írja ezt le.	kayræm ēēryo æst læ
Can you translate this for me?	Lefordítaná ezt nekem?	læfawrdēētonnaa æst nækæm
Please point to the phrase in the book.	Kérem, mutassa meg ezt a kifejezést a könyvben.	kayræm mootosh-sho mæ æst o keefæyæzaysht o kurn^Yvbæn
Just a minute. I'll see if I can find it in this book.	Egy pillanat. Megnézem, benne van-e a könyvben.	æd^Y peel-lonnot. mægnay zæm bæn-næ von-æ o kurn^Yvbæn
I understand.	Értem.	ayrtæm
I don't understand.	Nem értem.	næm ayrtæm
Do you understand?	Ön érti?	urn ayrtee

Can ...?

Can I have ...?	Kaphatok ...?	kophottawk
Can we have ...?	Kaphatunk ...?	kophottoonk
Can you show me ...?	Megmutatná ...?	mægmoototnaa
I can't.	Nem tudok.	næm toodawk
Can you tell me ...?	Megmondaná ...?	mægmawndonnaa
Can you help me, please?	Segítene nekem?	shæghēētænæ nækæm
Can you direct me to ...?	Elvezetne a ...?	ælvæzætnæ o

Wanting

I'd like ...	Szeretnék ...	sæarætnayk
We'd like ...	Szeretnénk ...	sæarætnaynk
Please give me ...	Kérem, adjon ...	kayræm od^Yawn*
Please give me this/that.	Kérem, adjon ezt/azt.	kayræm od^Yawn æst/ost
Please bring me ...	Kérem, hozzon ...	kayræm hawz-zawn

* j after d is pronounced like gy (d^Y).

lease bring me nis/that.	**Hozzon kérem ezt/ azt.**	hawz-zawn kayræm æst/ost
m hungry.	**Éhes vagyok.**	ayhæsh vod^yawk
m thirsty.	**Szomjas vagyok.**	sawmyosh vod^yawk
m tired.	**Fáradt vagyok.**	faarot vod^yawk
m lost.	**Eltévedtem.**	æltayvædtæm
m looking for ...	**A ...-t keresem.**	o....-t kæræshæm
's important.	**Fontos.**	fawntawsh
's urgent.	**Sürgős.**	shewrgūrsh
lurry up!	**Siessen!**	sheeæsh-shæn

t is/There is ...

t is ...	**Van ...**	von
s it ...?	**Van ...?**	von
t isn't ...	**Nincs ...**	neench
here is/There are ...	**Van .../Vannak ...**	von.../von-nok
s there/Are there ...?	**Van .../Vannak ...?**	von.../von-nok
here isn't any.	**Ez/Az nincs.**	æz/oz neench
here aren't any.	**Ezek/Azok nincsenek.**	æzæk/ozzawk neenchænæk

few common words

ig/small	**nagy/kicsi**	nod^y/keechee
heap/expensive	**olcsó/drága**	awlchaw/draago
ood/bad	**jó/rossz**	yaw/rawss
etter/worse	**jobb/rosszabb**	yawb/rawss-sob
ght/wrong	**helyes/helytelen**	hæ^yæsh/hæ^ytælæn
asy/difficult	**egyszerű/bonyolult**	æd^ysærēw/bawn^yawloolt
ght/heavy	**könnyű/nehéz**	kurn^yēw/næhayz
ull/empty	**teli/üres**	tælee/ewræsh

free/occupied	szabad/foglalt	sobbod/fawglolt
open/shut	nyitva/zárva	n\\ᵛeetvo/zaarvo
old/young	öreg/fiatal	urræg/feeottol
old/new	régi/új	rayghee/ōōᵛ
quick/slow	gyors/lassú	dᵛawrsh/losh-shōō
beautiful/ugly	szép/csúnya	sayp/chōōnᵛo
warm/cold	meleg/hideg	mælæg/heedæg
never/always	soha/mindig	shawho/meendeeg
early/late	korán/későn	kawraan/kayshū̄rn
here/there	itt/ott	eet/awt
near/far	közel/távol	kurzæl/taavawl
left/right	bal/jobb	bol/yawb
first/last	első/utolsó	ælshū̄r/ootawlshaw
now/then	ekkor/akkor	æk-kawr/ok-kawr
immediately/later	azonnal/később	ozzawn-nol/kayshū̄rb

Some prepositions ...

at	-kor (time)	-kawr
	-nál/-nél (place)	-naal/-nayl
on	-rá/-ra/-re/-on/	-raa/-ro/-ræ/-awn
	-en/-ön	-æn/-urn
in	-ban/-ben	-bon/-bæn
before (time)	előtt	ælū̄rt
before (place)	előtt	ælū̄rt
after	után	ootaan
behind	mögött	murgurt
to	felé/oda	fælay/awdo
from	-ból/-ből	-bāwl/-būrl
with	-val/-vel	-vol/-væl

---

* English prepositions are often rendered by suffixes in Hungarian. See p. 7.

without	**nélkül**	na**y**lkewl
inside	**belül**	bælewl
outside	**kívül**	kéēvewl
through	**keresztül**	kæræstewl
towards	**felé**	fælay
up	**fent**	fænt
down	**lent**	lænt
above	**felett**	fælæt
below	**alatt**	ollot
over	**fölött**	furlurt
under	**alatt**	ollot
until	**eddig/addig**	æd-deeg/od-deeg
for	**-ért**	-ayrt
between	**között**	kurzurt
during	**közben**	kurzbæn
since	**óta**	āw̄to

... and a few more useful words

and	**és**	aysh
or	**vagy**	vod**y**
but	**de**	dæ
not	**nem**	næm
nothing	**semmi**	sæm-mee
none	**egyik sem**	æd**y**eek sæm
very	**nagyon**	nod**y**awn
soon	**hamarosan**	hommorrawshon
perhaps	**talán**	tollaan
already	**már**	maar
again	**ismét**	eeshmayt
also	**is**	eesh

Arrival

You've arrived. Whether you come by train, plane, car or
Danube steamer, you'll have to go through passport and
customs formalities. (All except Austrian and Finnish
nationals require a visa in addition to their passport.) If
you didn't obtain one in advance through your travel agency
or a Hungarian consulate, you can get one at road crossing
points, river ports and at Budapest airport.

Customs officials and police on duty at crossing points speak
some English and German.

Note: rail travellers *cannot* have a visa issued on the spot.

Passport control

Here's my passport.	**Tessék, az útlevelem.**	tæsh-shayk oz ōōtlævæ-læm
I'll be staying…	**… maradok.**	… morroddawk
a few days	**Néhány napig**	nayhaanᵞ noppeeg
a week	**Egy hétig**	ædᵞ hayteeg
2 weeks	**2 hétig**	2 hayteeg
a month	**Egy hónapig**	ædᵞ hāwnoppeeg
I don't know yet.	**Még nem tudom.**	mayg næm toodawm
I'm here on holiday.	**A szabadságomat töltöm itt.**	o sobbodshaagawmot turlturm eet
I'm here on business.	**Üzleti úton vagyok.**	ewzlætee ōōtawn vodᵞawk
I'm just passing through.	**Csak átutazóban vagyok.**	chok aatootozzāwbon vodᵞawk

If the going gets hard, say:

| I'm sorry, I don't understand. | **Sajnálom, de nem értem.** | shoynaalawm dæ næm ayrtæm |
| Does anyone here speak English? | **Beszél itt valaki angolul?** | bæsayl eet vollokkee ongawlool |

CAR/BORDER FORMALITIES: see page 146

23

Customs

After collecting your baggage, leave by the green exit if you
have nothing to declare or by the red exit if you have goods
on which you must pay duty. Spot checks are frequently
made in the green channel.

The chart shows what main items you may take into Hungary duty-free.*

Cigarettes		Cigars		Tobacco	Spirits	Wine
250	or	50	or	250 g	1 l. and	2 l.

Narcotics and obscene publications will be confiscated, with
more severe penalties reserved.

I've nothing to declare.	**Nincs elvámolni valóm.**	neench ælvaamawlnee vollāwm
I've a ...	**Van egy ...**	von æd^y
carton of cigarettes bottle of whisky	**karton cigarettám üveg viszkim**	kortawn tseegorrættaam ewvvæg veeskeem
This is a gift.	**Ez ajándék.**	æz oyaandayk
It's for my personal use.	**Ez a személyes használatomat szolgálja.**	æz o sæmay^yæsh hosnaalottawmot sawlgaalyo
This is not new.	**Ez nem új.**	æz næm ōō^y

Kérem az útlevelét.	Your passport, please.
Önnek vízumra van szüksége. Legyen szíves jöjjön velem.	You need a visa. Come with me, please.
Kérem, nyissa ki ezt a táskát.	Please open this bag.
Ezért vámot kell fizetnie.	You'll have to pay duty on this.
Van még egyéb csomagja is?	Have you any more luggage?

* All allowances subject to change without notice.

ARRIVAL

Baggage – Porters

Porters are in short supply, though with perseverence you should be able to locate one. You'll generally find baggage trolleys. Against an extra tip, your taxi driver will help you.

Porter!	**Hordár!**	hawrdaar
Please take these bags.	**Kérem,vigye ezeket a bőröndöket.**	kayræm veed^Yæ æzækæt o bŪrrurndurkæt
That's my ...	**Ez az én ...**	æz oz ayn
bag/luggage suitcase	**táskám/csomagom bőröndöm**	taashkaam/chawmoggawm bŪrrurndurm
There's one piece missing.	**Egy csomag hiányzik.**	æd^Y chawmog heeaan^Y- zeek
Take these bags to the ...	**Kérem, vigye ezeket a csomagokat ...**	kayræm veed^Yæ æzækæt o chawmoggawkot
bus	**az autóbuszhoz**	oz oootāwbooss-hawz
taxi	**a taxihoz**	o toxeehawz
luggage lockers	**a csomagmegőrzőbe**	o chawmogmægŪrrzŪrbæ
Where are the baggage trolleys?	**Hol vannak a podgyász kézi- kocsik?**	hawl von-nok o pawd^Yaass kayzeekawcheek

Changing money

You'll find currency exchange facilities at the airport, major railway stations and all entry points for road traffic. If you arrive after hours, your hotel will be able to change a certain amount of dollars, pounds sterling or some other foreign currencies for you. Keep all receipts.

See page 134 for details of money and currency exchange as well as banking hours.

Where's the nearest currency exchange?	**Hol tudok valutát beváltani?**	hawl toodawk vollootaat bævaaltonnee
Can you change these traveller's cheques (checks)?	**Beváltják ezeket a traveller's csekkeket?**	bævaaltyaak æzækæt o trovvæl-lærs chæk- kækæt

TIPPING: see page 1

want to change ...ome ...	... akarok beváltani.	... okkorrawk bævaal-tonnee
ollars	Dollárt	dawl-laart
ounds sterling	Angol fontot	ongawl fawntawt
Can you change this to forints?	Átváltaná ezt forintra?	aatvaaltonnaa æst fawreentro

Directions—Finding a room

Tourist information offices are to be found at Budapest international airport, major railway stations and border crossing points. They are often able to book you a hotel room if you arrive without a reservation. Some staff members may speak English or German.

How do I get to his address?	Hogy jutok el ide?	hawd^y yootawk æl eedæ
How do I get to his hotel?	Hogy jutok el ehhez a szállodához?	hawd^y yootawk æl æh-hæz o saal-lawdaahawz
Is there a bus into town?	Van autóbuszjárat a városba?	von ooootāwboosyaarot o vaarawshbo
Where can I get a taxi?	Hol kapok taxit?	hawl koppawk toxeet
Where can I hire a car?	Hol lehet autót bérelni?	hawl læhæt oootāwt bayrælnee
Have you a map of the town?	Van térképe a városról?	von tayrkaypæ o vaarawshrāwl
Could you book me a hotel room, please?	Kérem, foglaljon részemre egy szobát.	kayræm fawglolyawn rayssæmræ æd^y sawbaat
In the town centre near the station	a központban az állomás mellett	o kurzpawntbon oz aal-lawmaash mæl-læt
single room double room	egy egyágyas szobát egy kétágyas szobát	æd^y æd^{y}aad^{y}osh sawbaat æd^y kaytaad^{y}osh sawbaat
ot too expensive	nem túl drágát	næm tōōl draagaat
Where is the hotel located?	Hol található a szálloda?	hawl tollaalhottāw o saal-lawdo

CHECKING IN: see page 30

Car rental

Car hire firms have offices at Budapest international airport and major railway stations. You can also hire a vehicle through a tourist office or your hotel. You must be at least twenty-one years of age and have held a full driving licence for more than one year. See the section beginning on page 142 for information on driving in Hungary.

You'll usually find someone at the agency who speaks English but if not, use the following phrases to specify your requirements.

I'd like to hire a ... car.	Egy ... kocsit szeretnék bérelni.	ædͨ ... kawcheet særætnayk bayrælnee
large/small	nagyot/kicsit	nodͨawt/keecheet
I'd like it for ...	... szeretném.	... særætnaym
a day/4 days a week/2 weeks	Egy napra/4 napra Egy hétre/2 hétre	ædͨ nopro/4 nopro ædͨ haytræ/2 haytræ
What's the charge per ...?	Mennyi a bérleti díj ...?	mæn^yee o bayrlætee dēēͨ
day/week	naponként/hetenként	noppawnkaynt/ hætænkaynt
Does that include mileage?	A bérleti díjban a kilométer járulék is benne van?	o bayrlætee dēēͨbon o keelawmaytær yaaroolayk eesh bæn-næ von
What's the charge per kilometre?	Mennyi a járulék kilométerenként?	mæn^yee o yaaroolayk keelawmaytærænkaynt
Is petrol (gas) included?	Ebben benn van az üzemanyag költsége?	æb-bæn bæn von oz ewzæmon^yog kurltshaygæ
I want full insurance.	Casco biztosítást kérek.	koshkaw beeztawshēē-taasht kayræk
I'll be doing about 200 kilometres.	Körülbelül 200 kilométert utazom a kocsival.	kurrewbælewl 200 keelawmaytært ootozzawm o kawcheevol
What's the deposit?	Mennyi a garanciális letét?	mæn^yee o gorrontseeaaleesh lætayt
I've a credit card.	Rendelkezem hitelkártyával.	rændælkæzæm heetælkaart^yaavol

SIGHTSEEING: see page 75

ARRIVAL

Taxi

Metered vehicles both state-owned and private are available in Budapest and all larger towns. When they are free, the rooftop *Taxi* sign is lit. It's advisable to state your destination before entering the cab, as a driver may refuse trips which are too long or out of the way. For reasons of crime prevention (attacks on drivers) your taxidriver will want to phone in your name and passport number to his control centre if you are going beyond city limits. It's customary to give a tip in addition to the amount shown on the meter.

Where can I get a taxi?	Hol kapok taxit?	hawl koppawk toxeet
Please get me a taxi.	Kérem, szerezzen egy taxit.	kayræm særæz-zæn æd^y toxeet
What's the fare to ...?	... -ig mennyi a viteldíj?	...-eeg mæn^yee o veetældēē^y
Take me to ...	Kérem, vigyen el ...	kayræm veed^yæn æl
this address	erre a címre	ær-ræ o tsēēmræ
the airport	a repülőtérre	o ræpewlūrtayr-ræ
the station	a vasútállomásra	o voshōōtaal-lawmaashro
the ... Hotel	a ... szállóba	o ... saal-lāwbo
the city centre	a városközpontba	o vaarawshkurzpawntbo
Turn ... at the next corner.	Forduljon ... a következő sarkon.	fawrdoolyawn ... o kurvætkæzūr shorkawn
left	balra	bolro
right	jobbra	yawbro
Stop here, please.	Kérem, itt álljon meg.	kayræm eet aalyawn mæg
I'm in a hurry.	Sietek.	sheeætæk
Could you drive more slowly, please?	Kérem, hajtson lassabban.	kayræm hoytshawn loshshob-bon
Would you help me carry my bags?	Kérem, segítsen vinni a podgyászt.	kayræm shægheetshæn veennee o pawd^yaast
Would you please wait for me?	Kérem, várjon.	kayræm vaaryawn

TIPPING: see page 1

Hotel—Other accommodation

Hotel rooms are often in short supply, both in the capital and in popular tourist areas such as around Lake Balaton. Whenever possible, make your bookings well in advance, though your home travel agency, and take along written confirmation so as to avoid any misunderstandings on the spot. The busiest periods are the summer holiday season and any time when trade fairs, exhibitions or major international conferences are being held, particularly in Budapest. Travel agencies in your own country will probably be able to give you the precise dates of such events. Otherwise you may like to write to one of the foreign agencies of *Ibusz*, the Hungarian national tourist organization. They are located in the following cities in western Europe: Brussels, Cologne, Frankfurt, London, Paris, Rome, Stockholm and Vienna. There is also an *Ibusz* office in New York. Your home travel agency will be able to give your their addresses.

Students might ask their national student travel service for details of inexpensive accommodation available in Hungary. You should take along an international student identity card if you intend to make use of such facilities.

Should you arrive in the country without prearranged accommodation, there are several offices you can turn to for assistance in finding a room. Tourist information offices are maintained at virtually all entry points. Local travel agencies may also make reservations for you. If hotels are full, they may be able to put you up in private homes. A booking fee is charged for on-the-spot reservations.

Rates are up to 30 per cent lower outside the main summer tourist season. A room for two works out appreciably cheaper than two single rooms.

CAMPING: see page 90

Szálloda
(**saal**-lawdo)

Hotels large and small go under this name (though the foreign word "hotel" is also used quite widely). They are graded by stars, from 5-star de-luxe establishments to 1-star budget hotels.

Only two or three top-rank international hotels in the capital are air-conditioned. Very few have swimming pools or saunas. Hotels are clean and standards of service acceptable, depending on the category of hotel. Most 3-, 4- and 5-star hotels offer shopping arcades, tourist and airline offices and a variety of sightseeing programs.

Motel
(**mawt**æl)

These are relatively rare in Hungary. Most are to be found along the shores of Lake Balaton as well as at some principal road junctions.

Fizetővendég-szolgálat
(**fee**zætūrvæn-dayg**sawl**gaalot)

This is the term for private accommodation, a service operated by most travel agencies both in Budapest and throughout the country. In Budapest, rates overlap with those of modest hotels, but in the countryside they are usually very moderate. You may have the choice of room only or with breakfast included. Bathroom facilities, generally shared, are available.

Along major roads and in holiday centres you will also see numerous signs for private accommodation reading *Szoba kiadó* or, in German, *Fremdenzimmer*. Both are the equivalent of the English "Bed and Breakfast". Feel free to knock on the door yourself, phrase book in hand— there's no need to go through an agency for this type of accommodation.

HOTEL

Checking in—Reception

My name is ...	... vagyok.	... vod^yawk
I've a reservation.	Már foglaltam szobát.	maar fawgloltom sawbaat
We've reserved two rooms, one single and a double.	Két szobát foglaltunk, egy egyágyasat és egy kétágyasat.	kayt sawbaat fawgloltoonk æd^y æd^yaad^yoshot aysh æd^y kaytaad^yoshot
Here's the confirmation.	Itt a visszaigazolásuk.	eet o vess-so-eegozzawlaashook
I'd like a ...	Szeretnék ...	særætnayk
single room	egyágyas szobát	æd^yaad^yosh sawbaat
double room	kétágyas szobát	kaytaad^yosh sawbaat
room with a bath	fürdőszobás szobát	fewrdūrsawbaash sawbaat
room with a shower	egy szobát zuhannyal	æd^y sawbaat zoohan^yol
room with a balcony	erkélyes szobát	ærkay^yæsh sawbaat
room with a view	szobát szép kilátással	sawbaat sayp keelaataash-shol
in the front	az utcai oldalon	oz oottsoee awldollawn
at the back	a hátsó oldalon	o haatshāw awldollawn
facing the lake	amelyik a tóra néz	ommæ^yeek o tāwro nayz
facing the courtyard	az udvari oldalon	oz oodvorree awldollawn
It must be quiet.	Egy csendes szobát kérek.	æd^y chændæsh sawbaat kayræk
I'd like a room a bit higher up/lower down.	A szobát egy kissé feljebb/lejjebb szeretném.	o sawbaat æd^y keesh-shay fælyæb/læ^y-yæb særætnaym
Is there ...?	Van ...?	von
central heating	központifűtés	kurzpawnteefēwtaysh
a radio in the room	rádió a szobában	raadeeāw o sawbaabon
a TV set in the room	TV a szobában	tayvay o sawbaabon
room service	felszolgálás a szobában	fælsawlgaalaash o sawbaabon
hot water	meleg víz	mælæg vēēz
running water	hideg víz	heedæg vēēz
a private toilet	külön W.C.	kewlurn vaytsay

In the higher-category hotels, most of the staff at the reception desk speak some English or German.

How long?

We'll be staying …	… maradunk.	… morroddoonk
overnight only	Csak erre az éjszakára	chock ær-ræ oz ay^{V}ssokkaaro
a few days	Néhány napig	nayhaan^V noppeeg
a week (at least)	(Legalább) egy hétig	(lægollaab) æd^V hayteeg
I don't know yet.	Még nem tudom.	mayg næm toodawm

How much?

What's the price …?	Mennyibe kerül …?	mæn^{V}eebæ kærewl
per night	egy éjszakára	æd^V ay^{V}ssokkaaro
per week	egy hétre	æd^V haytræ
for bed and breakfast	a szoba reggelivel	o sawbo ræg-gæleevæl
without meals	étkezés nélkül	aytkæzaysh naylkewl
for half board	napi két étkezéssel	noppee kayt aytkæzaysh-shayl
Does that include …?	Ez magában foglalja …?	æz moggaabon fawglolyo
service	a kiszolgálási díjat	o keessawlgaalaashee deeyot
resort tax	az üdülőhelyi illetéket	oz ewdewlūrhæ^{V}ee eel-lætaykæt
Is there any reduction for children?	Van kedvezmény a gyerekek után?	von kædvæzmayn^V o d^{V}ærækæk ootaan

Decision

May I see the room?	Megnézhetem a szobát?	mægnayzhætæm o sawbaat
I asked for a room with a bath.	Egy fürdőszobás szobát rendeltem.	æd^V fewrdūrsawbaash sawbaat rændæltæm
Do you have anything …?	Volna egy … szobájuk?	vawlno æd^V … sawbaayook
better/bigger	jobb/nagyobb	yawb/nod^{V}awb
cheaper/quieter	olcsóbb/csendesebb	awlchawb/chændæshæb
That's fine. I'll take it.	Ez jó lesz. Ezt kiveszem.	æz yāw læs. æst keevæsæm

NUMBERS: see page 175

HOTEL

Registration

Upon arrival at a hotel, motel or private boarding house, you'll have to fill in a registration form *(bejelentőlap)*. If it doesn't carry an English translation, ask:

What does this mean? **Ez mit jelent?** æz meet yælænt

If you don't understand what he's saying, show him this section:

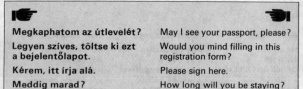

Megkaphatom az útlevelét?	May I see your passport, please?
Legyen szíves, töltse ki ezt a bejelentőlapot.	Would you mind filling in this registration form?
Kérem, itt írja alá.	Please sign here.
Meddig marad?	How long will you be staying?

What's my room number?	**Mi a szoba számom?**	mee o sawbo saamawm
Where can I park my car?	**Hol hagyhatom a kocsimat?**	hawl hod^yhottawm o kawcheemot
I'd like to leave this in your safe.	**Ezt a széfjükben szeretném hagyni.**	æzt o sayfyewkbæn særætnaym hod^ynee
Will you have my luggage sent up?	**Felvitetné a csomagjaimat?**	fælveetætnay o chawmod^yoeemot
Will you please wake me up at ...?	**Kérem ébresszen fel ... órakor.**	kayræm aybræs-sæn fæl... awrokawr

The bill (check)

Bills are usually paid weekly or, of course, upon departure if you stay less than a week. A 10-15 per cent service charge is generally included in the bill, but you may like to ask:

Is service included? **A felszolgálási díj benne van az árban?** o fælsawlgaalaashee dee^y bæn-næ von oz aarbon

Tipping is practically a must in Hungary. See inside back cover.

TELLING THE TIME: see page 178

Service, please!

Now that you are safely installed, meet some members of the hotel staff:

bellboy	kifutó	keefootāw
maid	szobalány	sawbollaan^y
manager	szálloda igazgató	saal-lawdo eegozgottāw
porter	hordár	hawrdaar
switchboard operator	telefonközpontos	tælæfawnkurzpawntawsh
waiter	pincér	peentsayr
waitress	pincérnő	peentsayrnūr

If you want to address members of the staff, you don't use the actual names shown above, but a general introductory phrase:

Excuse me ...	Elnézést ...	ælnayzaysht

General requirements

Please ask the maid to come up.	Kérem, küldje fel a szobalányt.	kayræm kewld^yæ fæl o sawbollaan^yt
Who is it?	Ki az?	kee oz
Just a minute.	Egy pillanat.	æd^y peel-lonnot
Come in!	Jöjjön be!	yur^y-yurn bæ
Please bring us ...	Kérem, hozzon nekünk ...	kayræm hawz-zawn nækewnk
2 cups of coffee	2 csésze kávét	2 chayssæ kaavayt
a sandwich	egy szendvicset	æd^y sændveechæt
Can we have breakfast in our room?	Reggelizhetünk a szobában?	ræg-gæleez-hætewnk o sawbaabon
What's the voltage here?	Milyen a feszültség?	mee^yæn o fæsewltshayg
Is there a bath on this floor?	Van fürdőszoba ezen az emeleten?	von fewrdūrsawbo æzæn oz æmælætæn
Can you get me a babysitter?	Tudnának egy bébiszittert szerezni?	toodnaanok æd^y baybeesseet-tært særæznee

May I have a/an/some ...?	Kaphatok ...?	kophottawk
ashtray	egy hamutálcát	æd^Y hommooltaaltsaat
bath towel	egy fürdőtörülközőt	æd^Y fewrdürturrewlkurzürt
extra blanket	egy plusz takarót	æd^Y plooss tokkorrāwt
envelopes	egy borítékot	æd^Y bawrēētaykawt
(more) hangers	vállfákat	vaalfaakot
hot-water bottle	ágymelegítőt	aad^{Y}mælægheētürt
ice cubes	jégkockákat	yaygkawtskaakot
needle and thread	tűt, cérnát	tēwt tsayrnaat
reading lamp	egy olvasólámpát	æd^Y awlvoshāwlaampaat
soap	szappant	sop-pont
writing paper	levélpapírt	lævaylpoppēērt
Where's the ...?	Hol van ...?	hawl von
bathroom	a fürdőszoba	o fewrdürsawbo
cocktail lounge	a koktél bár	o kawktayl baar
dining room	az étterem	oz ayt-tæræm
emergency exit	a vészkijárat	o vayskee^{Y}aarot
hairdresser's	a fodrász	o fawdraass
telephone	a telefon	o tælæfawn
television room	a TV szoba	o tayvay sawbo
toilet	a W.C.	o vaytsay

Breakfast

The Hungarian breakfast is a very substantial affair and is considered one of the most important meals of the day. It may consist of rolls and butter, jam, salami, cheese and eggs. Some even like a dish of excellent goulash or some stew to start off the day. If this is too much for you, just specify what you would like from the following list.

I'd like breakfast, please.	Reggelizni szeretnék.	ræg-gæleeznee særæt-nayk
I'll have some ...	Kérek ...	kayræk
cocoa	kakaót	kokkoāwt
coffee	kávét	kaavayt
with whipped cream	tejszínhabbal	tæ^{Y}ssēēnhob-bol
with milk	tejjel	tæ^Y-yæl
juice	gyümölcslét	d^{Y}ewmurlchlayt
grapefruit	grépfrutot	graypfrootawt
orange	narancslét	norronchlayt

EATING OUT: see page 38

milk	tejet	tæ^yæt
hot	melegen	mælægæn
cold	hidegen	heedægæn
tea	egy teát	æd^y tayaat
with milk	tejjel	tæ^y-yæl
with lemon	citrommal	tseetrawm-mol

May I have a/some …?	Kaphatok …?	kophottawk
boiled egg	főtt tojást	fūrt taw^yaasht
hard	kemény tojást	kæmayn^y taw^yaasht
medium	közepes tojást	kurzæpæsh taw^yaasht
soft	lágy tojást	laad^y taw^yaasht
bread	kenyeret	kæn^yæræt
butter	vajat	voyot
cheese	egy adag sajtot	æd^y oddog shoytawt
crescent rolls	kiflit	keefleet
fried eggs	tükör tojást	tewkurr taw^yaasht
ham and eggs	sonkát tojással	shawnkaat taw^yaash-shol
honey	mézet	mayzæt
jam	egy adag lekvárt	æd^y oddog lækvaart
rolls	péksüteményt	paykshewtæmayn^yt
salami	egy adag szalámit	æd^y oddog sollaameet
scrambled eggs	tojásrántottát	taw^yaashraantawt-taat
toast	tósztot	tāwstawt
yoghurt	egy joghurtot	æd^y yawghoortawt

Would you bring me some …?	Kérem, hozzon nekem …?	kayræm hawz-zawn nækæm
cream	tejszínt	tæ^ysseent
lemon	citromot	tseetrawmawt
pepper	borsot	bawrshawt
salt	sót	shāwt
sugar	cukrot	tsookrawt
(a glass of) water	(egy pohár) vizet	(æd^y pawhaar) veezæt
hot water	forróvizet	fawr-rāwveezæt

Difficulties

But perhaps there's something wrong…

The … doesn't work.	A … nem működik.	o … næm mēwkurdeek
heating	fűtés	fēwtaysh
light	világítás	veelaaghēētaash
radiator	fűtőtest	fēwtūrtæsht
radio	rádió	raadeeāw

shower	**zuhany**	zoohon[y]
tap	**csap**	chop
television	**TV**	tayvay
toilet	**W.C.**	vaytsay
ventilator	**ventillátor**	vænteel-laatawr

The washbasin is clogged.	**A mosdó el van dugulva.**	o mawshdaw æl von doogoolvo
The window is jammed.	**Az ablak be van szorulva.**	oz oblok bæ von sawroolvo
The blind is stuck.	**A roló fennakadt.**	o rawlaw fænokkodt
These aren't my shoes.	**Ez nem az én cipőm.**	æz næm oz ayn tseepürm
This isn't my laundry.	**Ez nem az én fehérnemüm.**	æz næm oz ayn fæhayrnæmewm
There's no hot water.	**Nincs melegvíz.**	neench mælægveez
My room has not been made up.	**Nem rakták rendbe a szobámat.**	næm roktaak rændbæ o sawbaamot
I've left the key in my room.	**A szobában felejtettem a kulcsomat.**	o sawbaabon fælæ[y]-tættæm o koolchawmot
The bulb is burnt out.	**Kiégett a körte.**	keeaygæt o kurrtæ
The ... is broken.	**Eltörött ...**	ælturrurt
lamp	**a lámpa**	o laampo
plug	**a dugasz**	o doogoss
shutter	**a zsalu**	o zholloo
socket	**a konnektor**	o kawnæktawr
switch	**a kapcsoló**	o kopchawlaw
venetian blind	**a redőny**	o rædürn[y]
window shade	**az ablakroló**	oz oblokrawlaw
Can you get it repaired?	**Meg tudja javíttatni?**	mæg toodyo yovveetotnee

Telephone—Mail—Callers

Can you get me London 123 4567?	**Kérem, hívja fel a London 123 4567 számot!**	kayræm heevyo fæl o lawndawn 123 4567 saamawt
Has anyone phoned for me?	**Keresett valaki?**	kæræshæt vollokkee

POST OFFICE AND TELEPHONE: see pages 137–141

Is there any mail for me?	Van a részemre posta?	von o rayssæmræ pawshto
Are there any messages for me?	Érkezett a részemre valami üzenet?	ayrkæzæt o rayssæmræ vollommee ewzænæt
Do you sell stamps?	Postabélyegük van?	pawshtobbay^{y}ægewk von
Would you please post this for me?	Kérem, feladná ezt nekem?	kayræm fælodnaa æst nækæm

Checking out

May I have my bill?	Kérem, a számlámat.	kayræm o saamlaamot
I must leave at once.	Rögtön indulnom kell.	rurgturn eendoolnawm kæl
We'll be checking out soon/around noon.	Korán elutazunk./ Dél körül utazunk el.	kawraan ælootozzoonk/ dayl kurrewl ootozzoonk æl
I'm leaving early tomorrow. Please have my bill ready.	Holnap korán utazom el. Kérem, készítsék el a számlámat.	hawlnop kawraan ootozzawm æl. kayræm kayssēētshayk æl o saamlaamot
Is everything included?	Ebben minden szerepel?	æb-bæn meendæn særæpæl
You've made a mistake in this bill, I think.	Azt hiszem, hibásan állította össze a számlát.	ost heessæm heebaashon aal-lēētawt-to urs-sæ o saamlaat
When's the next ... to Vienna?	Mikor indul a következő ... Bécsbe?	meekawr eendool o kurvætkæzūr ... baychbæ
bus/plane/train	autóbusz/repülő/ vonat	oootāwbooss/ræpewlūr/ vawnot
Would you get me a taxi?	Hívna egy taxit?	hēēvno æd^y toxeet
Would you please have somebody bring down our luggage?	Kérem, küldjön valakit, aki leviszi a csomagjainkat.	kayræm kewld^{y}urn vollokkeet okkee læveessee o chawmogyo-eenkot
We're in a great hurry.	Borzasztóan sietünk.	bawrzostāwon sheeætewnk
Here's my forwarding address.	Ez a következő címem.	æz o kurvætkæzūr tsēēmæm
It's been a very enjoyable stay.	Nagyon jól éreztük itt magunkat.	nod^{y}awn yāwl ayræztewk eet moggoonkot

TAXI: see page 27

Eating out

There are many different types of places in which to enjoy meals and drink, from simple snackbars to luxury restaurants:

Bisztró
(beestrāw)

A small restaurant, generally offering reasonably priced standard meals and drinks, including coffee and tea, at any time during opening hours. Usually frequented by people in a hurry.

Büfé
(bewfay)

Found at railway and bus stations, in shopping centres and department stores, buffets serve hot and cold sandwiches, cakes, desserts and all kind of drinks including coffee and tea. Some are open round the clock. Prices are reasonable.

Csárda
(chaardo)

A country inn, usually offering regional food and drink specialities in the medium price range. In the evening, gypsy bands often provide romantic music to go with the meal. Found mainly on major highways.

Cukrászda
(tsookraazdo)

A pastry shop serving sandwiches, cakes, desserts, ice cream, soft drinks, coffee, tea and alcoholic drinks. Larger establishments have light or pop music, either taped or live. Prices tend to be rather high.

Étkező
(aytkæzūr)

A small inn, often with only a few tables, serving regional specialities, local wines and beer at modest prices.

Étterem
(ayt-tæræm)

The traditional restaurant, serving a wide range of dishes and drinks. These establishments are classified according to location, facilities and standard of service, with the category indicated on the menu (see page 40). Prices do not necessarily reflect quality of food, and the self-same dish may cost much more in a first-class restaurant than in a modest one. Gypsy bands often play at night. In a hotel *étterem*, price and quality depend on the category of the hotel.

Kifőzés (**keefűrzaysh**)	A small, low-priced inn, often a family concern, open mainly during the tourist season. First-class country food as well as local wine and beer are served. In the Lake Balaton area some of these establishments are famous for their gourmet creations.
Önkiszolgáló (**urnkeessawlgaalaw**)	A self-service snackbar-type establishment. Mostly located in town centres and near railway stations, they are inexpensive but not always too clean.
Snackbár ("snackbar")	A superior *önkiszolgáló* offering sandwiches, cakes and all kinds of drinks including espresso coffee and tea at slightly higher prices.
Vendéglő (**vændayglūr**)	A larger restaurant, usually with rustic décor, serving moderately priced meals and all kinds of drinks. Good gypsy music is often played at night.

Mainly for drinking

Borozó (**bawrawzāw**)	A wine bar, offering a variety of wines and some snacks. Prices vary widely.
Borpince (**bawrpeentsæ**)	A wine cellar, usually run by a wine-producing cooperative or farm. Exceptionally high-quality wines and light food are available at moderate prices.
Drinkbár ("drinkbar")	A bar, frequented mostly by tourists, serving mainly spirits (liquor). Prices are high.
Eszpresszó (**æspræss-sāw**)	A small coffee bar offering mainly espresso coffee but also some other non-alcoholic and alcoholic beverages at moderate prices. Light refreshments and ice-cream are also available.
Mulató (**moolottāw**)	A modest nightclub, with a minor floor show. The accent is on expensive imported spirits. Light snacks are available.
Söröző (**surrurzūr**)	A beer hall, with moderate prices. Some imported beers are available but at higher prices.
Tejbár/Tejivó (**tæ^Ybaar/tæ^Yeevāw**)	Milkbars go under either of these two names. In addition to milk and milk-based drinks, sandwiches, cakes and other snacks are available, all at very reasonable prices. Just the place for breakfast or a mid-morning snack.

EATING OUT

Meals and menus

By law, all eating places must offer at least two complete set menus (*napi menü*—**no**ppee **mæ**new) at low to moderate prices. These menus typically comprise a soup, a main course and dessert or fruit. However, many people prefer to order à la carte. As a rule, drinks are listed on a separate card and they may be served by a different waiter. Some top restaurants also offer special dishes for those on certain diets as well as smaller portions for children. It is customary to tip the waiter 8–10 per cent of the bill, depending on quality of service.

You will generally see one or more of the following explanatory notices on the bill of fare:

EATING OUT

I. osztályu étterem	First-class restaurant
II. osztályu étterem	Second-class restaurant
III. osztályu étterem	Third-class restaurant
Osztályon felüli étterem.	Top-class restaurant
Az árak köret nélkül értendők.	Prices do not include garnishes.
Az ételeket körettel szolgáljuk fel.	Meals are served with garnishes.
Az X—el jelölt ételek elfogytak.	Meals marked with X are no longer available.
... Ft. kötelező fogyasztás.	Minimum order: ... forints.

Meal times

Breakfast (*reggeli*—**ræg**-gælee): 7–10 a.m.

Lunch (*ebéd*—**æ**bayd): noon–2 or 3 p.m.

Dinner (*vacsora*—**vo**chawro): 7–10 or 11 p.m.

Restaurants in leading hotels will often serve à-la-carte meals in your room round the clock.

BREAKFAST: see page 34

Hungry

I'm hungry/I'm thirsty.	**Éhes vagyok/ Szomjas vagyok.**	ayhæsh vod^yawk/ sawmyosh vod^yawk
Can you recommend a good restaurant?	**Ajánlana egy jó éttermet?**	oyaanlonno æd^y yāw ayt-tærmæt
Are there any inexpensive restaurants around here?	**Találhatók a környéken olcsó éttermek?**	tollaalhottāwk o kurrn^yaykæn awlchāw ayttærmæk

To be sure of getting a table in a well-known restaurant it's advisable to reserve your table in advance by telephone.

I'd like to book a table for 4, please.	**4 fő részére szeretnék asztalt foglalni.**	4 fūr rayssayræ særætnayk ostolt fawglolnee
We'll come at 8.	**8 órakor jövünk.**	8 āwrokkawr yurvewnk

Asking and ordering

Good evening. I'd like a table for 2.	**Jó estét kívánok. 2 fő részére kérek egy asztalt.**	yāw æshtayt keevaanawk. 2 fūr rayssayræ kayræk æd^y ostolt
I've reserved a table for 4.	**4 fő részére rendeltem asztalt.**	4 fūr rayssayræ rændæltæm ostolt
Could we have a table ...?	**Lenne szabad asztaluk ...?**	læn-næ sobbod ostollook
in the corner	**a sarokban**	o shorrawkbon
by the window	**az ablaknál**	oz obloknaal
outside	**kinnt**	keent
on the terrace	**a teraszon**	o tærossawn
Are these seats taken?	**Ezek a helyek foglaltak?**	æzæk o hæ^yæk fawgloltok
Waiter!/Waitress!	**Pincér!/Pincérnő!**	peentsayr/peentsayrnūr
I'd/We'd like something to drink/ eat.	**Szeretnék/Szeretnénk valamit inni/ enni.**	særætnayk/særætnaynk vollommeet een-nee/ æn-nee
What are the set menus?	**Mi a mai menü?**	mee o moee mænew

NUMBERS: see page 175

EATING OUT

42

May I have the menu and the drinks card?	Kérem az étlapot és az itallapot.	kayræm oz aytloppawt aysh oz eetol-loppawt
Can you serve me straight away? I'm in a hurry.	Azonnali kiszolgálást kérek. Sietek.	ozzawn-nollee keessawlgaalaasht kayræk. sheeætæk
Could we have a plate for the child, please?	Hozna egy tányért a gyereknek?	hawzno æd^y taan^yayrt o d^yæræknæk
Do you have any local dishes?	Ajánlana valami helyi különlegességet?	oyaanlonno vollommee hæ^yee kewlurnlægæsh-shaygæt
What's this?	Ez mi?	æz mee
Could we have a/an/ some ..., please?	Kaphatunk ...?	kophottoonk

another chair	még egy széket	mayg æd^y saykæt
ashtray	egy hamutartót	æd^y hommootortāwt
bottle of ...	egy üveg ...-t*	æd^y ewvæg ...-t
fork	egy villát	æd^y veel-laat
glass	egy poharat	æd^y pawhorrot
glass of water	egy pohár vizet	æd^y pawhaar veezæt
knife	egy kést	æd^y kaysht
lighter	egy öngyújtót	æd^y urnd^yōō^ytāwt
matches	gyufát	d^yoofaat
plate	egy tányért	æd^y taan^yayrt
serviette	egy szalvétát	æd^y solvaytaat
spoon	egy kanalat	æd^y konnollot
toothpicks	fogpiszkálót	fawgpeeskaalāwt

Mit parancsol?	What would you like?
Szabad ezt ajánlanom?	May I recommend this?
Mit óhajt inni?	What would you like to drink?
Sajnos, nem szolgálhatunk ... val.	We don't have any ...
Parancsol ...-t?	Do you want ...?

---

* See Grammar section for word endings.

I'd like ...	Kérnék ...	kayrnayk
aperitif	egy aperitívet	æd^y opæreetēēvæt
appetizer	elöételt	æluraytælt
beer	sört	shurrt
bread	kenyeret	kæn^yæræt
butter	vajat	voyot
cheese	sajtot	shoytawt
chicken	csirkét	cheerkayt
chips (Br.)	sült burgonyát	shewlt boorgawn^yaat
coffee	kávét	kaavayt
dessert	édességet	aydæsh-shaygæt
fish	halat	hollot
French fries	sült burgonyát	sewlt boorgawn^yaat
fruit	gyümölcsöt	d^yewmurlchurt
fruit juice	gyümölcslét	d^yewmurlchlayt
game	vadas ételt	voddosh aytælt
goulash	gulyáslevest	goo^yaashlævæsht
ice-cream	fagylaltot	fod^yloltawt
ketchup	ketchupot	kæchurpurt
lemonade	limonádét	leemawnaadayt
lettuce	fejes-salátát	fæ^yaysh shollaataat
meat	húst	hōōsht
milk	tejet	tæ^yæt
mineral water	ásványvizet	aashvaan^yveezæt
mustard	mustárt	mooshtaart
noodles	metéltet	mætayltæt
oil	étolajat	aytawloyot
pepper	borsot	bawrshawt
potatoes	burgonyát	boorgawn^yaat
poultry	szárnyast	saarn^yosht
rice	rizst	reezht
rolls	péksüteményt	paykshewtæmayn^yt
saccharine	szaharint	sohorreent
salad	salátát	shollaataat
salt	sót	shāwt
sandwich	szendvicset	sændveechæt
soft drink	üditőitalt	ewdeetūr-eetolt
soup	levest	lævæsht
spaghetti	spagettit	shpoggæt-teet
sugar	cukrot	tsookrawt
tea	teát	tæaat
vegetables	főzeléket	fūrzælaykæt
vinegar	ecetet	ætsætæt
water	vizet	veezæt
wine	bort	bawrt

What's on the menu?

Our menu is presented according to courses. Under each heading you'll find an alphabetical list of dishes likely to be offered on a Hungarian menu, with their English equivalents. You can also show the book to the waiter. Should you want some soup, for example, show him the corresponding list and let him point to what's available. Use pages 41-44 for ordering in general.

In Hungary, a typical à-la-carte meal consists of soup, an entrée, the main course and then a dessert or cheese. Many enjoy an aperitif to start off with and accompany the meal with one or two matching wines. (If you prefer beer or mineral water, your choice will raise no eyebrows.) Invariably, the occasion is rounded off with a good, strong coffee and a fruit brandy.

Here, then, is our guide to good eating and drinking. Just turn to the section you want.

EATING OUT

Appetizers

Restaurants offer a rich choice of both international and typically Hungarian appetizers, both hot and cold. For a light meal it's quite acceptable to take a soup, then an appetizer, and skip the rest.

I'd like a …	… is kérnék.	… eesh kayrnayk
cold appetizer	Hideg előétel	heedæg ælūraytælt
hot appetizer	Meleg előétel	mælæg ælūraytælt
What would you recommend?	Mit ajánlana?	meet oyaanlonno

Cold appetizers

apró fánk	oprāw faank	small chicken fritter
bécsi hering-saláta	baychee hæreeng-shollaato	herring salad Vienna style (with vinegar)
dinnye koktél	deen^yæ kawktayl	melon cocktail
dinnye sonkával	deen^yæ shawnkaavol	melon with ham
francia saláta	frontseeo shollaato	Russian salad
halmajonéz	holmoyawnayz	fish with mayonnaise
jérce koktél	yayrtsæ kawktayl	chicken cocktail
kaszinó tojás	kosseenāw taw^yaash	eggs with mayonnaise
kaviár	kovveeaar	caviar
majonézes kukorica	moyawnayzæsh kookawreetso	sweetcorn with mayonnaise
orosz hússaláta	awrawss hōōsh-shollaato	Russian salad with meat
ráksaláta	raakshollaato	crab salad
töltött tojás kaviárral	turlturt taw^yaash kovveeaar-rol	eggs stuffed with caviar

alföldi saláta
(olfurldee shollaato)
salad Alföldi style ("Puszta salad"): slices of sausage in a vinaigrette sauce (oil, vinegar, herbs)

almás cékla
(olmaash tsayklo)
apple slices and diced beetroot in a vinaigrette sauce

fokhagymás majonézes fejes saláta
(fawkhod^ymaash moyawnayzæsh fæ^yæsh shollaato)
lettuce salad with garlic-flavoured mayonnaise

EATING OUT

gombafejek máj-krémmel töltve
(**gawm**boffæ\ek maa\kraymmæl **turl**tvæ)

mushrooms stuffed with liver paté

halsaláta szegedi módra
(**hol**shollaato **sæ**gædee **maaw**dro)

fish salad Szeged style: fish pieces, diced peppers, tomatoes and chives turned in oil and accompanied by lettuce and hard-boiled eggs

hideg fogas tartár-mártással
(**hee**dæg **faw**gosh tortaarmaartaash-shol)

kind of pike-perch with tartar sauce (mayonnaise with gherkins, chives, capers and olives)

paprika szeletek körözöttel töltve
(**po**preeko **sæ**lætæk kurrurzurt-tæl **turl**tvæ)

green peppers, sliced in four, filled with a mix of ewe's cheese, butter, mustard, paprika, caraway seeds and some beer

Hot appetizers

csirág csőben sütve
cheeraag **chür**bæn **shewt**væ

baked asparagus

libamáj rizottó
leebomaa\ reezawt-taw

goose-liver risotto

tálon sült tojás
taalawn shewlt **taw**\aash

fried eggs, meat slices

zöldbab csőben sütve
zurldbob **chür**bæn **shewt**væ

and vegetables fried string beans

hortobágyi húsos palacsinta
(**haw**rtawbaad\ee **hoo**shawsh pollo-cheento)

stuffed omelet Hortobágy style: filled with veal or pork meat and sour cream, then briefly gratinated

libamáj pástétom
(leebommaa\ paashtaytawm)

goose-liver paté mixed with butter and béchamel (white) sauce, spices and brandy, served in flaky-pastry shell

omlet debreceni módra
(awmlæt dæbrætsænee **maaw**dro)

omelet Debrecen stype: filled with lecsó (a mix of sliced green peppers, tomatoes, rice and spices) and dry sausage slices

veseszeletek para-dicsommal
(**væsh**æsælætæk porroddeechawm-mol)

kidney slices with tomato

Bread and other bakery products

"The Hungarians will even eat bread with bread" goes an old saying—which may give you an idea of the varied and tasty range of bakery products you can look forward to in this country. Most milk bars, beer halls and better restaurants automatically place a selection of them on your table when you order.

fodros fehér kalács (fawdrawsh fæhayr kollaach)	spongy white milk-bread, available as rolls or in slices
mazsolás kalács (mozhawlaash kollaach)	spongy white milk-bread with raisins
briás kifli (awreeaash keeflee)	large, flaky, crescent-shaped roll
paprikás stangli (popreekaash shtonglee)	paprika-seasoned bread finger, reddish in colour
sajtos pogácsa (shoytawsh pawgaacho)	bread cone with cheese
tepertős pogácsa (tæpærtūrsh pawgaacho)	crispy bread cone, slightly salted and peppered, with bacon pieces
túrós karika (tōōrawsh korreeko)	dough ring with curds

Soups

Richly flavoured soups are part of the Hungarian way of life. They are generally quite thick. In some regions soup may be served for breakfast.

I'd like some soup.	**Levest kérek.**	lævæsht kayræk
almaleves hidegen/ melegen	olmollævæsh heedægæn/ mælægæn	cold/hot apple soup
bajai halászlé	boyo-ee hollaaslay	fish and potato soup
burgonyakrémleves	boorgawn^yokraymlævæsh	cream of potato soup
csontleves	chawntlævæsh	bone consommé

erőleves húsgom-bóccal	**ærūrlævæsh hōōshgawm-bāwtstsol**	consommé with meat dumplings
gombaleves	**gawm**bollævæsh	mushroom soup
kalocsai halászlé	**kollawcho-ee ho**llaaslay	fish soup in red wine
paradicsomleves	**porroddee**chawmlævæsh	tomato soup
savanyútojás leves	shovvon^Vōōtaw^Vaash lævæsh	sour egg soup
spárgakrém leves	**shpaar**gokraym lævæsh	cream of asparagus soup
tejfeles bableves	tæ^Vfælæsh boblævæsh	bean soup with sour cream
vegyes gyümölcs-leves hidegen	væd^Væsh d^Vewmurlchlæ-væsh heedægæn	chilled fruit soup

Soup specialities

bakonyi betyárleves (bokkawn^Vee bæt^Vaarlævæsh)	"outlaw soup"—soup Bakony style: a mix of chicken, beef chunks, thin noodles, mushrooms and vegetables, richly spiced
gulyásleves (gooyaashlævæsh)	Hungarian goulash: a mix of beef chunks, pota-toes, onions, tomatoes and peppers, richly spiced with paprika, caraway seeds and garlic
Jókai bableves (yāwko-ee boblævæsh)	bean soup Jókai style (Jókai was a famous Hungarian writer): a mix of smoked pig's knuck-les, butter beans and carrots, seasoned with pepper, garlic, paprika and parsley
kunsági pandúrleves (koonshaaghee pondōōrlævæsh)	chicken or pigeon soup Kunság style: seasoned with paprika, grated nutmeg, ginger and garlic
magyaros bur-gonyaleves (mod^Vorrawsh boorgawn^Vollævæsh)	Hungarian potato soup: diced potatoes and onions with paprika
magyaros csirke-aprólék leves (mod^Vorrawsh cheer-kæoprāwlayk lævæsh)	Hungarian chicken giblet soup with mushrooms, diced potatoes, pepper rings and tomatoes
palócleves (pollāwtslævæsh)	a mix of mutton, French beans, potatoes and sour cream, seasoned with paprika, garlic and caraway seeds
szegedi halászlé (sægædee hollaaslay)	a mix of various kinds of fish (usually carp, pike and wels), tomato and pepper rings, with hot paprika seasoning

Fish

I'd like some fish.	**Halat szeretnék.**	hollot særætnayk
What fish do you recommend?	**Milyen halat ajánl?**	mee^yæn hollott oyaanl

csuka	chooko	pike
fogas	fawgosh	a local fish of the pike-perch family
harcsa	horcho	wels
kecsege	kæchægæ	sterlet
nyelvhal	n^yælvhol	sole
pisztráng	peestraang	trout
ponty	pawnt^y	carp
tőkehal	tūrkæhol	cod
tonhal	tawnhol	tunny (Am. tuna)

Fish specialities

csuka tejfölben sütve (chooko tæ^yfurlbæn shewtvæ)	pike fried and served with sour cream
fogas fehér bormár- ásban (fawgosh fæhayr bawrmaartaashbon)	*fogas* in a white-wine sauce
fogasszeletek Gundel módra (fawgoshsælætæk goondæl māwdro)	slices of *fogas* Gundel style (Gundel was a famous Hungarian restaurateur): breaded fillet of pike
halfatányéros (holfottaan^yayrawsh)	assorted fish, some breaded or fried, served on a wooden plate, accompanied by tartar sauce
harcsaszelet fűszermártásban (horchossælæt fēwsæmaartaashbon)	fillet of wels in a spicy sauce doused with white wine
kecsege tejszínes paprikás mártásban (kæchægæ tæ^ysēēnæsh popreekaash maartaashbon)	sterlet in a cream and paprika sauce

paprikás ponty
(popreekaash pawnt^y)

carp served in a paprika sauce

pisztráng tejszín mártásban
(peestraang tæ^ysseen maartaashbon)

trout baked in cream

rostélyos töltött ponty
(rawshtay^yawsh turlturt pawnt^y)

fried carp, stuffed with a mix of bread, fish liver or roe, egg and herbs

Other specialities from Hungary's lakes and rivers include:

békacomb gombával és rákkal
(baykotsawmb **gawm**baavol aysh **raak**-kol)

frog's legs with freshwater crab-meat and mushrooms

békacomb paprikásan
(baykotsawmb popreekaashon)

frog's legs in a paprika sauce

rákpörkölt
(raakpurrkurlt)

broiled crab

Sauces

The sauces that accompany Hungarian dishes are distinctively flavoured to enhance the pleasures of the palate. (Contrary to widespread belief, spicy-hot preparations are not typical of the national cuisine.)

almamártás	olmommaartaash	apple sauce
bakonyi gombamártás	bokkawn^yee gawmbommaartaash	mushroom sauce
ecetes torma	ætsætæsh tawrmo	horse-radish sauce
fehérhagyma mártás	fæhayrhod^ymo maartaash	onion sauce
fokhagymás mártás	fawkhod^ymaash maartash	garlic sauce
kapormártás	koppawrmaartaash	dill sauce
meggymártás	mæd^ymaartaash	morello sauce
paprikás mártás	popreekaash maartaash	paprika sauce
tárkonyos mártás	taarkawn^yawsh maartaash	tarragon sauce
vadasmártás	voddoshmaartaash	brown sauce

EATING OUT

Meat

I'd like some ...	... kérek.	... kayræk
beef	**Marhahúst**	morhohōōsht
lamb	**Bárányhúst**	baaraan^yhōōsht
pork	**Disznóhúst**	deesnawhōōsht
veal	**Borjúhúst**	bawryōōhōōsht

borda	bawrdo	chop
comb	tsawmb	leg
fasírozott	foshēērawzawt	meatballs
filé	feelay	fillet
kolbászfélék	kawlbaasfaylayk	sausages
lapocka	loppawtsko	shoulder
máj	maa^y	liver
nyelv	n^yælv	tongue
sonka	shawnko	ham
szalonna	sollawn-no	bacon

boiled	**főve**	fūrvæ
braised	**dinsztelve**	deenstælvæ
breaded	**rántva**	raantvo
fried	**sütve**	shewtvæ
grilled	**roston sütve**	rawshtawn shewtvæ
roasted	**sülve**	shewlvæ
stewed (quickly)	**főzve**	fūrzvæ
stewed (slowly)	**pörköltnek**	purrkurltnæk
underdone (rare)	**félig nyersen**	fayleeg n^yærshæn
medium	**közepesen kisütve**	kurzæpæshæn keeshewtvæ
well-done (fried)	**jól megsütve**	yāwl mægshewtvæ
well-done (boiled)	**jól megfőzve**	yāwl mægfūrzvæ

(side text) EATING OUT

Veal

borjúpaprikás
(bawryōōpopreekaash)
veal fricassée with onions, pepper rings, tomatoes and a seasoning of paprika and garlic

borjúpörkölt
(bawryōōpurkurlt)
a stew composed of veal chunks, onions, tomatoes, pepper rings, seasoned with paprika and garlic

lecsós borjúmáj rántva
(læchāwsh bawryōōmaa^y raantvo)
breaded veal liver, garnished with a mix of pepper slices, tomatoes, rice, spiced with paprika and garlic

Beef

alföldi marharos-
télyos
(olfurldee morhorrawsh-
tay^yawsh)

steak Alföldi style: with a rich sauce and stewed vegetables

cigányrostélyos
(tseegaan^y-
rawshtay^yawsh)

steak gypsy style: with a brown sauce and braised vegetables

csikós tokány
(cheekāwsh tawkaan^y)

strips or chunks of beef braised in a mix of bacon strips or bits, onion rings and sour cream and tomato concentrate

erdélyi tokány
(ærday^yee tawkaan^y)

a dish originating in Transylvania: virtually the same as *csikós tokány*, but without the sour cream

hortobágyi
rostélyos
(hawrtawbaad^yee
rawshtay^yawsh)

steak Hortobágy style: braised in a mix of stock and bacon bits and accompanied by a large semolina dumpling

Pork

erdélyi rakott-
káposzta
(ærday^yee
rokkawttkaapawsto)

a Transylvanian dish consisting of layers of cabbage interspersed with rice and minced spiced pork, covered with sour cream and baked in the oven

debreceni
fatányéros
(dæbrætsænee
fottaan^yayrawsh)

a Debrecen speciality, prepared only for parties of three or more, usually containing pork chops and choice fillets as well as some veal; garnished with lettuce

rablóhús nyárson
(roblāwhōōsh
n^yaarshawn)

alternating pieces of pork, onions, mushrooms, bacon and veal roasted and served on a skewer

tejfölös-gombás
sertésborda
(tæ^yfurlursh gawm-
baash shærtayshbawrdo)

pork chop with mushrooms and sour cream

töltött malac
újfalusi módra
(turlturt mollots
ōō^yfollooshee māwdro)

stuffed suckling-pig Újfalu style: with a mix of spiced minced meat, liver, egg and bread

Game and fowl

I'd like some game.	Vadasat szeretnék.	voddoshot særaætnayk
csirke	cheerkæ	chicken
fácán	faatsaan	pheasant
fogoly	fawgaw^y	partridge
galamb	gollomb	pigeon
kacsa	kocho	duck
kappan	kop-pon	capon
liba	leebo	goose
nyúl	n^yool	rabbit
őz	ūrz	venison
pulyka	poo^yko	turkey
vaddisznó	vod-deesnāw	wild boar
vadkacsa	vodkocho	wild duck
vadliba	vodleebo	wild goose

csabai szarvascomb (chobboee sorvoshtsawmb)	venison stuffed with spicy Csabai sausage served in a paprika sauce
fácán gesztenyével töltött gombával (faatsaan gætæn^y-ayvæl turlturt gawmbaavol)	pheasant with a mushroom and chestnut filling
fogoly szalonnában sütve (fawgaw^y sollawn-naabon shewtvæ)	partridge in a bacon envelope, served in a sauce of stock, tomato concentrate and seasoning
nyúlszeletek pirított szárnyasmájjal (n^yoolsælætæk peerēētawt saarn^yoshmaa^y-yol)	rabbit with roasted chicken liver
pulykacomb tejfeles gombamártással (poo^ykotsawmb tæ^yfælæsh gawmbommaartaash-shol)	turkey cutlet in a mushroom sauce
vaddisznó borókamártással (vod-deesnāw bawrāwkommaartaash-shol)	wild boar served in a juniper sauce

EATING OUT

Vegetables—Salads

Vegetables and salads are served along with the main course in set menus. Otherwise, you may order them separately from the bill of fare.

burgonya	boorgawn^yo	potatoes
fehérrépa	fæhayr-raypo	turnips
gomba	gawmbo	mushrooms
hagyma	hod^ymo	onions
káposzta	kaapawsto	cabbage
kelbimbó	kælbeembāw	Brussels sprouts
kelkáposzta	kælkaapawsto	cauliflower
kukorica	kookawreetso	type of sweetcorn
lencse	lænchæ	lentils
paprika	popreeko	pepper
paradicsom	porroddeechawm	tomatoes
saláta	shollaato	lettuce
sárgarépa	shaargorraypo	carrots
spárga	shpaargo	asparagus
spenót	shpænāwt	spinach
sültkrumpli	shewltkroomplee	chips (French fries)
uborka	oobawrko	cucumber
vegyesfőzelék	væd^yæshfūrzælayk	mixed vegetables
vegyesköret	væd^yæshkur-ræt	mixed vegetables (served along with the dish)
zeller	zæl-lær	celery
zöldbab	zurldbob	French beans
zöldborsó	zurldbawrshāw	peas

Some herbs and spices used in Hungarian cooking:

édeskömény	aydæshkurmayn^y	caraway seeds
édespaprika	aydæshpopreeko	mild paprika
fokhagyma	fawkhod^ymo	garlic
fűszerpaprika	fēwsærpopreeko	chillies
kakukkfű	kokkookfēw	thyme
komló	kawmlāw	hops
majoránna	moyawraan-no	marjoram
pirospaprika	peerawshpopreeko	strong paprika
rozmaring	rawzmorreeng	rosemary
sáfrány	shaafraan^y	crocus leaf
szegfűszeg	sægfēwsæg	cloves
szekfűbors	sækfēwbawrsh	allspice
szerecsendió	særæchændeeāw	nutmeg

EATING OUT

Desserts

The Hungarians have a decidedly sweet tooth and much to offer in the way of desserts.

I'd like a dessert, please.	**Egy adag deszertet kérek.**	æd^y oddog dæsærtæt kayræk
Something light, please.	**Valami könnyűt legyen szíves.**	vollommee kurn^yēwt læd^yæn sēēvæsh
Nothing more, thank you.	**Köszönöm, többet nem kérek.**	kursurnurm turb-bæt næm kayræk

almás palacsinta	olmaash pollocheento	apple pancake
aranygaluska	orron^ygollooshko	sweet dumpling
csokoládéfánk	chawkawlaadayfaank	chocolate doughnut
csúsztatott palacsinta	chōōstottawt pollocheento	multi-layer pancake
dobostorta	dawbawshtawrto	caramel-topped chocolate cream cake
gesztenyepüré tejszínhabbal	gæstæn^yæpewray tæ^yssēēnhob-bol	chestnut purée with whipped cream
Gundel palacsinta	goondæl pollocheento	pancake with nut-cream and raisin filling, flambéd
kapros túrós rétes	koprawsh tōōrāwsh raytæsh	curds strudel with dill
kapucineres felfújt	koppootseenæræsh fælfōō^yt	mocha soufflé
kecskeméti barackpuding	kæchkæmaytee borrotsk-"pudding"	apricot pudding with vanilla cream
képviselőfánk	kaypveeshælūrfaank	cream puff
máglyarakás	maag^yorrokkaash	apple and jam pudding
mákosrétes	maakawshraytæsh	poppy-seed strudel
mandula felfújt	mondoolo fælfōō^yt	almond soufflé
rakott palacsinta	rokkawt pollocheento	multi-layer pancakes with various fillings
somlói galuska	shawmlāwee gollooshko	sweet dumplings made with vanilla, nuts and chocolate, in an orange-and-rum sauce
sült derelye	shewlt dæræ^yæ	fried jam turn-over
szilvás rétes	seelvaash raytæsh	plum strudel
töltött alma	turlturt olmo	apple stuffed with vanilla, raisins and cream

Ice-cream

Ice-cream and parfaits are often available as desserts. In addition, pastry shops and milkbars serve a variety of imaginative ice-based creations, frequently including fruit, cream or fancy cakes. As a dessert, ice-cream is sometimes served with a fresh-fruit salad. Alternatively, it may be flambéd with rum. There will generally be a choice of flavours.

Have you any ice-cream?	**Van fagylaltjuk?**	von fod^ylolt^yook
banán	bonnaan	banana
citrom	tseetrawm	lemon
csokoládé	chawkawlaaday	chocolate
dió	deeāw	walnut
eper	æpær	strawberry
kávé	kaavay	coffee
málna	maalno	raspberry
meggy	maed^y	sour cherry
mogyoró	mawd^yawrāw	hazelnut
narancs	norronch	orange
pisztás	peestaash	pistachio
vanília	vonnēēleeo	vanilla
Could I have it flambéd?	**Kaphatok lángoló fagylaltot?**	kophottawk laangawlāw fod^yloltawt

Cheese

Though Hungary produces more than a hundred types of cheese, on the whole they range little in taste. Most are rather bland, but there are some spiced or smoked varieties. Imitation camembert, cheddar, Dutch edam and other foreign cheeses are also available in better restaurants.

Processed cheeses, conveniently packaged in tubes or the familiar individual triangular portions, may be flavoured with pepper, paprika or a variety of vegetable aromas.

I'd like some cheese.	**Sajtot szeretnék.**	shoytawt særætnayk
Do you have a cheese-board?	**Milyen sajt van?**	mee^yæn shoyt von

Fruit

Do you have fresh fruit?	Van friss gyümölcsük?	von freesh d^yewmurlchewk
What sort of fruit do you have?	Milyen gyümölcsük van?	mee^yæn d^yewmurlchewk von
'd like a fresh-fruit cocktail.	Friss gyümölcs-koktélt kérek.	freesh d^yewmurlchkawk-taylt kayræk
alma	olmo	apple
áfonya	aafawn^ya	blueberries
ananász	onnonnaas	pineapple
banán	bonnaan	banana
citrom	tseetrawm	lemon
császárkörte	chaassaarkurrtæ	type of pear
cseresznye	chæræsn^yæ	cherries
datolya	dottaw^yo	dates
dió	deeāw	walnuts
egres	ægræsh	gooseberries
eper	æpær	strawberries
fekete cseresznye	fækætæ chæræsn^yæ	heart cherries
fekete ribizli	fækætæ reebeezlee	blackcurrants
füge	fewgæ	figs
gesztenye	gæstæn^yæ	chestnuts
görögdinnye	gurrurgdeen^yæ	water melon
onatán alma	yawnottaan olmo	Jonathan apple
körte	kurrtæ	pear
nálna	maalno	raspberries
mandarin	mondoreen	tangerine
mandula	mondoolo	almonds
meggy	mæd^y	sour cherries
mogyoró	mawd^yawrāw	hazelnuts
narancs	norronch	orange
őszibarack	ūrseeborrotsk	peach
ribizli	reebeezlee	redcurrants
ringló	reenglāw	greengage
sárgabarack	shaargobborrotsk	apricot
sárgadinnye	shaargoddeen^yæ	honeydew melon
starking alma	shtorkeeng olmo	starking apple
szeder	sædær	mulberries
szilva	seelvo	plum
szőlő	sūrlūr	grapes

EATING OUT

The bill (check)

I'd like the bill, please.	**Kérem a számlát.**	kayræm o **saam**laat
We'd like to pay separately.	**Külön-külön kívánunk fizetni.**	**kew**lurn **kew**lurn **kēē**vaanoonk **fee**zætnee
What is this amount for?	**Ez mire vonatkozik?**	æz **mee**ræ **vaw**notkawzeek
You've made a mistake in this bill, I think.	**Azt hiszem, ez a számla hibás.**	ost **hees**sæm æz o **saam**lo **hee**bash
Is everything included?	**Minden szerepel a számlában?**	**meen**dæn **sæ**ræpæl o **saam**laabon

How much do I owe you?	**Mennyi a számla összege?**	mæn^Yee o **saam**lo urs**sæ**gæ
Do you accept traveller's cheques?	**Fizethetek traveller's csekkel?**	**fee**zæt-hætæk **trov**væl-lærs **chæk**-kæl
Can I pay with this credit card?*	**Fizethetek ezzel a hitelkártyával?**	**fee**zæt-hætæk æz-zæl o **hee**tælkaart^Yaavol
Thank you, this is for you.	**Köszönöm. Ez a magáé.**	**kur**surnurm. æz o **mog**gaa-ay
Keep the change.	**A többi a magáé.**	o **turb**-bee o **mog**gaa-ay
That was an excellent/ delicious meal.	**Az étel kiváló/ fínom volt.**	oz **ay**tæl **kee**vaalāw/ **fēē**nawm vawlt
We've enjoyed ourselves very much, thank you.	**Jól szórakoztunk.**	yāwl **sāw**rokkawztoonk

---

* In Hungary, credit cards are generally accepted in all establishments frequented by foreign tourists.

Complaints

But perhaps you'll have something to complain about:

That's not what I ordered.	**Nem ezt rendeltem.**	næm æst rændæltæm
I asked for...	**Én...-t rendeltem.**	ayn ...-t rændæltæm
I asked for a small portion (for the child).	**Egy kisadagot rendeltem (a gyereknek).**	æd^y keeshoddoggawt rændæltæm (o d^yæræknæk)
There must be some mistake.	**Itt valami félre-értés lesz.**	eet vollommee faylræayr-taysh læs
May I change this?	**Hozna valami mást helyette?**	hawzno vollommee maasht hæ^yæt-tæ
The meat is...	**A hús...**	o hōōsht
overdone	**agyonsütötték**	od^yawnshewturt-tayk
underdone	**csak félig sütötték meg**	chok fayleeg shewturt-tayk mæg
This is too...	**Ez nagyon...**	æz nod^yawn
bitter	**keserű**	kæshærēw
salty	**sós**	shāwsh
sour	**savanyú**	shovvon^yōō
sweet	**édes**	aydæsh
The food is cold.	**Ez az étel hideg.**	æz oz aytæl heedæg
It's not fresh.	**Ez nem friss.**	æz næm freesh
What's taking you so long?	**Mi tart ilyen sokáig?**	mee tort ee^yæn shawkaa-eeg
Have you forgotten our drinks?	**Az innivalókat elfelejtette?**	oz een-neevollāwkot ælfælæ^ytæt-tæ
The wine is too cold.	**A bor túl hideg.**	a bawr tōōl heedæg
The wine tastes of cork.	**Ez a bor dugóízű.**	æz o bawr doogāwēēzēw
The beer isn't chilled.	**A sör nincs behűtve.**	o shurr neench bæhēwtvæ
This beer is flat.	**Ez a sör állott.**	æz o shurr aal-lawt
This isn't clean.	**Ez nem tiszta.**	æz næm teesto
There's a draught here.	**Huzat van.**	hoozot von
Would you ask the headwaiter to come over?	**Kérem, hívja ide a főpincért!**	kayræm hēēvyo eedæ o fūrpeenchayrt

Drinks

| Give me the drinks card, please. | **Legyen szíves az itallapot idehozni!** | lædʸæn sēēvæsh oz eetol-loppawt eedæhawznee |

Beer

Both local beer (which is rather strong) and foreign brand are usually available. It may be sold by the bottle or on draught. A 3-decilitre glass is called a *pohár*, a half-litre mug a *korsó*.

I'd like a bottle of ... beer.	**Egy üveg ... sört kérnék.**	ædʸ ewvæg shurrt kayrnayk
German	**német**	naymæt
Hungarian	**magyar**	modʸor
Pilsen	**pilzeni**	peelzænee
dark/light	**barna/világos**	borno/veelaagawsh
A *pohár/korsó* of beer, please.	**Egy pohár/korsó sört kérek.**	ædʸ pawhaar/kawrshaw shurrt kayræk

---

EGÉSZSÉGÉRE!
(ægayssaygayræ)

CHEERS!

Wine

For its size, Hungary produces an impressive range of good wines.

What kind of wine do you have?	**Milyen boruk van?**	meeʸæn bawrook von
I'd like a... of wine.	**Egy... bort kérek.**	ædʸ ... bawrt kayræk
glass/bottle	**pohár/üveg**	pawhaar/ewvæg
A bottle of white/red wine, please.	**Egy üveg fehér/vörös bort kérek.**	ædʸ ewvæg fæhayr/vurrursh bawrt kayræk

FLUID MEASURES: see page 130

EATING OUT

Type of wine	Examples	Accompanies
sweet white wine	Balatonfüredi szemelt rizling, Csopaki olasz rizling, Akali zöldszilváni, Tokaji aszu	desserts and pastry, but also thick soups
light dry white wine	Badacsonyi kéknyelű, Badacsonyi szürkebarát, Badacsonyi zöldszilváni, Egri Leányka, Tokaji furmint, Tokaji szamorodni	fish meals, liver, lighter meat dishes, goulash and other stews, steaks, cold meats, fruit
light-bodied red wine	Vaskúti kadarka, Villányi burgundi, Villányi kadarka, Egri pinot noir	fish soups, veal, pork, lamb, ham, beef, fowl, game, cheese
full-bodied red wine	Egri bikavér, Villányi medoc noir, Tihanyi merlot	game, duck, cheese
sparkling wine (sweet)	Törley réserve, Pannonia	desserts and fruit
sparkling wine (dry)	Pompadur, Pannonia	fowl, game
sparkling wine (extra dry)	Pannonia dry	light cheese

Tokay wine

This world-famous wine comes from the area near the city of Tokaj, considered by many the country's most outstanding wine-growing region. Its excellence is attributed to the properties of the local soil, the mineral content of the water, the traditional production methods employed and, some local people insist, the peculiar quality of the sunshine there.

Tokay wines come in three different categories: *Tokaji furmint* (dry), *Tokaji szamorodni* (medium-sweet) and *Tokaji aszu* (full-bodied, very sweet). Tokay vintages are graded according to excellence on a scale of from 3 to 5 *puttonyos* or points.

Other alcoholic drinks

Cocktails and highballs are unfamiliar to most Hungarians, and you are unlikely to find any available in ordinary restaurants and drinking places. Imported spirits can be found in some better bars and restaurants.

Do you have any...?	Van...?	von
cognac	konyakjuk	kawn^yokyook
gin	dzsinjük	dzheenyewk
liqueur	likörjük	leekurr^yewk
rum	rumjuk	roomyook
vermouth	vermutjuk	værmootyook
whisky	viszkijük	veeskee^yewk
vodka	vodkájuk	vawdkaa^yook
A (double) whisky, please.	Egy (dupla) viszkit, kérek.	æd^y (dooplo) veeskeet kayræk
neat (straight)	tisztán	teestaan
on the rocks	jéggel kérem	yayg-gæl kayræm
with a little water	kevés vízzel	kævaysh veez-zæl
Give me a gin and tonic, please.	Egy adag dzsint kérek tonikkal.	æd^y oddog dzheent kayræk tawneek-kol
Just a dash of soda, please.	Csak egy csöpp szódával kérem.	chok æd^y churp sawdaavoll kayræm
2 rum-and-cokes, please.	2 rumot kérek kólával.	2 roomawt kayræk kawlaavol

For a change, you might like to try one of Hungary's excellent fruit brandies:

I'd like a glass of... brandy.	Kérek egy pohár... pálinkát.	kayræk æd^y pawhaar... paaleenkaat
apple	alma	olmo
apricot	barack	borrotsk
cherry	cseresznye	chæræsnæ
pear	körte	kurtæ
plum	szilva	seelvo

A potent concoction you are unlikely to want to order but may be offered is a "Puszta cocktail"—a mixture of three kinds of fruit brandies and vermouth, served with lemon and iced. Treat it with respect!

Soft drinks

Some international soft-drink brands are widely available, along with a variety of fruit juices. Bottled mineral water, usually sparkling, is on sale everywhere.

I'd like some…	… kérek.	… kayræk
apple juice	Almalevet	olmollævæt
apricot juice	Baracklét	borrotsklayt
cola drink	Kólát	ka̅w̅laat
fruit juice	Gyümölcslevet	d^yewmurlchlævæt
grapefruit juice	Grépfruit-lét	"grapefruit" layt
lemonade	Limonádét	leemawnaadayt
lemon juice	Citromlét	tseetrawmlayt
mineral water	Ásvány vizet	aashvaan^y veezæt
orange juice	Narancslét	norronchlayt
soda water	Szóda vizet	sa̅w̅do veezæt
tomato juice	Paradicsomlét	porroddeechawmlayt

Coffee and tea

As you come to notice the Hungarians drinking coffee at all hours of the day, you'll be able to believe that the nation's per-capita consumption is one of the world's highest. Coffee is drunk strong (espresso style), black, usually sweet and very hot—though you obviously need not follow the local custom if you prefer your coffee otherwise. At most places, even white breakfast coffee is based on espresso.

Tea in Hungary is generally found rather weak and tasteless by British and American visitors.

I'd like a small / large coffee.	Egy szimpla/dupla kávét kérek.	æd^y seemplo/dooplo kaavayt kayræk
A white coffee, please.	Egy tejeskávét kérek.	æd^y tæ^yæshkaavayt kayræk
A cup of tea, please.	Egy csésze teát kérek.	æd^y chayssæ tæaat kayræk
Please bring me some …	… kérem.	… kayræm
cream / milk	Krémmel/Tejjel	kraym-mæl/tæ^yyæl
lemon / sugar	Citrommal/Cukorral	tseetrawm-mol/tsookawr-rol

Eating light—Snacks

For a quick sit-down meal, go to a *bisztro, büfé, cukrászda, önkiszolgáló, tejivó* or *tejbár* (see pages 38–39).

I'll have one of those, please.	Egy ilyet kérek.	æd^y ee^yæt kayræk

biscuits	apró sütemény	opraw shewtæmayn^y
bread	kenyér	kæn^yayr
cakes	tea sütemény	tæo shewtæmayn^y
cheese	sajt	shoyt
chicken	csirke	cheerkæ
half a roasted chicken	fél gril csirke	fayl "grill" cheerkæ
chips	sült krumpli	shewlt kroomplee
chocolate	tábla csokoládé	taablo chawkawlaaday
frankfurters	pár virsli	paar veershlee
French fries	sült krumpli	shewlt kroomplee
fried doughnut	lángos	laangawsh
fried eggs	tükörtojás	tewkurrtaw^yaash
fried fish	sült hal	shewlt hol
fried potato slices	roseibni	rawshæeebnee
fried sausages	sült kolbász	shewlt kawlbaass
ham and eggs	sonkát tojással	shawnkaat taw^yaash-shol
ham sandwich	sonkás szendvics	shawnkaash sændveech
ice-cream	fagylalt	fod^ylolt
ketchup	ketchup	kæchurp
meat sandwich	húsos szendvics	hooshaws sændveech
mustard	mustár	moshtaar
salami sandwich	szalámis szendvics	sollaameesh sændveech
sandwich	szendvics	sændveech
scrambled eggs	rántotta	raantawt-to
sweetcorn	kukorica	kookawreetso

DRINKS: see page 60

Travelling around

Plane

Budapest Ferihegy is the country's only commercial airport. There are, therefore, no scheduled domestic flights. Airport staff mostly speak some English or German, but here are a few useful expressions, just in case:

Is there a flight to Vienna?	**Van Bécsbe járatuk?**	von baychbæ yaarottook
When is the next plane to London?	**Mikor indul a következő gép Londonba?**	meekawr eendool o kurvætkæzũr gayp lawndawnbo
Is it nonstop?	**Leszállás nélkül?**	læssaal-laash naylkewl
Can I make a connection to New York?	**Át tudok szállni egy Nju-jork-i gépre?**	aat toodawk saalnee æd^y n^{y}oo-yawrk-ee gaypræ
I'd like a ticket to Rome.	**Rómába kérek egy jegyet.**	rawmaabo kayræk æd^y yæd^{y}æt
What's the fare ...?	**Mennyibe kerül egy jegy ...?**	mæn^{y}eebæ kærewl æd^y yæd^y
single (one-way)	**egy irányban**	æd^y eeraan^{y}bon
return (roundtrip)	**oda-vissza**	awdo vees-so
economy class	**turista osztályon**	tooreeshto awstaa^{y}awn
first class	**első osztályon**	ælshũr awstaa^{y}awn
When is the departure time?	**Mikor indul a járat?**	meekawr eendool o yaarot
What time do I have to check in?	**Mikor kell bejelent-keznem?**	meekawr kæl bæ^{y}ælænt-kæznæm
What's the flight number?	**Mi a járat száma?**	mee o yaarot saamo
What time do we arrive?	**Mikor érkezünk meg?**	meekawr eendool o yaarot

ÉRKEZÉS	INDULÁS
ARRIVAL	DEPARTURE

TELLING THE TIME: see page 178

TRAVELLING AROUND

Train

The Hungarian State Railways maintain quite a dense rail network, partly electrified, with both first- and second-class seating. First-class compartments, marked I, are comfortable. Second-class compartments, marked II, are adequate but not always as clean as they might be; they are also likely to be rather crowded and noisy. Service is punctual. International connections are generally good.

Rail travel within Hungary is quite inexpensive and is an excellent way to get to see the country. Hungary is linked to the Inter Rail agreement which allows young people up to the age of 25 to travel throughout some thirty countries of Europe for one month at a low-cost flat-rate charge. Travel agents in all Western European countries have details.

For trips within Hungary, tickets can be purchased from railway stations and travel agencies. A variety of options exist—regular, excursion, trade-fair and student tickets.

The three main railway stations in Budapest are: *Nyugati* (West), *Déli* (South) and *Keleti* (East). At all of them, some staff speak a little English or German.

Type of trains

Nemzetközi gyorsvonat (næmzætkurzee d^{y}awrshvawnot)	International express with first- and second-class seating; advance reservation (at an extra charge) is highly advisable.
Sebesvonat (shæbæshvawnot)	Express train, stopping at major centres only.
Gyorsvonat (d^{y}awrshvawnot)	A domestic express train which stops more frequently.
Személyvonat (sæmay^{y}vawnot)	Slow train, stopping at all stations.
Helyiérdekű (hæ^{y}eeayrdækēw)	Suburban train, painted green, often integrated into the municipal public transport system.
Motorvonat (mawtawrvawnot)	Rail coach, diesel, comprising three or four cars, used for shorter distances.

To the railway station

Where's the railway station?	**Hol a vasútállomás?**	hawl o voshōōtaal-lawmaash
Taxi, please!	**Halló, taxi!**	hol-lāw toxee
Take me to the ... Station.	**Vigyen kérem a ... pályaudvarra.**	veed^yæn kayræm o ... paa^yo-oodvor-ro
East	**keleti**	kælætee
South	**déli**	daylee
West	**nyugati**	n^yoogottee
Which bus goes to the ... Station?	**Melyik busz megy a ... pályaudvarra?**	mæ^yeek booss mæd^y o ... paa^yo-oodvor-ro

FELVILÁGOSITÁS	INFORMATION
VALUTABEVÁLTÁS	CURRENCY EXCHANGE

Where's the ...?

Where is the ...?	**Hol van ...?**	hawl von
currency exchange office	**a valutabeváltó hely**	o vollootobbævaaltāw hæ^y
information office	**az információs iroda**	oz eenfawrmaatseeāwsh eerawdo
letter box	**a postaláda**	o pawshtollaado
lost-property (lost-and-found) office	**az elhagyott tárgyak irodája**	oz ælhod^yawt taard^yok eerawdaa^yo
luggage lockers	**a csomagmegőrző**	o chawmogmægürrzür
newsstand	**az újságos kioszk**	oz ōō^yshaagawsh keeawsk
platform 5	**az 5-ödik peron**	oz 5 urdeek pærawn
restaurant	**az étterem**	oz ayt-tæræm
snack bar	**a gyorsbüfé**	o d^yawrshbewfay
ticket office	**a jegypénztár**	o yæd^ypaynztaar
travel agency	**az utazási iroda**	oz ootozzaashee eerawdo
waiting room	**a váróterem**	o vaarāwtæræm
Where are the toilets?	**Hol vannak az illemhelyek?**	hawl von-nok oz eel-læmhæ^yæk

TAXI: see page 27

Inquiries

When is the ... train to Siófok?	Mikor megy ... vonat Siófokra?	meekawr mæd^y ... vawnot sheeāwfawkro
first	az első	oz ælshūr
last	a következő	o kurvætkæzūr
next	az utolsó	oz ootawlshāw
What time does the train for Pécs leave?	Mikor indul a vonat Pécsre?	meekawr eendool o vawnot paychræ
What's the fare to Szeged?	Mibe kerül egy jegy Szegedig?	meebæ kærewl æd^y yæd^y sægædeeg
Is it an express train?	Ez gyorsvonat?	æz d^{y}awrshvawnot
What time does the train arrive at Győr?	Mikor érkezik meg a vonat Győrből?	meekawr ayrkæzeek mæg o vawnot d^{y}ūrrbūrl
Does the train stop at Hévíz?	Megáll a vonat Hévízen?	mægaal o vawnot hayveezæn
Is there a dining car on the train?	Van ezen a vonaton étkezőkocsi?	von æzæn o vawnottawn aytkæzūrkawchee
What platform does the train for Vienna leave from?	A bécsi gyorsvonat melyik vágányról indul?	a baychee d^{y}awrsh- vawnot mæ^{y}eek vaagaan^{y}rāwl eendool

TRAVELLING AROUND

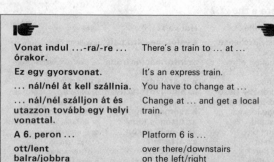

Vonat indul ...-ra/-re ... órakor.	There's a train to ... at ...
Ez egy gyorsvonat.	It's an express train.
... nál/nél át kell szállnia.	You have to change at ...
... nál/nél szálljon át és utazzon tovább egy helyi vonattal.	Change at ... and get a local train.
A 6. peron ...	Platform 6 is ...
ott/lent balra/jobbra	over there/downstairs on the left/right
Az ön vonata a ...-odik/ -edik vágányról indul.	Your train leaves from platform ...
... perces késéssel indul.	There's a delay of ... minutes.

NUMBERS: see page 175

Tickets

I'd like a ticket to Keszthely.	**Kérek egy jegyet Keszthelyre.**	kayræk ædᵞ yædᵞæt kæsthæᵞræ
Single (one-way)	**egy útra**	ædᵞ ōōtro
return (roundtrip)	**oda-vissza**	awdo vees-so
first class	**első osztályra**	ælshūr awstaaᵞro
second class	**második osztályra**	maashawdeek awstaaᵞro
I'd like to make a seat reservation.	**Szeretnék helyjegyet váltani.**	særætnayk hæᵞyædᵞæt vaaltonnee
I'd like a timetable, please.	**Kérek egy menetrendet.**	kayræk ædᵞ mænætrændæt

Első vagy második osztályra?	First or second class?
Egy útra vagy oda-vissza?	Single (one way) or return (roundtrip)?
10 éves korig a gyerekek félárú jeggyel utaznak.	It's half fare up to age 10.

Baggage—Porters

Porter!	**Hordár!**	hawrdaar
Take my luggage to the ... train.	**Kérem, vigye a csomagjaimat a ...-i vonathoz.**	kayræm veedᵞæ o chawmogᵞo-eemot o ...-ee vawnot-hawz
Can I have this luggage registered?	**Ezeket a podgyászokat szeretném feladni.**	æzækæt o pawdᵞassawkot særætnaym fælodnee
Where can I find a baggage trolley?	**Hol találhatok podgyász kézikocsit?**	hawl tollalhottawk pawdᵞass kazeekawcheet

BEJÁRAT	ENTRANCE
KIJÁRAT	EXIT
A VÁGÁNYOKHOZ	TO THE PLATFORMS

BAGGAGE and PORTERS: see also page 24

All aboard

English	Hungarian	Pronunciation
Does the train for Budapest leave from this platform?	A Budapestre menő vonat erről a peronról indul?	o boodoppæshtræ mænūr vawnot ær-rūrl o pærawr rāwl eendool
Is this the train for Debrecen?	Ez a debreceni vonat?	æz o dæbrætsænee vawnot
Is this seat taken?	Ez a hely foglalt?	æz o hæ^y fawglolt
I think that's my seat.	Azt hiszem, ez az én helyem.	ost heessæm æz oz ayn hæ^yæm
Would you mind looking after my luggage for a moment?	Vigyázna kérem egy percre a podgyászomra?	veed^yaazno kayræm æd^y pærtsræ o pawd-d^yaassawmro
Do you mind if I open/close the window?	Kinyithatnám/Becsukhatnám az ablakot?	keen^yeet-hotnaam/bæchook-hotnaam oz oblokkawt
Would you let me know before we get to Szeged?	Szólna, mielőtt Szegedre érkezünk?	sāwlno meeælūrt sægædræ ayrkæzewnk
What station is this?	Ez milyen állomás?	æz mee^yæn aal-lawmaash
How long does the train stop here?	Meddig áll itt a vonat?	mæd-deeg aal eet o vawnot
When do we get to the border?	Mikor, érkezünk a határra?	meekawr ayrkæzewnk o hottaar-ro

> **TILOS A DOHÁNYZÁS**
> NO SMOKING

> **DOHÁNYZÓ**
> SMOKING ALLOWED

Eating

Long-distance expresses, both domestic and international have dining cars which serve meals at normal hours. On some trains, alcoholic drinks and light refreshments are also served at a buffet, or an attendant may come round with baskets of supplies.

English	Hungarian	Pronunciation
Where's the dining car?	Merre van az étkezőkocsi?	mær-ræ von oz aytkæzūr-kawchee

MEAL TIMES: see page 40

Sleeping

Are there any free compartments in the sleeping car?	Van még szabad hely a hálókocsiban?	von mayg sobbod hæ^Y o haalāwkawcheebon
Are there any couchettes available?	Van még szabad kusettjük?.	von mayg sobbod kooshæt^{Y}ewk
Where's my berth?	Melyik az én ágyam?	mæ^{Y}eek oz ayn aad^{Y}om
Compartments 10 and 11, please.	A 10-es és 11-es fülkéket kérem.	o 10-æsh 11-æsh fewlkaykæt kayræm
I'd like an upper/lower berth.	Felső/Alsó ágyat kérek.	fælshūr/olshāw aad^{Y}ot kayræk
Would you make up our berths, please?	Kérem, vesse meg az ágyamat.	kayræm væsh-shæ mæg oz aad^{Y}ommot
Would you call me at 7 o'clock?	Kérem, keltsen fel 7 órakor.	kayræm kæltshæn fæl 7 āwrokkawr
Would you please bring me tea/coffee in the morning?	Kérem, reggel hozzon teát/kávét.	kayræm ræg-gæl hawzzawn tæaat/kaavayt

Lost property

We hope you'll never need this section during your journey, but just in case:

Where's the lost-property (lost-and-found) office?	Hol van a talált tárgyak irodája?	hawl von o tollaalt taard^{Y}ok eerawdaayo
I've lost my ...	Elvesztettem ...	ælvæstæt-tæm
handbag	a kézitáskámat	o kayzeetaashkaamot
passport	az útlevelemet	oz ōōtlævælæmæt
ring	a gyűrűmet	o d^{Y}ewrewmæt
ticket	a jegyemet	o yæd^{Y}æmæt
wallet	az irattárcámat	oz eerot-taartsaamot
watch	az órámat	oz āwraamot
I lost it in ...	... -ban/-ben hagytam el.*	...-bon/-bæn hod^{Y}tom æl
It's very valuable.	Nagyon értékes.	nod^{Y}awn ayrtaykæsh

See Grammar section for word endings.

Intercity coach (bus) services

Hungary has an extensive intercity coach network reaching
into all parts of the country. Vehicles are comfortable and
service is reasonably rapid, making bus travel the preferred
means of transport of many. Prices are on a par with those
for first-class rail travel. Most coaches are operated by the
Volán and Mavaut companies. They are generally painted
yellow.

TRAVELLING AROUND

Where can I get a coach to Esztergom?	Hol érem el az Esztergomba induló autóbuszt?	hawl ayræm æl oz æstærgawmbo eendoolāw oootāwboost
Which coach must I take for Tiszafüred?	Melyik busszal jutok el Tiszafüredre?	mæ^Veek boos-sol yootaw æl teessoffewrædræ
Where's the coach station?	Hol van az autóbusz állomás?	hawl von oz oootāwbooss aalawmaash
When is the ... coach to Győr?	Mikor indul ... busz Győrbe?	meekawr eendool ... boos d^Vūrrbæ
first	az első	oz ælshūr
last	az utolsó	oz ootawlshāw
next	a következő	o kurvætkæzūr
Do I have to change coaches?	Át kell közben szállnom?	aat kæl kurzbæn saalnawm
I'd like a timetable, please.	Kérek egy menetrendet.	kayræk æd^V mænætrændæt

Urban public transport

The nation's larger towns have well-organized public transport services consisting of bus, tram (streetcar) and/or suburban train networks. Buses are blue, trams yellow, and
suburban trains green. In addition, Budapest has an underground (subway) system.

Though the first underground (subway) on the continent of
Europe was built in Budapest, large-scale construction was
only taken up about 1950. There are now four lines in operation.

Modern, clean rolling stock serves the most important points throughout the capital. Stations are marked with a large M sign and a route number.

City buses, trams, suburban trains and the underground operate variously between 4 a.m. and midnight. On the underground, frequency of service is regulated to conform to passenger demand.

Smoking is prohibited on all urban public transport vehicles.

Tickets for buses, trams and the underground are on sale at termini, major news-stands, tobacconists' shops and post offices—but not on board the vehicles themselves. Tickets for suburban trains must be purchased at the railway station.

Rates for suburban trains vary according to the distance travelled. Buses, trams and the underground each charge a—slightly different—flat rate for a ticket which is valid only on the one vehicle (no transfers). You must punch your ticket in the automatic machine on board (or, for the underground, at the station entrance).

Season tickets, valid on all four forms of urban public transport, are available for one-month periods only. However, if you are likely to be making extensive use of public transport facilities you might still find that their convenience outweighs the extra cost, even for a stay of only a few days—particularly in Budapest.

Inspectors make spot-checks on tickets, and you can expect quite a hefty fine if yours is not in order.

Where can I buy a ticket for the ...?	Hol vehetek... jegyet?	hawl væhætæk ... yæd^{y}æt
bus	az autóbuszra	oz oootāwboosro
tram	a villamosra	o veel-lommawshro
suburban train	a H.É.V.-re	o hayv-ræ
underground (subway)	a metróra	o mætrāwro

A ... ticket, please.	Egy ... jegyet kérek.	æd^y ... yæd^{y}æt kayræk
bus/tram/ underground	autóbusz/villamos/ metró	oootawbooss/veel- lommawsh/mætraw
I'd like a season ticket, please.	Szeretnék egy bérletet váltani.	særætnayk æd^y bayrlæ- tæt vaaltonnee
Where's the nearest underground station?	Hol van a legköze- lebbi metró megálló?	hawl von o lægkurzælæb- bee mætraw mægaal- law

Boats

For a change of pace and viewpoint, you might like to take one of the passenger boats which ply the Danube and Tisza rivers all year round. Or, during the summer months, you can go for a relaxing cruise on Lake Balaton. From May to September there is a daily hydrofoil service on the Danube between Budapest and Vienna which takes about five hours. Also during the summer season, a number of river excursion boats operate on the Danube leaving from Budapest Central Docks (*Vigadó-tér*).

| A ... ticket to Vienna, please. | ... jegyet kérek Bécsbe. | ... yæd^{y}æt kayræk baychbæ |
| boat/hydrofoil | Hajó/Szárnyashajó | hoyaw/saarn^{y}oshhoyaw |

Other modes of transport

car	autó	oootaw
bicycle	kerékpár	kæraykpaar
moped (motorbike)	moped	mawpæd
motorcycle	motorkerékpár	mawtawrkæraykpaar
pedalo	vizibicikli	veezeebeetseeklee
rowing boat	evezős csónak	ævæzūrsh chawnok
sailing boat	vitorlás	veetawrlaash
scooter	robogó	rawbawgaw

Or perhaps you prefer:

hitch-hiking	autóstoppal utazni	oootawshtawp-pol ootoznee
horse-riding	lovagolni	lawvoggawlnee
walking	gyalogolni	d^{y}ollawgawlnee

Around and about—Sightseeing

In this section we are more concerned with cultural attractions. For entertainment, see page 81.

If you want to buy a guide book, ask:

see page 81

Can you recommend a good guide book on Budapest?	Ajánlana Budapestről egy jó utikalauzt?	oyaanlonno boodoppæsht-rūīl ædᵛ yāw ooteekollo-oozt
Is there a tourist office here?	Van itt utazási iroda?	von eet ootozzaashee eerawdo
Where's the tourist office?	Hol van az utazási iroda?	hawl von oz ootozzaashee eerawdo
What are the main points of interest?	Melyek a fő neveze-tességek?	mæᵛæk o fūr nævæ-zætæsh-shaygæk
We're here for …	… vagyunk itt.	… vodᵛoonk eet
only a few hours	Csak egy pár óráig	chok ædᵛ paar āwraaeeg
a day	Egy napig	ædᵛ noppeeg
3 days	3 napig	3 noppeeg
a week	Egy hétig	ædᵛ hayteeg
Can you recommend a sightseeing tour?	Ajánlana egy városnéző kőrútat?	oyaanlonno ædᵛ vaarawsh-nayzūr kūrrōōtot
Where does the bus start from?	Honnan indul az autóbusz?	hawn-non eendool oz oootāwbooss
Will it pick us up at the hotel?	A busz a szálló-dánál vesz fel bennünket?	o booss o saal-lawdaa-naal væs fæl bæn-newnkæt
Where do the cruises start from?	Honnan indul a kíránduló hajó?	hawn-non eendool o kēēraandoolāw hoyāw
What bus/underground do we take?	Melyik buszra/földalattira szálljunk fel?	mæᵛeek boosro/furld-ollot-teero saalyoonk fæl
How much does the tour cost?	Mennyibe kerül a városnéző kőrút?	mænᵛeebæ kærewl o vaarawshnayzūr kūrrōōt
What time does the tour start?	Mikor kezdődik a városnéző kőrút?	meekawr kæzdūrdeek o vaarawshnayzūr kurrōōt

SIGHTSEEING

TELLING THE TIME: see page 178

At what time do we get back?	Mikor érkezünk vissza?	meekawr ayrkæzewnk vees-so
Is lunch included in the tour price?	Az ebéd benne van az árban?	oz æbayd bæn-næ von oz aarbon
Is there an English-speaking guide?	Van angolul beszélő idegenvezetőjük?	von ongawlool bæsaylūr eedægænvæzætūr̄yewk
We'd like to hire a car for the day.	Gépkocsit szeret-nénk kölcsönözni egy napra.	gaypkawcheet særætnaynk kurlchurnurznee æd^y nopro
I'd like to hire a chauffeur-driven car.	Szeretnék bérelni egy kocsit sofőrrel.	særætnayk bayrælnee æd^y kawcheet shawfūrr-ræl
Can you get me an English-speaking chauffeur?	Kaphatnék egy angolul beszélő sofőrt?	kophotnayk æd^y ongawlool bæsaylūr shawfūrrt
I'd like to hire an English-speaking private guide.	Szeretnék külön, angolul beszélő idegenvezetőt kapni.	særætnayk kewlurn ongawlool bæsaylūr eedægænvæzætūrt kopnee
for half a day for a full day	fél napra egy napra	fayl nopro æd^y nopro
What will that cost me?	Mennyibe kerül?	mæn^Veebæ kæerewl
Is that price all-inclusive?	Az árban minden benne van?	oz aarbon meendæn bæn-næ von
Can I pay with ...?	Fizethetek ...?	feezæt-hætæk
this credit card traveller's cheques	hitelkártyával traveller's csekkel	heetælkaart^Vaavol trovvæl-lærs chæk-kæl
Where is/are the ...?	Hol van ...?	hawl von
airport	a repülőtér	o ræpewlūrtayr
art gallery	a képzőművészeti galéria	o kaypzūrmēwvayssætee gollayreeo
botanical gardens	a botanikus kert	o bawtonneekoosh kært
building	az épület	oz aypewlæt
business district	az üzleti negyed	oz ewzlætee næd^Væd
castle	a vár	o vaar
cathedral	a székesegyház	o saykæshæd^Vhaaz
caves	a barlang	o borlong
cemetery	a temető	o tæmætūr
chapel	a kápolna	o kaapawlno
church	a templom	o tæmplawm
city centre	a városközpont	o vaarawshkurzpawnt

concert hall	a hangversenyterem	o hongvværshæn^ytæræm
conference centre	a konferencia központ	o kawnfæræntseeo kurzpawnt
docks	a móló	o maᵂlaw
downtown area	a városközpont	o vaarawshkurzpawnt
exhibition	a kiállítás	o keeaal-leetaash
fortress	az erődítmény	oz ærᵘrdeetmayn ^y
fountain	a forrás	o fawr-raash
garden	a kert	o kært
lake	a tó	o taᵂ
law courts	a bíróság	o beeraᵂshaag
library	a könyvtár	o kurn^yvtaar
market	a piac	o peeots
memorial	az emlékoszlop	oz æmlaykawslawp
monument	az emlékmű	oz æmlaykmeᵂ
museum	a múzeum	o mooᵘzæoom
observatory	a csillagvizsgáló	o cheel-logveezhgaalaᵂ
old town	a régi város	o rayghee vaarawsh
opera house	az opera	oz awpæro
palace	a palota	o pollawto
park	a park	o pork
parliament building	a Parlament épülete	o porlommænt aypewlætæ
planetarium	a planetárium	o plonnætaareeoom
port	a kikötő	o keekurtᵘr
post office	a postahivatal	o pawshtoheevottol
ruins	a romok	o rawmawk
shopping centre	a bevásárló központ	o bævaashaarlaᵂ kurzpawnt
stadium	a stadion	o shtoddeeawn
statue	a szobor	o sawbawr
synagogue	a zsinagóga	o zheenoggaᵂgo
theatre	a színház	o seeᵉnhaaz
tomb	a síremlék	o sheeræmlayk
tower	a torony	o tawrawn^y
TV studios	a TV studio	o tayvay shtoodeeaᵂ
university	az egyetem	oz æd^yætæm
zoo	az állatkert	oz aal-lotkært

SIGHTSEEING

SZABAD BELÉPÉS	ADMISSION FREE
TILOS A FÉNYKÉPEZÉS	NO CAMERAS ALLOWED

Admission

Is ... open on Sundays?	A ... vasárnaponként nyitva van?	o ... voshaarnoppawnkaynt n^yeetvo von
When does it open/close?	Mikor nyit/zár?	meekawr n^yeet/zaar
How much is the entrance fee?	Mennyibe kerül a belépőjegy?	mæn^yeebæ kærewl o bælaypūryæd^y
Is there any reduction for ...?	... részére kedvezményes a belépőjegy?	... rayssayræ kædvæzmayn^yæsh o bælaypūryæd^y
children	Gyerekek	d^yærækæk
families	Családok	chollaadawk
the handicapped	Nyomorékok	n^yawmawraykawk
pensioners	Nyugdíjasok	n^yoogdēēyoshawk
students	Diákok	deeaakawk
Where can I get a ticket?	Hol lehet jegyet kapni?	hawl læhæt yæd^yæt kopnee
Can I buy a catalogue?	Kaphatok egy katalógust?	kophottawk æd^y kottollāw goosht
Have you any guide books in English?	Van angolnyelvű útikalauzuk?	von ongawln^yælvēw ōōteekollo-oozook
Is it all right to take pictures?	Szabad fényképezni?	sobbod fayn^ykaypæznee

Who—What—When?

What's that building?	Az az épület mi?	oz oz aypewlæt mee
Who was the ...?	Ki volt ...?	kee vawlt
architect	az építész	oz aypēētayss
artist	a művész	o mēwvayss
painter	a festő	o fæshtūr
sculptor	a szobrász	o sawbraass
Who built it?	Ki építette?	kee aypēētæt-tæ
When was it built?	Mikor épült?	meekawr aypewlt
Who painted this picture?	Ki festette ezt a képet?	kee fæshtæt-tæ æst o kaypæt
When did he live?	Mikor élt?	meekawr aylt
Where's the house in which ... lived?	Hol az a ház, amelyben ... élt?	hawl oz o haaz ommæ^ybæn ... aylt

Just the adjective you've been looking for ...

It's ...	Ez ...	æz
awful	borzasztó	bawrzostáw
beautiful	gyönyörű	d^yurn^yurrēw
fantastic	csodálatos	chawdaalottawsh
gloomy	borongós	bawrawngáwsh
horrible	rettenetes	ræt-tænætæsh
impressive	benyomást keltő	bæn^yawmaasht kæltūr
interesting	érdekes	ayrdækæsh
magnificent	pompás	pawmpaash
monumental	óriási	áwreeaashee
overwhelming	lenyűgöző	læn^yēwgurzūr
sinister	rosszhangulatú	rawshongoolottōō
strange	különös	kewlurnursh
superb	kiváló	keevaaláw
surprising	meglepő	mæglæpūr
ugly	csúnya	chōōn^yo

What's your special interest?

I'm interested in ...	Bennünket ... érdekel/ érdekelnek.*	bæn-newnkæt ... ayr- dækæl/ayrdækælnæk
antiques	a régiségek	o raygheeshaygæk
archaeology	az archeológia	oz orhæawláwgheeo
botany	a növénytan	o nurvayn^yton
coins	az érmék	oz ayrmayk
fine arts	a szépművészet	o saypmēwvayssæt
furniture	a bútorok	o bōōtawrawrk
geography	a földrajz	o furldroyz
geology	a földtan	o furldton
handicrafts	a mesterségek	o mæshtærshaygæk
history	a történelem	o turrtaynælæm
horticulture	a kertészet	o kærtayssæt
Hungarian literature	a magyar irodalom	o mod^yor eerawdollawm
languages	a nyelvek	o n^yælvæk
medicine	az orvostudomány	oz awrvawshtoodawmaan^y
music	a zene	o zænæ
natural history	a természettudo- mányok	o tærmayssæt-toodaw- maan^yawk
ornithology	a madártan	o moddaarton

* Use *érdekelnek* with words in the following list which end in **k**.

painting	**a művészetek**	o me̅w̅vayssætæk
philately	**a bélyeggyűjtés**	o bay^yægd^yew^ytaysh
pottery	**a fazekasság**	o fozzækosh-shaag
prehistory	**a történelem előtti kor**	o turrtaynælæm ælu̅rt-tee kawr
science	**a tudományok**	o toodawmaan^yawk
sculpture	**a szobrászat**	o sawbraassot
zoology	**az állatvilág**	oz aal-lotveelaag
Where's the ... department?	**Hol van a/az ...-i részleg?**	hawl von o/oz ...-ee rayslæg

Religious services

Over 80 per cent of all Hungarians are Roman Catholics Minorities include, notably, Protestants and members of the Eastern Orthodox church, and Jews.

Most churches are open to the public. If you visit a church for sightseeing purposes while a service is progress, stay in the rear part of the building so as not to disturb the worshippers. Mass may be said in either Hungarian or Latin.

If you are interested in taking photographs, don't forget to ask permission first.

Is there a ... near here?	**Van a közelben ...?**	von o kurzælbæn
Catholic church	**katolikus templom**	kottawleekoosh tæmplawm
mosque	**mecset**	mæchæt
Protestant church	**protestáns templom**	prawtæshtaansh tæmplawm
synagogue	**zsinagóga**	zheenoggaʷgo
At what time is ...?	**Mikor van ...?**	meekawr von
mass	**a mise**	o meeshæ
the service	**a szertartás**	o særtortaash
Where can I find a ... who speaks English?	**Hol találok egy angolul beszélő ...?**	hawl tollaalawk æd^y ongawlool bæsaylu̅r
minister	**plébánost**	playbaanawsht
priest	**papot**	poppawt
rabbi	**rabit**	robbeet

Relaxing

Cinema (movies)—Theatre

A visit to a Hungarian cinema will no doubt be quite an experience, as most foreign films are dubbed into the language of the country. You can expect a newsreel, perhaps a children's cartoon film and a feature film in addition to the main attraction. You'll find out what's showing from local newspapers and a special weekly movie magazine.

Cinemas are open every day of the week. Screening starts as early as 9 a.m., and some cinemas have late-night shows at about midnight.

Since showings are not continuous, you can purchase your ticket up to three days in advance for a specific time. Prices are very reasonable.

Theatre programmes and concerts generally start at 7 p.m. Theatres often close on Mondays.

Tickets can be purchased on the spot, but for a special event you would be wise to make your booking in advance, possibly through a ticket office in the centre of town or a tourist office. Theatre and concert tickets are also very advantageous, even for the National Opera House.

During summer, open-air performances are staged on Margaret Island *Margitsziget* in Budapest. At the same time of year Szeged, in the south of the country, is the scene of a music and opera festival, *Szegedi Ünnepi Játékok*.

Do you have an entertainment guide for ...?	Van ...-i programjuk?	von ...-ee **praw**gromyook
What's on at the cinema tonight?	Mi megy ma este a moziban?	mee mæd^y mo æshtæ o **maw**zeebon
What's on at the ... Theatre?	Mit játszanak a ... színházban?	meet **yaat**sonnok o ... **seen**haazbon

What sort of play is it?	Ez milyen darab?	æz mee^yæn dorrob
Who is it by?	Ki a szerző?	kee o særzūr
Where is …'s new film showing?	… új filmjét hol játszák?	… ōō^y feelmyayt hawl yaatsaak
Can you recommend a …?	Ajánlana egy …?	oyaanlonno æd^y
cartoon film	rajzfilmet	royzfeelmæt
comedy	bohózatot	bawhāwzottawt
documentary film	dokumentum filmet	dawkoomæntoom feelma
good film	jó filmet	yāw feelmæt
musical	zenés színdarabot	zænaysh sēendorrobbawt
play	darabot	dorrobbawt
revue	revüt	rævewt
something light	valami könnyűt	vollommee kurn^yewt
thriller (film)	bűnügyi filmet	bēwnewd^yee feelmæt
thriller (play)	bűnügyi darabot	bēwnewd^yee dorrobbawt
Western	vadnyugati filmet	vodn^yoogottee feelmæt
At which theatre is that new play by … being performed?	… új darabját hol adják?	… ōō^y dorrobyaat hawl odyaak
Who's in it?	Ki játszik benne?	kee yaatseek bæn-næ
Who's playing the lead?	Ki játsza a főszerepet?	kee yaatso o fūrsæræpæt
What time does the show begin?	Mikor kezdődik a darab?	meekawr kæzdūrdeek o dorrob
What time does it end?	Mikor van vége?	meekawr von vaygæ
Are there any tickets left for tonight?	Van még jegyük ma estére?	von mayg yæd^yewk mo æshtayræ
How much are the tickets?	Mibe kerülnek a jegyek?	meebæ kærewlnæk o yæd^yæk
I'd like to book 2 seats for next (Friday) evening.	(Péntek) estére szeretnék 2 jegyet rendelni.	(payntæk) æshtayræ særætnayk 2 yæd^yæt rændælnee
Can I have a ticket for the matinée on (Tuesday)?	Kaphatok egy jegyet a (keddi) matinéra?	kophottawk æd^y yæd^yæt o (kæd-dee) motteenayr
I'd like a seat in the stalls (orchestra)/circle (mezzanine).	A földszintre/Az erkélyre kérek egy jegyet.	o furldseentræ/oz ærkay^yræ kayræk æd^y yæd^yæt

ow much are the eats in the front ow?	**Mibe kerül a jegy az első sorban?**	meebæ kærewl o yæd^y oz ælshūr shawrbon
want 2 seats in the talls (orchestra).	**A földszintre kérek 2 jegyet.**	o furldseentræ kayræk 2 yæd^yæt
omewhere in the niddle.	**Valahova középre.**	vollohawvo kurzaypræ
May I have a rogramme, please?	**Kaphatok egy műsort?**	kophottawk æd^y mēw-shawrt
Vhere's the cloak-oom?	**Hol a ruhatár?**	hawl o roohawtaar

🖝   🖘

Sajnálom, minden jegyünk elkelt.	I'm sorry, we're sold out.
Csak az erkélyre van még néhány jegyünk.	There are only a few seats left in the circle (mezzanine).
Szabad a jegyét?	May I see your ticket?
Ez az Ön helye.	This is your seat.

RELAXING

Concert—Opera—Ballet

Vhere's the opera ouse?	**Hol az operaház?**	hawl oz awpærohaaz
Vhere's the concert all?	**Hol a hangver-senyterem?**	hawl o **hong**værshæn^y-tæræm
Vhat's on at the pera tonight?	**Mi megy ma az operában?**	mee mæd^y mo oz **awp**æ-raabon
Vho's singing?	**Ki énekel?**	kee aynækæl
Vho's dancing?	**Ki táncol?**	kee taantsawl
What time does the rogramme start?	**Mikor kezdődik a program?**	meekawr kæzdūrdeek o **prawg**rom
Vhat's the name of ne orchestra?	**Melyik zenekar játszik?**	mæ^yeek zænækor yaatseek
Vhat are they play-ng?	**Mit játszanak?**	meet yaatsonnok
Vho's the conductor?	**Ki vezényel?**	kee væzayn^yæl

Nightclub

Budapest has a number of nightclubs, several of them located in the larger hotels. Similar establishments can be found in lesser quantity in other major towns and, during the summer tourist season, along Lake Balaton.

They generally offer floor shows which, though entertaining, are rather more decorous than those found in some other capital cities—there's no striptease, for example. Music can be very good, and may include live jazz. Prices are predictably high.

Apart from light snacks, no meals are served.

Nightclub hours are from about 10 p.m. to 4 or 5 in the morning, six days a week. The closing day varies. Advance reservations are advisable for the select nightclubs in some five-star hotels, but elsewhere you should have no trouble finding a table.

Can you recommend a good nightclub?	Ajánlana egy jó éjszakai mulatót?	oyaanlonno $æd^y$ yāw ay^ysokko-ee moolottāwt
Is there a floor show?	Műsor van?	mēwshawr von
What time does the floor show start?	Mikor kezdődik a műsor?	meekawr kæzdūrdeek o mēwshawr
Is evening dress necessary?	Alkalmi öltözet szükséges?	olkolmee urlturzæt sewkshaygæsh

And once inside …

A table for 2, please.	Egy asztalt kérek 2 fő részére.	$æd^y$ ostolt kayræk 2 fūr rayssayræ
I've booked a table for 4.	4 fő részére foglaltam asztalt.	4 fūr rayssayræ fawgloltom ostolt
My name is …	… vagyok.	… vod^yawk
I phoned you earlier.	Az előbb telefonáltam Önöknek.	oz ælūrb tælæfawnaaltom urnurknæk
We haven't a reservation.	Nincs foglalásunk.	neench fawglollaashoonk

I'd like the drinks card, please.	**Az itallapot kérem.**	oz eetol-loppawt **kayræm**
We'd like a bottle of ...	**Egy üveg ... kérünk.**	æd^y **ewvaeg** ... **kayrewnk**
champagne	**pezsgőt**	**pæzhgūrt**
red wine	**vörösbort**	**vurrursbawrt**
white wine	**fehérbort**	**fæhayrbawrt**

Dancing

Would you like to dance?	**Van kedve táncolni?**	von **kædvæ taantsawlnee**
Where can we go dancing?	**Hol lehet táncolni?**	hawl **læhæt taantsawlnee**
Is there a discotheque in town?	**Van a városban diszkó?**	von o **vaarawshbon deeskāw**
Is there an entry fee?	**Belépőjegy van?**	**bælaypūryæd^y** von
There's a dance at the ... Hotel.	**A ... Hotelban lehet táncolni.**	o ... **hawtælbon læhæt taantsawlnee**
May I have this dance?	**Szabad felkérnem egy táncra?**	**sobbod fælkayrnæm æd^y taantsro**

Do you happen to play ... ?

Chess is a big favourite in Hungary. There is hardly a week without a major tournament being held somewhere.

| Do you play chess? | **Sakkozik?** | **shok-kawzeek** |

bishop	**futó**	**footāw**
castle (rook)	**bástya**	**baasht^yo**
king	**király**	**keeraa^y**
knight	**huszár**	**hoossaar**
pawn	**gyalog**	**d^yollawg**
queen	**vezér**	**væzayr**
Check!	**Sakk!**	shok
Checkmate!	**Matt!**	mot

RELAXING

Do you play draughts (checkers)?	**Játszik francia sakkot?**	yaatseek frontseeo shok-kawt
Do you play cards?	**Kártyázik?**	kaart^yaazeek
bridge	**bridzs**	breedzh
canasta	**kanaszta**	konnosto
gin rummy	**römi**	rurmee
poker	**póker**	pawkær

hearts	**kőr**	kūrr
diamonds	**káró**	kaaraw
clubs	**treff**	træf
spades	**pikk**	peek
ace	**ász**	aass
king	**király**	keeraa^y
queen	**felső**	fælshūr
jack (knave)	**alsó**	olshaw
joker	**dzsóker**	dzhawkær

Sports

The Hungarians are a sport-loving nation, and facilities for both watching and playing sports are widely available.

Soccer *(labdarugás)* is without a doubt the top spectator sport. Most towns have at least one team, and except in the height of summer you'll certainly be able to see a match whatever part of the country you happen to be in.

Basketball *(kosárlabda)* comes second in terms of popularity. It is played all year round, all over the country, in various leagues. The country boasts some 40,000 regular players.

Water polo *(vizilabda)* is another big favourite. The national team has won many international prizes. Main centres are the National Sports Pool *(Nemzeti Sportuszoda)* on Margaret Island and the Komjáti Swimming Pool *(Komjáti Uszoda)*, both in Budapest.

Horse racing *(lóverseny)* is widely organized during the season, with several meetings a week. The Budapest race-course (track) is called *Budapesti ügető*. Bets can be placed at state-run offices (see page 88).

Sailing *(vitorlázás)* is popular on Lake Balaton and Lake Velence. Regattas and races take place on both lakes between May and October.

Table tennis *(asztalitenisz)* claims around 100,000 regular club players throughout the country, and you should not have too much difficulty in gaining access to a club's facilities during your visit.

Fencing *(vívás)* has a good number of adherents in the country. Its practitioners have made their mark in the field of international competition.

The daily sports paper *Népsport* contains details of what's on in the sporting world—including chess—throughout the country. Any local sports fan with some knowledge of English will be delighted to translate for you and help you find what you want.

Is there a football game on anywhere this Saturday?	Most szombaton lesz valahol futbalmeccs?	mawsht sawmbottawn læs vollohawl footbol mæch
I'd like to see a basketball match.	Szeretnék megtekinteni egy kosárlabdamérkőzést.	særetnayk mægtækeentænee æd^y kawshaarlobdomayrkūrzaysht
Who's playing?	Ki játszik?	kee yaatseek
What's the admission charge?	Mibe kerül a belépőjegy?	meebæ kærewl o bælaypūr-yaed^y
Can you get me 2 tickets?	Szerezne nekem 2 jegyet?	særæznæ nækæm 2 yæd^{y}æt
Where's the Budapest race-course?	Hol találom a budapesti ügetőpályát?	hawl tollawlawm o boodoppæshtee ewgætūrpaa-^{y}aat
Where are the tennis courts?	Hol találok teniszpályát?	hawl tollaalawk tæneespaa^{y}aat
Can I hire rackets?	Bérelhetek ütőket?	bayrælhætæk ewtūrkæt

Where can I play table tennis?	Hol lehet ping-pongozni?	hawl læhæt peeng-pawngawznee
What's the charge per ...?	Mennyi a bérleti díj ...?	mæn^{y}ee o bayrlætee dēē^y
day	naponta	noppawnto
game	játszmánként	yaatsmaankaynt
hour	óránként	āwraankaynt
Is there a swimming pool near here?	Van a környéken uszoda?	von o kurrn^{y}aykæn oossawdo
Is it outdoors or indoors?	Nyitott, vagy fedett?	n^{y}eetawt vod^y fædæt
Can one swim in the lake/river?	Szabad úszni a tóban/folyóban?	sobbod ōōsnee o tāwbon/faw^{y}āwbon
Is there any good fishing around here?	Hol lehet a környéken jól horgászni?	hawl læhæt o kurrn^{y}aykær yāwl hawrgaasnoo
Do I need a licence?	Kell hozzá engedély?	kæl hawz-zaa ængæday^y
Where can I get one?	Hol lehet a horgászengedélyt beszerezni?	hawl læhæt o hawrgaass-ængæday^{y}t bæssæræznee

Betting

Betting on horses and soccer matches is legal and widespread. There is also a state lottery *(lottó)* every week.

The government betting authority, *Sportfogadási és Lottó Igazgatóság* maintains offices in most towns through which you can place your bets on horse races and soccer matches. They also sell lottery tickets. Forms for betting on soccer matches, as well as lottery tickets, can also be obtained from tobacconists', larger news-stands and street vendors. Winnings are paid out in local currency, after deduction of a profits tax.

| Where's the nearest betting shop? | Hol a legközelebbi fogadó iroda? | hawl o lægkurzælæb-bee fawgoddāw eerawdo |

On the beach

Landlocked Hungary may not have a sea coastline, but bathing, boating and sailing facilities are numerous along lake shores and river banks. The approximately 230-square-mile (600-square-kilometre) Lake Balaton is a special favourite, and its shallow waters are generally quite safe, provided normal precautions are taken. Note that power boats are not allowed on Balaton, so you'll have to go elsewhere for water-skiing (the Danube, Tisza and other rivers).

Is it safe for swimming?	Itt biztonságos az úszás?	eet beeztawnshaagawsh oz ōōssaash
Is there a lifeguard?	Mentőszolgálat van?	mæntūrsaawlgaalot von
Is it safe for children?	Gyerekek részére biztonságos?	d^{y}ærækæk rayssayræ beeztawnshaagawsh
The lake is very calm.	A tó nagyon nyugodt.	o tāw nod^{y}awn n^{y}oogawdt
Are there any dangerous currents?	Nincsenek veszélyes örvények?	neenchænæk væssay^{y}æsh urrvayn^{y}æk

MAGÁN STRAND	TILOS A FÜRDÉS
PRIVATE BEACH	NO BATHING

What's the temperature of the water?	Mennyi a víz hőmérséklete?	mæn^{y}ee o vēēz hūrmayrshayklætæ
I'd like to hire a/an/some...	Szeretnék bérelni egy	særætnayk bayrælnee æd^y
air mattress	gumimatracot	goomeemotrotsawt
deck chair	nyugágyat	n^{y}oogaad^{y}ot
kayak	kajakot	koyokkawt
rowing boat	evezős csónakot	ævæzūrsh chāwnokkawt
sailing boat	vitorláshajót	veetawrlaashhoyāwt
skin-diving equipment	búvárfelszerelést	bōōvaarfælsærælaysht
water skis	vizisít	veezeeshēēt
What's the charge per hour?	Mibe kerül óránként?	meebæ kærewl āwraankaynt

Camping—Countryside

Camping facilities are available at about 200 sites, the majority of which are clustered around Lake Balaton, South-West of Budapest. They are graded in three categories according to the amenities and services they offer. First- and second-class sites have shops, restaurants, showers, toilets and electrical outlets for campers. Tents and cabins can be rented at first-class sites.

If you wish to have the freedom of camping but a little more comfort, you can rent a holiday home sleeping from two to six people. Here you'll be able to enjoy various extra services including laundry, catering, shopping and some sports facilities. Some units have their own little gardens.

Most camping sites and holiday-home centres operate from May to October.

Foreign visitors generally find rates very advantageous, and members of internationally affiliated camping and caravaning clubs often enjoy reductions. Bills can be paid in local currency.

Lists of camping sites and holiday homes detailing facilities and rates can be obtained from local and foreign branches of Ibusz (see page 28 for addresses abroad), most hotels, the Hungarian Motoring Association *(Magyar Autóklub)* or the Hungarian Camping and Caravaning Club *(Magyar Kemping és Karaván Klub)*.

CAMPING: see also page 106

Is there a camping site near here?	**Van a közelben kemping?**	von o kurzælbæn kæmpeeng
Have you room for a tent/caravan (trailer)?	**Van helyük egy sátor/lakókocsi részére?**	von hæᵛewk ædᵛ shaa-tawr/lokkāwkawchee rayssayræ
Where can we rent a holiday home?	**Hol bérelhetnénk egy nyaralót?**	hawl bayrælhætnaynk ædᵛ nᵛorrollāwt

May we light a fire?	**Szabad tüzet gyújtani?**	sobbod tewzæt d^yōō-tonnee
Is this drinking water?	**Ivóvíz van?**	eevāwvēēz von
Are there any shops on the site?	**Vannak üzletek a kemping területén?**	von-nok ewzlætæk o kæmpeeng tærewlætayn
Are there any ...?	**Vannak ...?**	von-nok
baths	**fürdőszobák**	fewrdūrssawbaak
kitchens	**konyhák**	kawn^yhaak
laundry facilities	**mosódák**	mawshāwdaak
showers	**zuhanyozók**	zoohon^yawzāwk
toilets	**vécék**	vaytsayk
What's the charge ...?	**Mennyibe kerül ...?**	mæn^yeebæ kærewl
per day	**naponta**	noppawnto
per person	**személyenként**	sæmay^yænkaynt
for a car	**gépkocsinként**	gaypkawcheenkaynt
for a tent	**sátranként**	shaatronkaynt
for a caravan	**lakókocsinként**	lokkāwkawcheenkaynt
Do you known anyone who can put us up for the night?	**Ismer valakit, akinél éjszakára megszállhatunk?**	eeshmær vollokkeet okkeenayl ay^yssokkaaro mægsaalhottoonk

TÁBOROZNI TILOS	**TILOS LAKÓKOCSIVAL PARKIROZNI**
NO CAMPING	NO CARAVANS (TRAILERS)

Landmarks

barn	**a csűr**	o chēwr
beach	**a part**	o port
bridge	**a híd**	o hēēd
brook	**a patak**	o pottok
building	**az épület**	oz aypewlæt
canal	**a csatorna**	o chottawrno
castle	**a vár**	o vaar
church	**a templom**	o tæmplawm
cliff	**a szikla**	o seeklo
cottage	**a tanya**	o ton^yo
crossroads	**a keresztút**	o kæræstōōt
farm	**a gazdaság**	o gozdoshaag
ferry	**a komp**	o kawmp
field	**a szántóföld**	o saantāwfurld

forest	**az erdő**	oz aerdūr
fortress	**az erődítmény**	oz aerūrdēētmayn^y
hamlet	**a kunyhó**	o koon^yhāw
highway	**az országút**	oz awrsaagōōt
hill	**a domb**	o dawmb
house	**a ház**	o haaz
hut	**a menedékház**	o maenaedayk-haaz
inn	**a vendéglő**	o vaendayglūr
lake	**a tó**	o tāw
marsh	**a mocsaras**	o mawchorrosh
moorland	**a legelő**	o laegaelūr
mountain	**a hegy**	o haed^y
path	**az ösvény**	oz urshvayn^y
peak	**a csúcs**	o chōōch
pond	**a tavacska**	o tovvochko
pool	**a víztároló**	o vēēztaarawlāw
railway line	**a vasúti pálya**	o voshōōtee paa^yo
river	**a folyó**	o faw^yāw
road	**az út**	oz ōōt
ruin	**a rom**	o rawm
spring	**a forrás**	o fawr-raash
stream	**a folyam**	o faw^yom
swamp	**a mocsár**	o mawchaar
tower	**a torony**	o tawrawn^y
track	**a földút**	o furldōōt
tree	**a fa**	o fo
valley	**a völgy**	o vurld^y
village	**a falu**	o folloo
vineyard	**a szölő**	o surlūr
water	**a víz**	o vēēz
waterfall	**a vízesés**	o vēēzaeshaysh
well	**a kút**	o kōōt
wood	**a liget**	o leegaet

What's the name of that river?	**Mi a folyó neve?**	mee o faw^yāw naevae
How high is that mountain?	**Milyen magas az a hegy?**	mee^yaen moggosh oz o haed^y

… and if you're tired of walking, you can always try hitch-hiking *(autóstoppal utazni)*:

Can you give me a lift to …?	**Elvinne …-ba/-be/ -ra/-re?***	aelveen-nae …-bo/-bae/ -ro/-rae

*See Grammar section for word endings.

Making friends

Introductions

A few phrases to get you started:

How do you do?	Jónapot kívánok.	yāwnoppawt kēēvaanawk
How are you?	Hogy van?	hawd^y von
Fine, thank you. And you?	Jól, köszönöm. És Ön?	yāwl kursurnurm. aysh urn
I'd like you to meet a friend of mine.	Szeretném bemutatni az egyik barátomat.	særætnaym bæmoototnee oz æd^yeek borraatawmot
May I introduce ...?	Bemutathatom ...?	bæmootot-hotawm
John, this is ...	John, ez ...	dzhawn æz
My name is ...	A nevem ...	o nævæm
Glad to know you.	Örülök, hogy megismerhetem.	urrewlurk hawd^y mægeeshmærhætæm
... sends his/her best regards.	... szívélyesen üdvözli.	... sēēvayl^yæssæn ewdvurzlee
It's nice to see you (again).	Örülök hogy (újra) találkozunk.	urrewlurk hawd^y(ōō^yro) tollaalkawzoonk

Follow-up

How long have you been here?	Mióta van itt?	meeāwto von eet
We've been here a week.	Egy hete vagyunk itt.	æd^y hætæ vod^yoonk eet
Is this your first visit?	Most vannak itt először?	mawsht von-nok eet ælūrssurr
No, we came here last year.	Nem, már tavaly is itt voltunk.	næm maar tovvoy eesh eet vawltoonk
Are you enjoying your stay?	Jól érzik magukat?	yāwl ayrzeek moggookot
Yes, I like ... very much.	Igen ... nagyon tetszik.	eegæn ... nod^yawn tætseek
I like the countryside a lot.	Nagyon szeretem a vidéket.	nod^yawn særætæm o veedaykæt

This is a very interesting town.	Ez nagyon érdekes város.	æz nod^yawn ayrdækæsh vaarawsh
Are you on your own?	Egyedül van?	æd^yædewl von
I'm with ...	... vagyok.	... vod^yawk
my husband	A férjemmel	o fayrryæm-mæl
my wife	A feleségemmel	o fælæshaygæm-mæl
my family	A családommal	o chollaadawm-mol
my children	A gyerekeimmel	o d^yærækæeem-mæl
my parents	A szüleimmel	o sewlæeem-mæl
some friends	Néhány barátommal	nayhaan^y borraatawm-mol
Where do you come from?	Honnan jön?	hawn-non yurn
Where are you staying?	Hol lakik?	hawl lokkeek
I'm a student.	Diák vagyok.	deeaak vod^yawk
What are you studying?	Mit tanul?	meet tonnool
I'm here on business.	Hivatalosan vagyok itt.	heevottollawshon vod^yawk eet
What kind of business are you in?	Mi a foglalkozása?	mee o fawglolkawzaasho
I hope we'll meet again.	Remélem, hamarosan.	ræmaylæm hommorawshon

The weather

The Hungarians love to talk about it—in fact, they like to blame most things that go wrong on the weather!

What a lovely day!	Gyönyörű napunk van!	d^yurn^yurrēw noppoonk von
What awful weather!	Micsoda pocsék idő van!	meechawdo pawchayk eedūr von
Isn't it cold/hot today!	Nincs hideg/meleg?	neench heedæg/mælæg
Do you think it will ... tomorrow?	Mit gondol, holnap ...?	meet gawndawl hawlnop
clear up	kiderül	keedærewl
rain	esik	æsheek
snow	havazik	hovvozzeek
be sunny	süt a nap	shewt o nop

Invitations

My wife/My husband and I would like you to join us for dinner.	Feleségemmel/Férjemmel együtt szeretnénk ha velünk vacsoráznának.	fælæshaygæm-mæl/**fayr**-yæm-mæl æd^{y}ewt sæærætnaynk ho vælewnk vochawraaznaanok
Can you come to dinner tonight?	Eljönne ma este vacsorára?	ælyurn-næ mo æshtæ vochawraaro
Can you come over for a drink this evening?	Átjönne ma este egy italra?	aatyurn-næ mo æshtæ æd^y eetolro
There's a party. Are you coming?	Összejövetelünk van. Eljön?	urs-sæ^{y}urvætælewnk von. ælyurn
That's very kind of you.	Nagyon kedves Öntől.	nod^{y}awn kædvæsh urn-tūrl
Great! I'd love to come.	Nagyszerű. Szívesen eljönnék.	nod^{y}særēw. sēēvæshæn ælyurn-nayk
What time shall we come?	Mikor jöjjünk?	meekawr yur^y-yewnk
May I bring a friend/ girl friend?	Egy barátomat/ barátnőmet is elhozhatom?	æd^y borraatawmot/ borraatnūrmæt eesh ælhawz-hottawm
I'm afraid we've got to go now.	Azt hiszem, most már mennünk kell.	ost **heess**æm mawsht maar mæn-newnk kæl
Next time, you must come to visit us.	Legközelebb feltétlenül látogassanak meg.	lægkurzælæb fæl-taytlænewl laataw-gosh-shonnok mæg
Thanks for the evening.	Köszönet az estéért.	kursurnæt oz æshtayayrt
I/We enjoyed it very much.	Nagyon élveztem/ élveztünk.	nod^{y}awn aylvæztæm/ aylvæztewnk

Dating

May I get you a drink?	Meghívhatom egy italra?	mæghēēvhottawm æd^y eetolro
Would you like a cigarette?	Parancsol egy cigarettát?	porronchawl æd^y tsee-gorræt-taat
Excuse me, could you give me a light?	Bocsánat, van tüze?	bawchaanot von tewzæ

Are you waiting for someone?	Vár valakire?	vaar vollokkeeræ
Leave me alone, please!	Kérem, hagyjon békén!	kayræm hod^Yawn baykayr
Are you free this evening?	Ráérne ma este?	raaayrnæ mo æshtæ
I'm sorry, I already have an engagement this evening.	Sajnálom, de ma estére már van programom.	shoynaalawm dæ mo æshtayræ maar von prawgrommawm
Would you like to go out with me tomorrow night?	Eljönne velem holnap este?	ælyurn-næ vælæm hawlnop æshtæ
Would you like to go dancing?	Lenne kedve táncolni?	læn-næ kædvæ taan-tsawlnee
I know a good discotheque.	Tudok egy jó diszkót.	toodawk æd^Y yāw deeskāwt
Do you know a good discotheque?	Ismer egy jó diszkót?	eeshmær æd^Y yāw deeskāwt
Shall we go to the cinema?	Menjünk moziba?	mæn^Yewnk mawzeebo
Would you like to go for a drive?	Van kedve autózni egyet?	von kædvæ ooootāwznee æd^Yæt
Where shall we meet?	Hol találkozzunk?	hawl tollaalkawz-zoonk
I'll pick you up at your hotel.	A szállodájánál majd felveszem.	o saal-lawdaa^Yaanaal moyc fælvæsæm
I'll call for you at 8.	8 órakor magáért jövök.	8 āwrok-kawr moggaa-ayrt yurvurk
May I take you home?	Hazakisérhetem?	hozzokkeeshayrhætæm
Can I see you again tomorrow?	Holnap újra láthatom?	hawlnop ōō^Yro laat-hottawm
Thank you, it's been a very enjoyable evening.	Köszönöm. Nagyon szép este volt.	kursurnurm. nod^Yawn sayp æshtæ vawlt
What's your telephone number?	Mi a telefonszáma?	mee o tælæfawnsaamo
What time is your last bus/train?	Mikor indul az utolsó autóbusza/villamosa?	meekawr eendool oz ootawlshāw oooetāwboosso/veel-lommawsho

Shopping guide

This shopping guide is designed to help you find what you want with ease, accuracy and speed. It features:

1. a list of all major shops, stores and services (p. 98)
2. some general expressions required when shopping to allow you to be selective and specific (p. 100)
3. full details of the shops and services most likely to concern you. Here you'll find advice, alphabetical lists of items and conversion charts, as listed under the headings below.

		Page
Bookshop	books, newspapers, magazines, stationery	104
Camping	camping equipment	106
Chemist's (drugstore)	medicines, first-aid supplies, cosmetics, toilet articles	108
Clothing	clothes, shoes, accessories	112
Electrical appliances	radios, tape-recorders, records, shavers, batteries, etc.	119
Hairdresser	men's and ladies' hairdressers', beauty salon	121
Jeweller— Watch shop	jewellery, watches, watch repairs	123
Laundry—Dry cleaning	usual facilities	126
Photography	cameras, accessories, film, developing	127
Provisions	this section is confined to basic items required for picnics	129
Souvenirs	souvenirs, gifts, fancy goods, local specialities	131
Tobacconist	smokers' supplies	132

Shops—Stores—Services

Most shops are open from 10 a.m. to 6 p.m. (department stores from 9 a.m. to 7 p.m.), Monday–Friday, and from 9 a.m. to 2 p.m., Saturday, without a break. Some tobacconists' and most pastry shops also stay open on Sunday. Grocers' and dairy shops may start as early as 6 a.m.

Price tags in Hungarian shops show the price you actually pay. No tax is added, and discounts are not negotiable.

Intertourist shops, found in most main centres, are likely to have a wider range of goods on sale than you'll see elsewhere. Payment must be made in hard currency. Imported items such as whisky, perfumes, cigarettes and appliances will often be less expensive in these shops than at home.

Where's the nearest ...?	Hol van a legközelebbi ...?	hawl von o lægkurzælæb-bæ
antique shop	régiség-kereskedés	raygheeshayg-kæræshkædaysh
art gallery	képzőművészeti galéria	kaypzūrmēwvaysætee gollayreeo
baker	pék	payk
barber	borbély	bawrbay^y
beauty salon	kozmetikai szalon	kawzmæteeko-ee sollawn
bookshop	könyvesbolt	kurn^{y}væshbawlt
butcher	hentes	hæntæsh
camera shop	fotószaküzlet	fawtāwsokkewzlæt
candy store	édességbolt	aydæsh-shaygbawlt
chemist	gyógyszertár	d^{y}awd^{y}særtaar
confectioner	cukrászda	tsookraasdo
dairy shop	tejbolt	tæ^{y}bawlt
delicatessen	csemegebolt	chæmægæbawlt
department store	áruház	aaroohaaz
drugstore	illatszerbolt	eel-lotsærbawlt
dry-cleaner	vegytisztító	væd^{y}teestēētāw
fishmonger	halkereskedés	holkæræshkædaysh
florist	virágüzlet	veeraaghewzlæt
furrier	szőrme üzlet	sūrrmæ ewzlæt
greengrocer	zöldségesbolt	zurldshaygæshbawlt
grocer	élelmiszerbolt	aylælmeessærbawlt
hairdresser (ladies')	női-fodrászat	nūr-ee-fawdraassot
hairdresser (men's)	férfi-fodrászat	fayrfee-fawdraassot

hardware store	vasüzlet	voshewzlæt
Intertourist shop	Intertourist bolt	"intertourist" bawlt
jeweller	ékszerész	ayksærayss
laundry	mosoda	mawshawdo
liquor store	szeszes italok	sæsæsh eetollawk
market	piac	peeots
newstand	újságárus	$\overline{oo}^y$shaagaaroosh
off-licence	szeszes italok	sæsæsh eetollawk
optician	látszerész	laatsærayss
pastry shop	cukrászda	tsookraasdo
pharmacy	gyógyszertár	$d^y\overline{aw}d^y$særtaar
photo shop	fotószaküzlet	fawt$\overline{aw}$sokkewzlæt
shoemaker (repairs)	cipőjavító	tseep$\overline{ur}$-yov$\overline{ee}$t$\overline{aw}$
shoe shop	cipőbolt	tseep$\overline{ur}$bawlt
souvenir shop	szuvenírbolt	soovæn$\overline{ee}$rbawlt
sports shop	sportszerkereskedés	shpawrtsærkæræshkædaysh
stationer	papírüzlet	popp$\overline{ee}$rewzlæt
supermarket	szupermarket	soopærmaarkæt
sweet shop	édességbolt	aydæsh-shaygbawlt
tailor	szabó	sobb$\overline{aw}$
tobacconist	dohánybolt	dawhaan^{y}bawlt
toy shop	játéküzlet	yaataykewzlæt
travel agency	utazási iroda	ootozzaashee eerawdo
vegetable store	zöldségbolt	zurldshaygbawlt
watchmaker	órás	$\overline{aw}$raash
wine merchant	bor szaküzlet	bawr sokkewzlæt

..and some other useful addresses:

bank	bank	bonk
currency exchange office	valuta beváltó hely	vollooto bævaalt$\overline{aw}$ hæ^y
dentist	fogorvos	fawgawrvawsh
doctor	orvos	awrvawsh
filling station	töltőállomás	turlt$\overline{ur}$aal-lawmaash
hospital	kórház	k$\overline{aw}$rhaaz
library	könyvtár	kurn^{y}vtaar
lost property (lost-and found) office	talált tárgyak hivatala	tollaalt taard^{y}ok heevotollo
police station	rendőrség	rænd$\overline{ur}$rshayg
post office	posta	pawshto
telegraph office	távirda	taaveerdo
tourist office	turista ügynökség	tooreeshto ewd^{y}nurkshayg

SHOPPING GUIDE

Where?

Where's there a good ...?	**Hol van egy jó ...?**	hawl von æd^y yāw
Where can I find a ...?	**Hol találok egy ...?**	hawl tollaalawk æd^y
Where can I buy ...?	**Hol kapok ...?**	hawl koppawk
Can you recommend an inexpensive ...?	**Ajánlana egy olcsó ...?**	oyaanlonno æd^y awlchāw
Where's the main shopping area?	**Hol a bevásárlóközpont?**	hawl o bævaashaarlāw-kurzpawnt
Is it far from here?	**Messze van innen?**	mæs-sæ von een-næn
How do I get there?	**Hogy jutok el oda?**	hawd^y yootawk æl awdo
Where's the courtesy desk?	**Hol a vevőszolgálat?**	hawl o vævūrsawlgaalot

Service

Can you help me?	**Segítene?**	shægēētænæ
I'm just looking round.	**Csak nézelődök.**	chok nayzælūrdurk
I want ...	**Szükségem van egy ...**	sewkshaygæm von æd^y
Can you show me some ...?	**Mutatna néhány ...?**	moototno nayhaan^y
Do you have any ...?	**Kapható ...?**	kophottāw

That one

Can you show me ...?	**Láthatnám ...?**	laathotnaam
that one	**azt**	ost
those	**azokat**	ozzawkot
the one in the window	**azt ott a kirakatban.**	ost awt o keerokkotbon
It's over there.	**Ott van.**	awt von

KIÁRUSÍTÁS SALE	**VÉGKIÁRUSÍTÁS** CLEARANCE

Defining the article

'd like a ... one.	**...-ra/-re van szükségem.***	... -ro/-ræ von **sewk-shaygæm**
t must be ...	**...-ra/-re gondolok.***	... -ro/-ræ **gawndawlawk**

big	**nagy**	nod^y
cheap	**olcsó**	awlchāw
dark	**sötét**	shurtayt
good	**jó**	yāw
heavy	**nehéz**	næhayz
large	**nagy**	nod^y
light (colour)	**világos**	veelaagawsh
light (weight)	**könnyű**	kurn^{y}ew
oval	**ovális**	awvaaleesh
rectangular	**négyzetes**	nayd^{y}zætæsh
round	**kerek**	kæræk
small	**kicsi**	keechee
soft	**puha**	pooho
square	**négyszögű**	nayd^{y}surgew

I don't want anything too expensive.	**Nem valami drága holmira gondolok.**	næm vollommee draago hawlmeero gawndawlawk

Preference

Haven't you anything ...?	**Nincs valami ...?**	neench vollommee
better/cheaper	**jobb/olcsóbb**	yawb/awlchāwb
larger/smaller	**nagyobb/kisebb**	nod^{y}awb/keeshæb
Can you show me some more?	**Mutatna még másfélét is?**	moototno mayg maashfaylayt eesh

How much?

How much is this?	**Mibe kerül?**	meebæ kærewl
Please write it down.	**Kérem, írja le.**	kayræm ēēryo læ
I don't want to spend more than ...	**Nem akarok többet mint ...-t költeni.**	næm okkorrawk turb-bæt meent ...-t kurltænee

* See Grammar section for word endings.

Decision

I'll take it.	**Ezt megveszem.**	æst mægvæsæm
No, I don't like it.	**Nem, nem tetszik.**	næm næm tætseek

Ordering

Can you order it for me?	**Megrendelné a részemre?**	mægrændælnay o ray-sæmræ
How long will it take?	**Meddig kell várni?**	mæd-deeg kæl vaarnee
I'd like it as soon as possible.	**A lehető leggyorsabban szeretném megkapni.**	o læhætūr lægd^{y}awr-shob-bon sæærætnaym mægkopnee

Delivery

Please deliver it to the … Hotel.	**Kérem, szállítsa le a … szállodába!**	kayræm saal-lēētsho læ o … saal-lawdaabo
Please send it to this address.	**Kérem, küldje el erre a címre!**	kayræm kewld^{y}æ æl ær-ræ o tsēēmræ
Will I have any difficulty with the customs?	**Nem lesz problémám a vámnál?**	næm læs prawblaymaam o vaamnaal

Paying

How much is it?	**Mibe kerül?**	meebæ kærewl
Can I pay with traveller's cheques?	**Fizethetek traveller's csekkel?**	feezæt-hætæk trovvæl-lærs chæk-kæl
Do you accept credit cards?	**Hitelkártyát elfogadnak?**	heetælkaart^{y}at æl-fawgodnok
Do you accept …?	**Elfogadnak …?**	ælfawgodnok
U.S. dollars	**amerikai dollárt**	ommæreeko-ee dawl-laart
Canadian dollars	**kanadai dollárt**	konnoddo-ee dawl-laart
pounds sterling	**angol fontot**	ongawl fawntawt
Can I please have a receipt?	**Kaphatok egy elismervényt?**	kophottawk æd^y æleesh-mærvayn^{y}t
Haven't you made a mistake in the bill?	**Nem állította tévesen össze a számlát?**	næm aal-lēētawt-to tayvæ-shæn urs-sæ o saamlaat
Will you please wrap it?	**Becsomagolva kéri?**	bæchawmoggawlvo kayree

CHANGING MONEY: see page 135

SHOPPING GUIDE

Anything else?

No thanks, that's all.	**Nem, köszönöm. Ez minden.**	næm **kursurnurm**. æz **meendæn**
Yes, please show me ...	**Igen, kérem mutassa meg nekem a ...**	eegæn kayræm **mootoshsho** mæg nækæm o
Could I have a carrier bag, please?	**Kérnék egy szatyrot.**	kayrnayk æd^y sot^{y}rawt
Thank you.	**Köszönöm.**	kursurnurm
Goodbye.	**Viszontlátásra.**	veessawntlaataashro

☞　　　　　　　　　　　　　　　　　　🖐

Segíthetek ...?	Can I help you?
Mit parancsol?	What are you looking for?
Milyen ... parancsol?	What ... would you like?
színt/fazont minőséget/mennyiséget	colour/shape quality/quantity
Sajnálom, ilyent nem tartunk.	I'm sorry, we haven't any.
Elfogyott.	We're out of stock.
Megrendeljük az Ön részére?	Shall we order it for you?
Összesen ... forintba kerül kérem.	That's ... forints, please.
A pénztár ott van.	You pay over there.
Hitelkártyát/Traveller's csekket nem fogadunk el.	We don't accept credit cards/ traveller's cheques.

Dissatisfied

Can you please exchange this?	**Kicserélné ezt?**	keechæraylnay æst
I want to return this.	**Ezt vissza akarom váltani.**	æst vees-so okkorrawm vaaltonnee
I'd like a refund.	**Kérem a vételár visszatérítését.**	kayræm o vaytælaar vees-sottayreetayshayt
Here's the receipt.	**Itt az elismervény.**	eet oz æleeshmærvayn^y

Bookshop—Stationer's—Newsstand

In Hungary, books and stationery items are usually sold in separate shops. Newspapers and magazines are sold at newsstands and at post offices. Western dailies and newsmagazines are available at major hotels and some kiosks in the capital.

Where's the nearest ...?	Hol a legközelebbi ...?	hawl o lægkurzælæb-bee
bookshop	könyvesbolt	kurn^Yvæshbawlt
newsstand	újságáruda	ōō^Yshaagaaroodo
stationer's	papír és írószer-kereskedés	poppēēr aysh ēērāwssær-kæræshkædaysh
Where can I buy an English-language newspaper?	Hol kapok angol-nyelvű újságot?	hawl koppawk ongawl-n^Yælvew ōō^Yshaagawt
I'd like a/an/some ...	Kérnék ...	kayrnayk
address book	egy címregisztert	aed^Y tsēēmrægheestært
ballpoint pen	egy golyóstollat	æd^Y gaw^Yāwshtawl-lot
book	egy könyvet	æd^Y kurn^Yvæt
box of paints	egy doboz festéket	æd^Y dawbawz fæshtaykæt
carbon paper	másolópapírt	maashawlāwpoppēērt
cellophane tape	ragasztó szalagot	roggostāw solloggawt
crayons	krétát	kraytaat
dictionary	egy szótárt	æd^Y sāwtaart
English-Hungarian	angol-magyar	ongawl-mod^Yor
pocket dictionary	zsebszótárt	zhæbsāwtaart
drawing paper	rajzpapírt	royzpoppēērt
drawing pins	rajzszeget	royzsægæt
envelopes	néhány borítékot	nayhaan^Y bawrēētaykawt
eraser	radírt	roddēērt
exercise book	egy füzetet	æd^Y fewzætæt
fountain pen	egy töltőtollat	æd^Y turltürtawl-lot
glue	ragasztót	roggostāwt
grammar book	egy tankönyvet	æd^Y tonkurn^Yvæt
guide book	egy útikalauz	æd^Y ooteekollo-oozt
ink	tintát	teentaat
black/blue/red	fekete/kék/piros	fækætæ/kayk/peerawsh
magazine	egy képes folyóiratot	æd^Y kaypæsh faw^Yāweerottawt
map	egy térképet	æd^Y tayrkaypæt
of the town	egy várostérképet	æd^Y vaarawshtayrkaypæ
road map	egy térképet	æd^Y tayrkaypæt

newspaper	egy ... újságot	æd^Y ... $\overline{oo}^Y$shaagawt
American	amerikai	ommæreeko-ee
English	angol	ongawi
notebook	egy jegyzetfüzetet	æd^Y yæd^{Y}zætfewzætæt
note paper	jegyzetpapírt	yæd^{Y}zætpoppēērt
paperback	egy zsebkönyvet	æd^Y zhæbkurn^{Y}væt
paper napkins	csomagolópapírt	chawmoggāwlawpoppēērt
paste	ragasztót	roggostāwt
pen	egy tollat	æd^Y tawl-lot
pencil	egy ceruzát	æd^Y tsæroozaat
pencil sharpener	egy ceruza-hegyezőt	æd^Y tsæroozohæd^{Y}æzūrt
picture book	egy képeskönyvet	æd^Y kaypæshkurn^{Y}væt
playing cards	kártyát	kaart^{Y}aat
postcards	levelező-lapokat	lævælæzūr-loppawkot
rubber	radírt	roddēērt
ruler	egy vonalzót	æd^Y vawnolzāwt
sketchpad	egy vázlatfüzetet	æd^Y vaazlotfewzætæt
string	zsineget	zheenægæt
thumbtacks	rajzszeget	royzsægæt
tissue paper	selyempapírt	shæ^{Y}æmpoppēērt
typewriter ribbon	írógépszalagot	ēērāwgaypsolloggawt
typing paper	gépíró-papírt	gaypēērāw-poppēērt
wrapping paper	papír szalvétákat	poppēēr solvaytaakot
writing pad	egy jegyzettömböt	æd^Y yæd^{Y}zæt-turmburt

Where's the guidebook section?	Hol találom az útikalauzrészleget?	hawl tollaalawm oz ooteekollo-oozrayslægæt
Where do you keep the English books?	Hol tartják az angolnyelvű könyveket?	hawl tort^{Y}aak oz ongawl-n^{Y}ælvēw kurn^{Y}vækæt
Have you any of ...'s books in English?	Angol nyelven megvan ... valamelyik műve?	ongawl n^{Y}ælvæn mægvon ... vollommæ^{Y}eek mēwvæ

Here are some Hungarian authors whose books are available in English translation. In accordance with Hungarian usage, we have given the writer's surname first.

Arany János
Jókai Mór
József Attila

Mikszáth Kálmán
Petőfi Sándor
Rejtő Jenő*

* In English translation, Rejto's works are published under the name P. Howard.

Camping

Here we're concerned with items of equipment you may need.

I'd like a/an/ some ...	Szeretnék ...	særætnayk
bottle opener	egy üvegnyitót	æd^y ewvaegn^yeetāwt
bucket	egy vödröt	æd^y vurdrurt
camp bed	egy tábori ágyat	æd^y taabawree aad^yot
can opener	egy konzervnyitót	æd^y kawnzærn^yeetāwt
candles	gyertyákat	d^yært^yaakot
chair	egy széket	æd^y saykæt
folding chair	egy összecsukható széket	æd^y urs-sæchook-hottāw saykæt
clothes-pegs	ruhaakasztó csipeszeket	rooho-okkostāw cheepæsækæt
corkscrew	egy dugóhúzót	æd^y doogāwhōōzāwt
crockery	edényeket	ædayn^yækæt
cutlery	evőeszközöket	ævūræskurzurkæt
deck chair	egy nyugágyat	æd^y n^yoogaad^yot
first-aid kit	egy elsősegély-dobozt	æd^y ælshūrshægay^y-dawbawzt
fishing tackle	egy horgász-felszerelést	æd^y hawrgaasfælsæræ-laysht
flashlight	egy zseblámpát	æd^y zhæblaampaat
frying pan	egy tepsit	æd^y tæpsheet
groundsheet	egy pokrócot	æd^y pawkrāwtsawt
hammer	egy kalapácsot	æd^y kolloppaachawt
hammock	egy függőágyat	æd^y fewg-gūraad^yot
ice-bag	egy hűtőtáskát	æd^y hewtūrtaashkaat
kerosene	petróleumot	pætrāwlæoomawt
kettle	egy fazekat	æd^y fozzækot
lamp	lámpát	laampaat
lantern	egy lámpást	æd^y laampaasht
matches	gyufát	d^yoofaat
mattress	egy matracot	æd^y motrotsawt
air mattress	egy gumimatracot	æd^y goomeemotrotsawt
methylated spirits	főzőspirituszt	fūrzūrshpeereetoost
nails	szeget	sægæt
pail	egy vödröt	æd^y vurdrurt
paraffin	petróleumot	pætrāwlæoomawt
penknife	egy zsebkést	æd^y zhæbkaysht
picnic case	egy kiránduló táskát	æd^y keeraandoolāw taashkaat
plastic bags	nájlonszatyrot	næ^ylawnsot^yrawt

CAMPING: see also page 90

pot	egy fazekat	æd^Y fozzækot
pressure cooker	egy kuktát	æd^Y kooktaat
rope	kötelet	kurtælæt
rucksack	egy hátizsákot	æd^Y haateezhaakawt
saucepan	egy nyeles serpenyőt	æd^Y n^Yælæsh shær-pæn^Yūrt
scissors	egy ollót	æd^Y awl-lāwt
screwdriver	egy dugóhúzót	æd^Y doogāwhōōzāwt
sheath knife	egy tőrt	æd^Y tūrrt
sleeping bag	egy hálózsákot	æd^Y haalāwzhaakawt
stewpan	egy serpenyőt	æd^Y shærpæn^Yūrt
stove	egy kályhát	æd^Y kaa^Yhaat
string	zsineget	zheenægæt
table	egy asztalt	æd^Y ostolt
folding table	egy összecsukható asztalt	æd^Y urs-sæchook-hottāw ostolt
tent	egy sátrat	æd^Y shaatrot
tent pegs	sátorcölöpöket	shaatawrtsurlurpurkæt
tent pole	egy sátorrudat	æd^Y shaatawr-roodot
tin opener	egy konzervnyitót	æd^Y kawnzærvn^Yeetāwt
tongs	egy fogót/egy csipeszt	æd^Y fawgāwt/æd^Y chee-pæst
tool kit	egy szerszámosládát	æd^Y særsaamawshlaadaat
torch	egy zseblámpát	æd^Y zhæblaampaat
vacuum flask (bottle)	egy hőpalackot	æd^Y hūrpollotskawt
water carrier	egy vizhordót	æd^Y veezhawrdāwt
wood alcohol	faszeszt	fossæst

SHOPPING GUIDE

Crockery

cups	csészék	chayssayk
mugs	bögrék	burgrayk
plates	tányérok	taan^Yayrawk
saucers	csészealjak	chayssæolyok

Cutlery

forks	villák	veel-laak
knives	kések	kayshæk
spoons	kanalak	konnollok
teaspoons	teáskanalak	tæaashkonnollok
(made of) plastic	műanyag ...	mēwon^Yog
(made of) stainless steel	rozsdamentes acél ...	rawzhdommæntæsh otsayl

Chemist's—Drugstore

In Hungarian, the name for a chemist's shop, or drugstore, is *patika* (**po**tteeko) or *gyógyszertár* (**d**ʸ**a̅w̅d**ʸsærtaar). Their range of wares is restricted to pharmaceutical and related products—they do not sell the wide range of goods found in most British or American pharmacies.

Outside normal hours, pharmacies open on a rota basis—in larger centres there will always be at least one on night and weekend duty. An illuminated sign in each pharmacy window tells you where you can get service after hours.

For cosmetics and toiletries, go to an *illatszerbolt* (**eel**lotsærbawlt), and for photo supplies, to a *fotószaküzlet* (**faw**ta̅w̅sokewzlæt).

This section is divided into two parts:

1 Medicine, first aid, etc.
2 Toilet articles, cosmetics, etc.

General

Where's the nearest (all-night) chemist's?	Hol a legközelebbi (éjjel-nappali) patika?	hawl o lægkurzælæb-bee (ayʸ-yæl-**nop**-pawlee) potteeko
What time does the chemist's open/close?	Mikor nyit/zár a patika?	meekawr nʸeet/zaar o potteeko

1 Medicines—First aid

I want something for...	Kérek valami gyógyszert ... ellen.	kayræk vollommee dʸa̅w̅dʸsært ... æl-læn
a cold	megfázás	mægfaazaash
a cough	köhögés	kurhurgaysh
a hangover	másnaposság	maashnoppawsh-shaag
hay fever	szénanátha	saynonnaat-ho
insect bites	rovarcsípés	rawvorcheepaysh
sunburn	napszúrás	nopso̅o̅raash
travel sickness	utazási rosszullét	ootozzaashee raws-sool-layt
an upset stomach	gyomorrontás	dʸawmawr-rawntaash

DOCTOR: see page 162

SHOPPING GUIDE

Can I get it without a prescription?	Ezt recept nélkül is megkaphatom?	æst rætsæpt naylkewl eesh mægkop-hottawm
Shall I wait?	Várjak?	vaaryok
I'd like a/an/some ...	Kérnék ...	kayrnayk
adhesive plaster	sebtapaszt	shæbtoppost
antiseptic ointment	fertőtlenítő kenőcsöt	fæertürtlænēetür kænürchurt
aspirins	aszpirint	ospeereent
bandage	kötszert	kurtsært
calcium tablets	mésztablettát	maystoblæt-taat
clinical thermometer	egy hőmérőt	æd^y hürmayrürt
contraceptives	fogamzásgátlót	fawgomzaashgaatlāwt
corn pads	tyúkszemírtót	t^{y}ooksæmēertāwt
cotton wool	vattát	vot-taat
cough drops	köhögés elleni cseppeket	kurhurgaysh æl-lænee chæp-pækæt
disinfectant	fertőtlenítőt	fæertürtlænēetürt
ear drops	fülcseppeket	fewlchæp-pækæt
ear plugs	füldugót	fewldoogāwt
eye drops	szemcseppeket	sæmchæp-pækæt
first-aid kit	egy elsősegély-csomagot	æd^y ælshürshægay^y-chawmoggawt
gauze	gézt	gayzt
insect repellent	rovarírtót	rawvorrēertāwt
iodine	jódot	yāwdawt
laxative	hashajtót	hoshhoytāwt
nose drops	orrcseppeket	awrchæp-pækæt
painkiller	fájdalomcsillapítót	faa^{y}dollawmcheel-loppēetāwt
sanitary towels	egészségügyi vattát	ægayss-shayghews^{y}ee vot-taat
sleeping pills	altatót	oltottawt
stomach pills	gyomorfájás elleni tablettákat	d^{y}awmawrfaa^{y}aash æl-lænee toblæt-taakot
tampons	tampont	tompawnt
throat lozenges	toroköblítő tablettát	tawrawkurblēetür toblæt-taat
tranquillizers	nyugtatót	n^{y}oogtottāwt
vitamin pills	vitamin tablettákat	veetommeen toblæt-taakot

SHOPPING GUIDE

| MÉREG! | CSAK KÜLSŐLEG! |
| POISON! | DO NOT SWALLOW! |

2 Toilet articles—Cosmetics

I'd like a/an/some ...	Kérnék ...	kayrnayk
acne cream	egy pattanás elleni krémet	æd^y pot-tonnaash ællenee kraymæt
after-shave lotion	egy borotva kölnit	æd^y bawrawtvo kurlneet
astringent	egy borotvatapasztimsót	æd^y bawrawtvotopposteemshāwt
bath essence	egy fürdősampont	æd^y fewrdūrshompawnt
bath salts	fürdősót	fewrdūrshāwt
cologne	egy kölnit	æd^y kurlneet
cream	egy krémet	æd^y kraymæt
for dry/normal/greasy skin	száraz/normál/zsíros bőrre	saaroz/nawrmaal/zhēērawsh būrr-ræ
cleansing cream	egy tisztító krémet	æd^y teestēētāw kraymæ
cuticle cream	egy bőrkrémet	æd^y būrrkraymæt
foot cream	egy lábkrémet	æd^y laabkraymæt
foundation cream	egy alapozó krémet	æd^y olloppawzāw kraymæt
hand cream	egy kézkrémet	æd^y kayzkraymæt
moisturizing cream	egy nedvesítő krémet	æd^y nædvæshēētūr kraymæt
night cream	egy éjjeli krémet	æd^y ay^y-yælee kraymæ
cuticle remover	egy bőreltávolítót	æd^y būrræltaavawlēētāwt
deodorant	egy dezodort	æd^y dæzawdawrt
emery board	egy anyósnyelvet	æd^y on^yawshn^yælvæt
eyeliner	egy szemkihúzót	æd^y sæmkeehōōzāwt
eye pencil	egy szemöldökceruzát	æd^y sæmurldurktsæroozaa
eye shadow	egy szemkifestőt	æd^y sæmkeefæshtūrt
face pack	egy arcpakolást	æd^y ortspokkawlaasht
face powder	egy arcpúdert	æd^y ortspōōdært
foot powder	egy lábpúdert	æd^y laabpōōdært
lipsalve	egy ajakkrémet	æd^y oyok-kraymæt
lipstick	egy rúzst	æd^y rōōzht
make-up kit	egy make-up dobozt	æd^y "make-up" dawbawzt
make-up	make-up eltávolítót	"make-up" æltaavawlēētāwt
make-up remover pads	make-up eltávolító tamponokat	"make-up" æltaavawlēētāwt tompawnawkot
mascara	egy maszkarát	æd^y moskorraat
nail brush	egy körömkefét	æd^y kurrurmkæfayt
nail clippers	egy körömvágót	æd^y kurrurmvaagāwt
nail file	egy körömreszelőt	æd^y kurrurmræsælūrt

ail polish	körömlakkot	kurrurmlok-kawt
ail-polish remover	körömlakk lemosót	kurrurmlok læmawshāwt
ail scissors	egy körömollót	æd^y kurrurmawl-lāwt
aper handkerchiefs	papírzsebkendőt	poppēērzhæbkændūrt
erfume	kölnit	kurlneet
owder	púdert	pōōdært
zor	egy borotvát	æd^y bawrawtvaat
zorblades	borotvapengéket	bawrawtvoppængaykæt
ouge	egy rúzst	æd^y rōōzht
having brush	egy borotvaecsetet	æd^y bawrawtvoæchætæt
having cream	egy borotvakrémet	æd^y bawrawtvokraymæt
having soap	egy borotvaszap-pant	æd^y bawrawtvossop-pont
oap	egy szappant	æd^y sop-pont
un-tan cream	egy napozókrémet	æd^y noppāwzāwkraymæt
un-tan oil	egy napolajat	æd^y noppawloyot
alcum powder	egy hintőport	ædy heentūrpawrt
oilet paper	w.c. papírt	waytsay poppēērt
oothbrush	egy fogkefét	æd^y fawgkæfayt
oothpaste	egy fogkrémet	æd^y fawgkraymæt
weezers	egy csipeszt	æd^y cheepæst

or your hair

obby pins	hullámcsattokat	hool-laamchot-tawkot
omb	egy fésűt	æd^y fayshēwt
urlers	hajcsavarokat	hoychovvorrawkot
ye	hajfestéket	hoyfæshtaykæt
air brush	egy hajkefét	æd^y hoykæfayt
air pins	hajtűket	hoytēwkæt
acquer	egy hajlakkot	æd^y hoylok-kawt
il	egy brilantint	æd^y breelonteent
etting lotion	hajlakkot	hoylok-kawt
hampoo	egy sampont	æd^y shompawnt
for dry/greasy hair	száraz/zsíros hajra	saaroz/zhēērawsh hoyro
for dandruff	korpásodás ellen	kawrpaashāwdaash æl-læn

or the baby

aby food	bébi eledelt	baybee ælædælt
ib	egy előkét	æd^y ælūrkayt
ummy (comforter)	egy cumit	æd^y tsoomeet
eeding bottle	egy cumis üveget	æd^y tsoomeesh ewvægæt
appies (diapers)	pelenkákat	pælænkaakot
ubber teat	egy cumit üvegre	æd^y tsoomeet ewvægræ

Clothing

If you want to buy something specific, prepare yourself in advance. Look at the list of clothing on page 116. Get some idea of the colour, material and size you want. They're listed on the next few pages.

General

I'd like ... for a 10-year-old boy.	Egy ...-t kérek 10 éves fiú részére.	æd^y ...-t kayræk 10 ayvæsh feeōō rayssayræ
It's for a 6-year-old girl.	Egy 6 éves leány részére lesz.	æd^y 6 ayvæsh læaan^y rayssayræ læs
I want something like this.	Valami ilyet kérek.	vollommee ee^{y}æt kayræk
I like the one in the window.	Az tetszik, ami a kirakatban van.	oz tætseek ommee o kee-rokkotbon von
How much is that per metre?	Mibe kerül métere?	meebæ kærewl maytæræ

1 centimetre = 0.39 in.	1 in. = 2.54 cm
1 metre = 39.37 in.	1 ft. = 30.5 cm
10 metres = 32.81 ft.	1 yd. = 0.91 m

Colour

Do you have something in ...?	Van ... színűben?	von ... sēēnéwbæn
I'd like something lighter/darker.	Valami sötétebbet/ világosabbat szeretnék.	vollommee shurtaytæb-bat veelaagawshob-bot sæ-rætnayk
I want something to match this.	Valami ehhez illőt keresek.	vollommee æh-hæz eel-lūī kæræshæk
I don't like the colour.	A színe nem tetszik.	o sēēnæ næm tætseek

beige	**drapp**	drop
black	**fekete**	fækætæ
blue	**kék**	kayk
navy blue	**tengerkék**	tængærkayk
sky blue	**égszínkék**	aygseenkayk
brown	**barna**	borno
dark brown	**sötétbarna**	shurtaytborno
light brown	**világosbarna**	veelaagawshborno
golden	**arany**	oron^y
green	**zöld**	zurld
bottle green	**palackzöld**	pollotskzurld
lime green	**citromzöld**	tseetrawmzurld
olive green	**olivazöld**	awleevozzurld
grey	**szürke**	sewrkæ
lilac	**lila**	leelo
orange	**narancssárga**	norronchshaargo
pink	**rózsaszín**	rawzhosseen
red	**vörös**	vurrursh
crimson	**karmazsinvörös**	kormozheenvurrursh
purple	**bíbor**	beebawr
scarlet	**skarlátvörös**	shkorlaatvurrursh
silver	**ezüst**	æzewsht
turquoise	**türkiz**	tewrkeez
violet	**ibolyakék**	eebaw^{y}okkayk
white	**fehér**	fæhayr
yellow	**sárga**	shaargo
golden yellow	**aranysárga**	orron^{y}shaargo
lemon	**citromsárga**	tseetrawmshaargo
light ...	**világos ...**	veelaagawsh
dark ...	**sötét ...**	shurtayt

sima	**csíkos**	**pöttyös**	**kockás**	**mintás**
(sheemo)	(cheekawsh)	(purt^{y}ursh)	(kawtskaash)	(meentaash)

Material

Have you anything in ...?	**... anyaguk van?**	... on^{y}oggook von
Do you have any better quality?	**Valami jobb minőségü árújuk nincs?**	vollommee yawb meenur-shaygew aarooyook neench

I'd like a cotton blouse.	Egy pamutblúzt keresek.	æd[y] pommootblōōzt kæræshæk
Is that ...?	Az ...?	oz
handmade	kéziszöyésű	kayzeessurvayshēw
imported	importált	eempawrtaalt
made here	belföldi gyártású	bælfurldee d[y]aartaashōō
What's it made of?	Miből van?	meebūrl von

cambric	batiszt	botteest
camelhair	teveszőr	tævæssūrr
chiffon	sifon	sheefawn
corduroy	kordbársony	kawrdbaarshawn[y]
cotton	pamut	pommoot
felt	filc	feelts
flannel	flanel	flonnæl
gabardine	gabardin	gobbordeen
lace	csipke	cheepkæ
leather	bőr	būrr
linen	vászon	vaassawn
rayon	műselyem	mēwshæ[y]æm
rubber	gumi	goomee
quilting	tűzdelt	tēwzdælt
satin	szatén	sottayn
silk	selyem	shæ[y]æm
suede	antilop	onteelawp
taffeta	taft	toft
terrycloth	frotír	frawtēēr
tulle	tüll	tewl
velvet	bársony	baarshawn[y]
velveteen	gyapjúbársony	d[y]opyōōbaarshawn[y]
wool	gyapjú	d[y]opyōō
worsted	kamgarn-szövet	komgorn-survæt

Is it ...?	Ez ...?	æz
colourfast	színtartó	sēēntortāw
crease-proof	gyűrődésmentes	d[y]ēwrūrdayshmæntæsh
easy-care	tiszta könnyen kezelhető	teesto kurn[y]æn kæzælhætūr
pure cotton	tiszta pamut	teesto pommoot
shrink-resistant	méret tartó	mayræt tortāw
synthetic	műanyag	mēwon[y]og
wash-and-wear	nem kell vasalni	næm kæl vosholnee

Sizes

In Europe, sizes vary somewhat from country to country, and even within one country, so these charts must be taken as an approximate guide only.

Ladies

	Dresses/Suits						
American	8	10	12	14	16	18	20
British	30	32	34	36	38	40	42
Continental	36	38	40	42	44	46	48

	Stockings						Shoes			
American ⎫ British ⎭	8	8½	9	9½	10	10½	6 4½	7 5½	8 6½	9 7½
Continental	0	1	2	3	4	5	37	38	40	41

Gentlemen

	Suits/Overcoats						Shirts			
American ⎫ British ⎭	36	38	40	42	44	46	15	16	17	18
Continental	46	48	50	52	54	56	38	41	43	45

	Shoes								
American ⎫ British ⎭	5	6	7	8	8½	9	9½	10	11
Continental	38	39	41	42	43	43	44	44	45

A good fit?

I take size 38.	**38-ast kérek.**	38-osht **kayræk**
May I try it on?	**Felpróbálhatom?**	**fæl**prāwbaalhottawm
It fits very well.	**Nagyon jól áll.**	nod^{y}awn yāwl aal
It's too ...	**Túl ...**	tōōl
short/long	**rövid/hosszú**	**rur**veed/**haws**-sōō
tight/loose	**feszes/bő**	**fæ**sæsh/būr
How long will it take to alter?	**Meddig tart az átalakítása?**	**mæd**-deeg tort oz **aat**-ollokkēētaasho

Clothes and accessories

I'd like a/an/some …	Szeretnék …	særætnayk
anorak	egy anorákot	æd^y onnawraakawt
bath robe	egy fürdőköpenyt	æd^y fewrdürkurpæn^yt
blazer	egy blézert	æd^y blayzært
blouse	egy blúzt	æd^y blōozt
bra	egy melltartót	æd^y mæltortāwt
braces	egy nadrágtartót	æd^y nodraagtortāwt
briefs	egy rövid alsónadrágot	æd^y rurveed olshaw-nodraagawt
cap	egy sapkát	æd^y shopkaat
cardigan	egy kardigánt	æd^y kordeegaant
coat	egy kabátot	æd^y kobbaatawt
dress	egy ruhát	æd^y roohaat
dressing gown	egy pongyolát	æd^y pawnd^yawlaat
evening gown	egy estélyi ruhát	æd^y æshtay^yee roohaat
frock	egy öltönyt	æd^y urlturn^yt
fur coat	egy szőrmekabátot	æd^y sūrrmækobbaatawt
gloves	egy pár kesztyűt	æd^y paar kæst^yēwt
handkerchief	egy zsebkendőt	æd^y zhæbkændūrt
hat	egy kalapot	æd^y kolloppawt
house coat	egy házikabátot	æd^y haazeekobbaatawt
jacket	egy zakót	æd^y zokkāwt
jeans	egy farmernadrágot	æd^y formærnodraagawt
jersey	egy kötöttkabátot	æd^y kurturtkobbaatawt
jumper	egy pulóvert	æd^y poolāwvært
leather trousers	egy bőrnadrágot	æd^y būrrnodraagawt
lingerie	valami alsóneműt	vollommee olshawnæmewt
mackintosh	egy esőkabátot	æd^y æshūrkobbaatawt
nightdress	egy hálóinget	æd^y haalāweengæt
overcoat	egy felöltőt	æd^y fælurltūrt
panties	egy harisnyana-drágot	æd^y horreeshn^yo-nodraagawt
pants	egy nadrágot	æd^y nodraagawt
pants suit	egy nadrágkosz-tümöt	æd^y nodraagkawstewmurt
pantyhose	egy harisnya-nadrágot	æd^y horreeshn^yo-nodraagawt
pullover	egy pulóvert	æd^y poolāwvært
pyjamas	egy pizsamát	æd^y peezhommaat
raincoat	egy esőkabátot	æd^y æshūrkobbaatawt
scarf	egy sálat	æd^y shaalot
shirt	egy inget	æd^y eengæt
shorts	egy sortot	æd^y shawrtawt
skirt	egy szoknyát	æd^y sawkn^yaat

slip	egy alsószoknyát	æd^Y olshāwsawkn^Yaat
socks	egy pár zoknit	æd^Y paar zawkneet
sports jacket	egy sportkabátot	æd^Y shpawrtkobbaatawt
stockings	egy pár harisnyát	æd^Y paar horreeshn^Yaat
suit (man's)	egy férfiöltönyt	æd^Y fayrfeeurlturn^Yt
suit (woman's)	egy női ruhát	æd^Y nūr-ee roohaat
suspenders (Am.)	egy nadrágtartót	æd^Y nodraagtortāwt
sweater	egy pulóvert	æd^Y poolāwvært
swimsuit	egy fürdőruhát	æd^Y fewrdūrroohaat
tie	egy nyakkendőt	æd^Y n^Yok-kændūrt
tights	egy harisnya-nadrágot	æd^Y horreeshn^Yo-nodraagawt
topcoat	egy nagykabátot	æd^Y nod^Ykobbaatawt
track suit	egy tréningruhát	æd^Y trayneengroohaat
trousers	egy nadrágot	æd^Y nodraagawt
T-shirt	egy atléta trikót	æd^Y otlayto treekāwt
undershirt	egy trikót	æd^Y treekāwt
vest (Am.)	egy mellényt	æd^Y mæl-layn^Yt
vest (Br.)	egy trikót	æd^Y treekāwt
waistcoat	egy mellényt	æd^Y mæl-layn^Yt

belt	öv	ūrv
buckle	csatt	chot
button	gomb	gawmb
collar	gallér	gol-layr
elastic	gumi	goomee
pocket	zseb	zhæb
press-stud	patentgomb	pottæntgawmb
safety pin	biztosítótű	beeztawsheetāwtew
zip (zipper)	cipzár	tseepzaar

And for those handy with the needle:

crochet hook	horgolótű	hawrgawlāwtew
crochet thread	horgoló cérna	hawrgawlāw tsayrno
knitting needles	kötőtűk	kurtūrtewk
sewing cotton	varrófonál	vor-rāwfawnaal
sewing needles	varrótűk	vor-rawtewk
sewing thread	varrócérna	vor-rāwtsayrno
thimble	gyűszű	d^Yewssew
wool	gyapjú	d^Yopyōō

Shoes

I'd like a pair of ...	Szeretnék egy pár ...	særætnayk æd^y paar
boots	csizmát	cheezmaat
galoshes	sárcipőt	shaartseepürt
hiking boots	turista bakkancsot	tooreeshto bok-konchawt
sandals	szandált	sondaalt
shoes	cipőt	tseepürt
slippers	papucsot	poppoochawt
sneakers	tornacipőt	tawrnotseepürt
tennis shoes	teniszcipőt	tæneestseepürt
These are too ...	Ez túl ...	æz tōōl
large/small	nagy/kicsi	nod^y/keechee
narrow/wide	keskeny/széles	kæshkæn^y/saylæsh
Do you have the same in ...?	Volna ugyanez ...?	vawlno ood^yonnæz
beige/brown	drappban/barnában	drop-bon/bornaabon
black/white	feketében/fehérben	fækætaybæn/fæhayrbæn
rubber/leather	gumiból/bőrből	goomeebāwl/bürrbürl
cloth/suede	szövetből/antilopból	survætbürl/onteelawpbāwl
Is it genuine leather?	Ez tiszta bőrből van?	æz teesto bürrbürl von
I'd like ...	Szeretnék ...	særætnayk
pair of insoles	egy pár talpbetétet	æd^y paar tolpbætaytæt
shoe horn	egy cipőkanalat	æd^y tseepürkonnollot
shoe laces	egy cipőfűzőt	æd^y paar tseepürfēwzürt
shoe polish	egy doboz cipőkrémet	æd^y dawbawz tseepür-kraymæt
shoe trees	néhány kaptafát	nayhaan^y koptoffaat

Shoe repairs

Can you repair these shoes?	Meg tudná javítani ezt a cipőt?	mæg toodnaa yovvēētonnee æst o tseepürt
I want them soled and heeled.	Talpaltatni és sarkaltatni szeretném.	tolpoltotnee aysh shorkoltotnee særætnaym
When will they be ready?	Mikorra lesz kész?	meekawr-ro læss kayss

Electrical appliances and accessories

In Hungary, 220 volts, 50 cps, AC current is universal. Plugs are different from American and British ones, so you'll need to have the plugs changed on any appliances you bring from home.

I'd like a plug for this.	Ehhez kérek egy dugaszt.	æh-hæz **kay**ræk æd^y **doo**gost
Do you have a battery for this?	Van ehhez elemjük?	von æh-hæz **æl**æmyewk
This is broken. Can you repair it?	Eltört. Megtudják javítani?	**æl**turt. **mæg**tood^yaak **yov**vēētonnee
When will it be ready?	Mikor lesz kész?	**mee**kawr læss kayss
I'd like a/an/some ...	Szeretnék ...	**sæ**rætnayk
adaptor	egy adaptert	æd^y **od**doptært
amplifier	egy erősítőt	æd^y **æ**rūrshēētūrt
blender	egy keverőt	æd^y **kæ**værūrt
bulb	egy villanykörtét	æd^y **veel**-lon^ykurrtayt
calculator	egy kalkulátort	æd^y **kol**koolaatawrt
clock	egy órát	æd^y **aw**raat
alarm clock	egy ébresztőórát	æd^y **ay**bræstūraawraat
wall clock	egy faliórát	æd^y **fol**leeawraat
extension cord	egy hosszabbítót	æd^y **haws**-sob-bēētawt
hair dryer	egy hajszárítót	æd^y **hoy**saarēētawt
iron	egy vasalót	æd^y **vosh**ollawt
kettle	egy fazekat	æd^y **fozz**ækot
plug	egy dugaszt	æd^y **doo**gost
radio	egy rádiót	æd^y **raa**deeawt
car radio	egy autórádiót	æd^y **ooo**tawraadeeawt
portable radio	egy hordozható rádiót	æd^y **haw**rdawz-hottaw **raa**deeawt
record player	egy lemezjátszót	æd^y **læ**mæzyaatsawt
shaver	egy borotvát	æd^y **baw**rawtvaat
speakers	hangfalakat	**hong**follokkot
tape recorder	egy magnetofont	æd^y **mog**nætawfawnt
cassette tape recorder	egy kazettás magnót	æd^y **kozz**æt-taash **mog**nawt
television set	egy tévékészüléket	æd^y **tay**vaykayssewlaykæt
portable TV set	egy hordozható tévét	æd^y **haw**rdawz-hottaw **tay**vayt
toaster	egy kenyérpirítót	æd^y **kæn**^yayrpeerēētawt
transformer	egy transzformátort	æd^y **tron**sfawrmaatawrt

SHOPPING GUIDE

Record shop

Do you have any records by ...?	**Van ...-tól/-től valamilyen lemezük?***	von ...-tāwl/-tūrl vollo-mee^yæn læmæzewk
May I listen to this record/cassette?	**Meghallgathatnám ezt a lemezt/kazettát?**	mæghollgot-hotnaam æst o læmæzt/kozzæt-taat
I want a cassette.	**Egy kazettát kérek.**	æd^y kozzæt-taat kayræk
I'd like a new stylus.	**Egy új gramofontűt kérek.**	æd^y ōō^y grommawfawntēwt kayræk

LP (33 rpm)	**nagylemez**	nod^ylæmæz
EP (45 rpm)	**kislemez**	keeshlæmæz
mono	**mono**	mawnaw
stereo	**sztereo**	stæræaw

chamber music	**kamara zene**	kommorro zænæ
classical music	**klasszikus zene**	klos-seekoosh zænæ
folk music	**népzene**	naypzænæ
instrumental music	**zenekari muzsika**	zænækorree moozheeko
jazz	**dzsessz**	dzhæs
light music	**könnyűzene**	kurn^yēwzænæ
orchestral music	**zenekari darab**	zænækorree dorrob
pop music	**popzene**	pawpzænæ
rock music	**rockzene**	rawkzænæ
sacred music	**egyházi zene**	æd^yhaazee zænæ

Here are the names of a few popular recording artists (surnames first, Hungarian style):

Bende Zsolt	**Kovács Kati**
Házy Erzsébet	**Sass Sylvia**
Koncz Zsuzsa	**Zalatnai Sarolta**

* See Grammar section for word endings.

Hairdresser's—Beauty salon

Hairdressers' work usually from 7 a.m. to 9 p.m., Monday–Friday, and from 7 a.m. to 7 p.m., Saturday.

Is there a ladies' hairdresser/beauty salon in the hotel?	Van a szállodában fodrászat/kozmetikai szalon?	von o saal-lāwdaabon fawdraassot/kawzmæteeko-ee sollawn
Can I make an appointment for (Friday)?	Mikor jöhetek (pénteken)?	meekawr yurhætæk (payntækæn)
I'd like a shampoo and set.	Hajmosást kérek berakással.	hoymawshaasht kayræk bærokkaash-shol

in a bun	befonva	bæfawnvo
with curls	fürtösítve	fewrtursheetvæ
a cut	hajvágás	hoyvaagash
with a fringe	lófarokkal	lāwforrawk-kol
page-boy style	fiúsra vágva	feeōōshro vaagvo
a permanent wave	tartós hullám	tortāwsh hool-laam

I want a ...	Kérek egy ...	kayræk æd^y
bleach	szőkítést	sūrkeetaysht
blow-dry	hajszárítást	hoyssaareetasht
colour rinse	bemosást	bæmawshaasht
cut and set	hajvágást és berakást	hoyvaagaasht aysh bærokkaasht
dye	festést	fæshtaysht
shampoo	hajmosást	hoymawshaasht
for dry hair	száraz hajra	saaroz hoyro
for greasy hair	zsíros hajra	zhēērawsh hoyro
tint	színezést	seenæzaysht
the same colour	ugyanilyen színűre	ood^{y}onnee^{y}æn seenéwræ
a darker colour	sötétebb színre	shurtaytæb seenræ
a lighter colour	világosabb színre	veelaagawshob seenræ
Do you have a colour chart?	Van színtáblájuk?	von seentaablaa^{y}ook

I don't want any hair-spray.	Hajlakkot nem kérek.	hoylok-kawt næm kayræk
I want a ...	Kérek egy ...	kayræk æd^y
face pack	arcpakolást	ortspokkawlaasht
manicure	manikűrt	monneekēwrt
pedicure	pedikűrt	pædeekēwrt

DAYS OF THE WEEK: see page 181

SHOPPING GUIDE

122

Under the hair dryer, you might want to say:

It's too hot.	Ez túl forró.	æz tōōl fawr-rāw
A bit warmer, please.	Egy kissé forróbbra kérem.	ædᵞ keesh-shay fawr-rāwbro kayræm
Do you have any magazines?	Van valami olvasnivalójuk?	von vollommee awlvoshneevollāwᵞook

At the barber's

I'm in a hurry.	Sietek.	sheeætæk
I'd like a shave.	Egy borotválást kérek.	ædᵞ bawrawtvaalaasht kayræk
I want a haircut, please.	Egy hajvágást kérek.	ædᵞ hoyvaagaasht kayræk
Cut it short, please.	Rövidre kérem.	rurveedræ kayræm
Don't cut it too short.	Ne vágja túl rövidre.	næ vaagyo tōōl rurveedræ
A razor cut, please.	Egy borotva-hajvágást kérek.	ædᵞ bawrawto-hoyvaagaasht kayræk
Don't use the electric clippers.	Ne használja a villanyborotvát.	næ hosnaalyo o veellonᵞbawrawtvaat
That's enough off.	Már eleget levett.	maar ælægæt lævæt
A little more off the ...	Még egy kicsit le lehet venni ...	mayg ædᵞ keecheet læ læhæt væn-nee
back	hátul	haatool
neck	a nyaknál	o nᵞoknaal
sides	kétoldalt	kaytawldolt
top	felül	fælewl
I'd like some hair lotion.	Hajszeszt kérek.	hoysæst kayræk
Please don't use any oil.	Kérem, ne használjon olajat.	kayræm næ hosnaalyawn awloyot
Would you please trim my ...?	Kérem, vágja le a ...	kayræm vaagyo læ o
beard	szakállamat	sokkaal-lommot
moustache	bajuszomat	boyoossawmot
sideboards (sideburns)	pajeszomat	poyæssawmot

TIPPING: see page 1

Jeweller's—Watchmaker's

Major department stores, some small shops and private craftsmen sell costume jewellery, watches and items of folk art. The sale of gold and silver objects as well as precious stones is limited to branches of the *Óra és Ékszerbolt* chain and Intertourist shops. You may have to pay in hard currency.

Can you repair this watch?	Meg tudják ezt az órát javítani?	mæg **tood**Yaak æst oz a̅w̅raat yovvēētonnee
It's too slow.	Sokat késik.	shawkot kaysheek
It's too fast.	Nagyon siet.	nodYawn sheeæt
The ... is broken.	Eltört ...	ælturrt
glass	az üvegje	oz ewvægyæ
spring	a rugója	o roogaw Yo
strap	a szíja	o sēē Yo
winder	a felhúzója	o fælhōōzaw Yo
The battery is flat.	Kimerült az elem.	keemærewlt oz ælæm
I want this watch cleaned.	Szeretném az órát kitisztíttatni.	særætnaym oz a̅w̅raat keeteestēēt-totnee
When will it be ready?	Mikorra lesz kész?	meekawr-ro læss kayss
Could I see that?	Megnézhetném?	mægnayz-hætnaym
I'm just looking round.	Csak nézelödök.	chok nayzælurdurk
I'd like a small present for ...	Valami szerény ajándékot szeretnék ... részére.	vollommee særaynY oyaan-daykawt særætnayk ... rayssayræ
I don't want anything too expensive.	Nem túl drágára gondolok.	næm tōōl draagaaro gawndawlawk
I'd like something ...	Valami ... szeretnék.	vollommee ... særætnayk
better	jobbat	yawb-bot
cheaper	olcsóbbat	awlcha̅w̅b-bot
simpler	egyszerűbbet	æd Ysæræwb-bæt
Is this sterling silver?	Ez valódi ezüst?	æz volla̅w̅dee æzewsht
How many carats is this?	Ez hány karátos?	æz haanY korraatawsh

Look up the name of the article you wish to buy in the following list. The lists on the next page will tell you what it's made of.

I'd like a/an/some …	Szeretnék …	særætnayk
bangle	egy karperecet	æd^y korpærætsæt
bead necklace	egy gyöngynyakéket	æd^y d^Vurnd^Yn^Nokkaykæt
bracelet	egy karkötőt	æd^y korkurturt
brooch	egy brost	æd^y brawsht
buckle	egy csattot	æd^y chot-tawt
chain	egy nyakláncot	æd^y n^Yoklaantsawt
cigarette case	egy cigaretta-tárcát	æd^y tseegorræt-tottaartsaat
cigarette lighter	egy öngyújtót	æd^y urnd^Yoo^Ytawt
clock	egy órát	æd^y awraat
alarm clock	egy ébresztőórát	æd^y aybræstur-awraat
electric alarm clock	egy villany ébresztőórát	æd^y veel-lon^Y aybræstur-awraat
kitchen clock	egy konyhai órát	æd^y kawn^Yho-ee awraat
wall clock	egy faliórát	æd^y folleeawraat
costume jewellery	divatékszert	deevottayksært
cross	egy keresztet	æd^y kæræstæt
cuff links	inggombot	eeng-gawmbawt
cutlery	evőeszközt	ævur-æskurzt
ear clips	fülcsiptetőt	fewlcheeptæturt
earrings	fülbevalót	fewlbævollawt
jewel box	egy ékszeres dobozt	æd^y ayksæræsh dawbawzt
music box	egy zenedobozt	æd^y zænædawbawzt
napkin ring	egy szalvéta gyűrűt	æd^y solvayto d^Yewrewt
necklace	egy nyakláncot	æd^y n^Yoklaantsawt
pendant	egy függőt	æd^y fewg-gurt
pin	egy tűt	æd^y tewt
powder compact	egy púdertartót	æd^y poodærtortawt
ring	egy gyűrűt	æd^y d^Yewrewt
engagement ring	egy eljegyzési-gyűrűt	æd^y ælyæd^Yzayshee-d^Yewrewt
signet ring	egy pecsétgyűrűt	æd^y pæchaytd^Yewrewt
wedding ring	egy házassági gyűrűt	æd^y haazosh-shaaghee d^Yewrewt
rosary	egy olvasót	æd^y awlvoshawt
serviette ring	egy szalvéta gyűrűt	æd^y solvayto d^Yewrewt
silverware	valami ezüst tárgyat	vollommee æzewsht taard^Yot
snuff box	egy dohány szelencét	æd^y dawhaan^Y sælæntsayt
tie pin	egy nyakkendő tűt	æd^y n^Yok-kændur tewt

watch	egy órát	æd^y $\overline{aw}$raat
pocket watch	egy zsebórát	æd^y zhæbæ$\overline{aw}$raat
quartz watch	egy kvartz órát	æd^y kvorts $\overline{aw}$raat
stopwatch	egy stopperórát	æd^y shtawp-pæræ$\overline{aw}$raat
wristwatch	egy karórát	æd^y korræ$\overline{aw}$raat
watch strap	egy óraszíjat	æd^y $\overline{aw}$rossēē^{y}ot
What kind of stone is this?	Ez milyen kő?	æz mee^{y}æn kū̄r

amethyst	ametiszt	ommæteest
diamond	gyémánt	d^{y}aymaant
emerald	smaragd	shmorrogd
pearl	igazgyöngy	eegozd^{y}urnd^y
ruby	rubin	roobeen
sapphire	zafir	zoffeer
tiger's-eye	macskaszem (kvarc)	mochkossæm (kvorts)
topaz	topáz	tawpaaz
turquoise	türkiz	tewrkeez

| What's it made of? | Miből van? | meebūrl von |

alabaster	alabástrom	ollobaashtrawm
amber	borostyánkő	bawrawsht^{y}aankū̄r
brass	sárgaréz	shaargorrayz
copper	réz	rayz
coral	korál	kawraal
crystal	kristály	kreeshtaa^y
ebony	ébenfa	aybænfo
enamel	zománc	zawmaants
glass	üveg	ewvæg
cut glass	csiszolt üveg	cheessawlt ewvæg
gold	arany	orron^y
gold plate	aranyfüst	orron^{y}fewsht
ivory	elefántcsont	ælæfaantchawnt
jade	ékszer	ayksær
mother-of-pearl	gyöngyház	d^{y}urnd^{y}haaz
nickel silver	alpakka	olpok-ko
pewter	ón	$\overline{aw}$n
platinum	platina	plotteeno
silver	ezüst	æzewsht
silver plate	ezüstlemez	æzewshtlæmæz
stainless steel	rozsdamentes acél	rawzhdomæntæsh otsayl

Laundry—Dry cleaning

If your hotel doesn't have its own laundry or dry-cleaning service, you'll have to go to a *Patyolat* (**pot**ʸawlot), an establishment which handles both laundry and dry cleaning. It may take some time, but it will certainly be quite inexpensive. Some of these shops offer express service for removing spots and stains while you wait.

Where's the nearest ...?	**Hol találom a legközelebbi ...?**	hawl **t**ollaalawm o **læg**-kurzælæb-bee
dry cleaner	**száraz vegytisztítót**	saaroz væd ʸteestēētāwt
laundry	**mosodát**	mawshawdaat
I want these clothes ...	**Ezeket a ruhákat akarom ...**	æzækæt o roohaakot okkorrawm
cleaned	**kitisztíttatni**	keeteestēēt-totnee
washed and ironed	**kimosatni és kivasaltatni**	keemawshotnee aysh keevosholtotnee
When will it be ready?	**Mikor lesz kész?**	meekawr læss kayss
I need it ...	**... szükségem van rájuk.**	... sewkshaygæm von raaʸook
today	**Mára**	maaro
tomorrow	**Holnapra**	hawlnopro
before Friday	**Péntekre**	payntækræ
as soon as possible	**Minél hamarabb**	meenayl hommorrob
Can you mend this?	**Kijavítanák?**	keeyovvēētonnaak
Can you sew on this button?	**Felvarrná ezt a gombot?**	fælvornaa æst o gawmbawt
Can you get this stain out?	**Kivennék ezt a foltot?**	keevæn-nayk æst o fawltawt
Can this be invisibly mended?	**Meg lehet ezt láthatatlanul javítani?**	mæg læhæt æst laathototlonnool yovvēētonnee
Is my laundry ready?	**Kész van a mosnivalóm?**	kayss von o mawshneevollāwm
My name is ...	**... vagyok.**	... vodʸawk
This isn't mine.	**Ez nem az enyém.**	æz næm oz ænʸaym
There's one piece missing.	**Egy darab hiányzik.**	ædʸ dorrob heeaanʸzeek

DAYS OF THE WEEK: see page 181

Photography

want an inexpensive camera.	Egy olcsó fényké-pezőgépet keresek.	æd^y awlchāw fayn^ykaypæ-zūrgaypæt kæræshæk
Do you sell home-movie cameras?	Filmfelvevőjük van?	feelmfælvævūr-yewrk
Show me the one in the window.	Mutassa meg a kirakatban lévőt.	mootosh-sho mæg o kee-rokkotbon layvūrt
I'd like to have some passport photos taken.	Néhány útlevél-fényképet szeretnék készíttetni.	nayhaan^y ōōtlævaylfayn^y-kaypæt særætnayk kay-ssēētætnee

Film

It would be advisable to take some film with you to Hungary since some sizes are not available (Polaroid and 127).

I'd like a film for his camera.	Ebbe a gépbe való filmet kérek.	æb-bæ o gaypbæ vollāw feelmæt kayræk
black-and-white film	fekete-fehér film	fækætæ fæhayr feelm
colour film	színes film	sēēnæsh feelm
slide film	dia-film	deeo-feelm
cartridge	filmpatron	feelmpotrawn
cassette	kazetta	kozzæt-to
roll film	tekercsfilm	tækærchfeelm
120	százhúsz	saazhōōss
135	százharmincöt	saazhormeentsurt
single 8	normál nyolc milliméteres	nawrmaal n^yawlts meelee-maytæræsh
super 8	szuper nyolc milliméteres	soopær n^yawlts meelee-maytæræsh
20/36 exposures	húsz/harmincöt képes	hōōss/hormeentsurt kay-pæsh
this size	ez a méret	æz o mayræt
this ASA/DIN number	ez az ASA/DIN cikkszám	æz oz osho/deen tseeksaam
artificial light type	mesterséges fényérzékeny	mæshtærshaygæsh fayn^yayrzaykæn^y
daylight type	nappali fényre érzékeny	nop-pollee fayn^yræ ayrzaykæn^y
fine grain	finomszemcsés	feenawmsæmchaysh
high speed	nagy érzékenységű	nod^y ayrzaykæn^yshaygēw

NUMBERS: page 175

SHOPPING GUIDE

Processing

How long will it take you to process this film?	**Mennyi ideig tart az előhívás?**	mæn^yee eedæeeg tort oz ælūrhēēvaash
How much will it cost?	**Mennyibe kerül?**	mæn^yeebæ kærewl
with a glossy/matt finish	**fényes/matt kikészítéssel**	fayn^yæsh/mot keekay-ssēētaysh-shæl
with/without border	**széllel/szél nélkül**	sayl-læl/sayl naylkewl
Will you please enlarge this?	**Kérem ezt kinagyítani.**	kayræm æst keenod^yēē-tonnee

Accessories

I want a/some ...	**Kérek ...**	kayræk
cable release	**egy kábeles kioldót**	æd^y kaabælæsh kee-awldāwt
filter red/yellow ultraviolet	**egy szűrőt vöröset/sárgát ultraviolát**	æd^y sēw̄rūrt vurrurshæt/shaargaat ooltrovveeawlaat
flash bulbs	**néhány vaku-izzót**	nayhaan^y vokkoo-eez-zāwt
flash cubes	**néhány vaku-kockát**	nayhaan^y vokkoo-kawtskaat
lens	**egy lencsét**	æd^y lænchayt
lens cap	**egy lencsevédőt**	æd^y lænchævaydūrt
light meter	**egy fénymérőt**	æd^y fayn^ymayrūrt
telephoto lens	**egy teleobjektívet**	æd^y tælæawbyæktēēvæt

Repairs

This camera doesn't work. Can you repair it?	**Ez a gép elromlott. Meg tudják javítani?**	æz o gayp ælrawmlawt. mæg tood^yaak yovvēē-tonnee
The film is jammed.	**Beszorult a film.**	bæsawroolt o feelm
There's something wrong with the ...	**... nem működik.**	... næm mēw̄kurdeek
exposure counter	**A kioldás számláló**	o keeawldaash saamlaalāw
film winder	**A filmtekerő**	o feelmtækærūr
light meter	**A fénymérő**	o fayn^ymayrūr
rangefinder	**A távolság beállító**	o taavawlshaag bæaal-lēētāw
shutter	**A zár**	o zaar

Provisions

Here's a basic list of food and drink that you might want on
a picnic or for the occasional meal in your hotel room.

I'd like some ...	Kérnék ...	kayrnayk
apple juice	almalét	olmollayt
apples	almát	olmaat
bananas	banánt	bonnaant
beer	sört	shurrt
biscuits (Br.)	kekszet	kæksæt
bread	kenyeret	kæn^yærræt
butter	vajat	voyot
cake	süteményt	shewtæmayn^yt
candy	édességet	aydæsh-shaygæt
cheese	sajtot	shoytawt
chocolate	csokoládét	chawkawlaadayt
coffee	kávét	kaavayt
cola drink	kólát	kaw̄laat
cold meat (a selection)	felvágottat	fælvaagawt-tot
cookies	kekszet	kæksæt
cooking fat	főzőzsírt	fūrzūrzhēērt
crackers	ropogós pálcát	rawpawgaw̄sh paaltsaat
cream	krémet	kraymæt
cucumbers	uborkát	oobawrkaat
eggs	tojást	taw^yaasht
flour	lisztet	leestæt
frankfurters	virslit	veershleet
grapefruit	grépfrutot	graypfrootawt
grapefruit juice	grépfrut levet	graypfroot lævæt
ham	sonkát	shawnkaat
ice-cream	fagylaltot	fod^yloltawt
lemons	citromot	tseetrawmawt
lettuce	fejes salátát	fæ^yæsh shollaataat
liver sausage	májas hurkát	maa^yosh hoorkaat
milk	tejet	tæ^yæt
mineral water	ásványvizet	aashvaan^yveezæt
mustard	mustárt	mooshtaart
oil	olajat	awloyot
orange juice	narancslevet	norronchlævæt
oranges	narancsot	norronchawt
pepper	borsot	bawrshawt
pickles	ecetes uborkát	ætsætæsh oobawrkaat
potato crisps (chips)	burgonya csipszet	boorgawn^yo cheepsæt
potatoes	burgonyát	boorgawn^yaat

rolls	péksüteményt	paykshewtæmayn^Yt
salad	salátát	shollaataat
salami	szalámit	sollaameet
salt	sót	sh<del>aw</del>t
sandwiches	szendvicset	sændveechæt
sausages	kolbászt	kawlbaast
spaghetti	spagettit	shpoggæt-teet
sugar	cukrot	tsookrawt
sweets	édességet	aydæsh-shaygæt
tea	teát	tæaat
tomato juice	paradicsomlevet	porroddeechawmlævæt
tomatoes	paradicsomot	porroddeechawmawt
yoghurt	joghurtot	yawghoortawt

basket	egy kosarat	æd^Y kawshorrot
bottle	egy üveget	æd^Y ewvægæt
bottle opener	egy üvegnyitót	æd^Y ewvægn^Yeet<del>aw</del>t
box	egy dobozt	æd^Y dawbawzt
corkscrew	egy dugóhúzót	æd^Y doog<del>aw</del>h<del>ooz</del><del>aw</del>t
matches	gyufát	d^Yoofaat
plastic bag	egy plasztik zacskót	æd^Y plosteek zochk<del>aw</del>t
shopping bag	egy bevásár-lótáskát	æd^Y bævaashaarl<del>aw</del>-taashkaat
tin	egy konzervet	æd^Y kawnzærvæt
tin (can) opener	egy konzervnyitót	æd^Y kawnzærvn^Yeet<del>aw</del>t
tinfoil	alufóliát	olloof<del>aw</del>leeaat
tube of ...	egy tubus ...-t	æd^Y tooboosh ...-t

Weights and measures

1 kilogram or kilo (kg) = 1000 grams (g)

100 g = 3.5 oz.	½ kg = 1.1 lb.
200 g = 7.0 oz.	1 kg = 2.2 lb.

1 oz. = 28.35 g
1 lb. = 453.60 g

1 litre (l) = 10 decilitres (dl) or 100 centilitres (cl)
or 1000 millilitres (ml)

1 l = 0.88 imp. quarts = 1.06 U.S. quarts
1 dl = approx. ⅛ pint
2 dl = approx. ⅓ pint

1 imp. quart = 1.14 l	1 U.S. quart = 0.95 l
1 imp. gallon = 4.55 l	1 U.S. gallon = 3.8 l

Souvenirs

Hungary is a land full of fascination for souvenir- and gift-hunters. At centres throughout the country the ancient traditions of woodcarving, embroidery, weaving, pottery and other folk arts are alive and flourishing. Modern designs are found alongside age-old motifs.

Other good buys include regional costumes, local paintings, gramophone records and picture books, not to forget the many excellent local wines, fruit brandies and foodstuffs.

If you are looking for the ultimate executive toy for your boss, try the pocket-sized Hungarian "magic cube". It's a variegated cube made up of interlocking elements which you must twist around in an attempt to line up all the squares of the same colour on the same face. The endless permutations can drive even advanced mathematicians to either distraction or obsession.

carpet	szőnyeg	surn ͮæg
carved bowl	faragott váza	forroggawt vaazo
carved box	faragott doboz	forroggawt dawbawz
carved walking-stick	faragott sétapálca	forroggawt shaytoppaaltso
embroidered blouse	hímzett blúz	heemzæt blooz
embroidered tablecloth	hímzett asztalterítő	heemzæt ostoltæreetur
embroidery (petit point)	hímzés	heemzaysh
fruit brandy	gyümölcspálinka	d ͮewmurlchpaaleenko
apricot brandy	barack pálinka	borrotsk paaleenko
cherry brandy	cseresznye pálinka	chæræsn ͮæ paaleenko
plum brandy	szilva pálinka	seelvo paaleenko
gramophone record	gramofonlemez	grommawfawnlæmæz
handicrafts	kézmüipari termék	kayzmeweeporree tærmayk
Herend china	herendi porcellán	hæræendee pawrtsælaan
magic cube	bűvös kocka	bewvursh kotsko
picture book	képes kalauz	kaypæsh kollo-ooz
pottery	fazekastárgyak	fozækoshtaard ͮok
rug	szőnyeg	surn ͮæg
rustic chair	faragott szék	forroggawt sayk
rustic jugs	falusi kancsók	follooshee konchawk
szűr (Hungarian cape)	szűr	sewr
Tokay wine	tokaji bor	tawkoyee bawr

Tobacconist

Cigarettes, cigars and tobacco are on sale in *Dohánybolt*
(**daw**haanᵞbawlt) and *Trafik* (**tro**ffeek) shops, in all *ÁBC*
(**aa**baytsay) and other department stores, and at most hotel
counters. Intertourist branches also sell smokers' supplies,
including foreign brands of cigarettes, against hard currency. Local cigarettes can be bought in packets of twenty or by
the carton of 200. There are no cigarette vending machines.

Smoking is strictly prohibited in all public transport vehicles
with the exception of trains, which have smokers' compartments. Cinemas, theatres and concert halls also ban smoking.

A packet of cigarettes, please.	**Kérek egy csomag cigarettát.**	kayræk ædᵞ chawmog tseegorræt-taat
I'd like a/an/some …	**Kérek …**	kayræk
cigar	**egy szivart**	ædᵞ seevort
cigars	**néhány szivart**	nayhaanᵞ seevort
cigarette case	**egy cigaretta tárcát**	ædᵞ tseegorræt-to taartsaat
cigarette holder	**egy szipkát**	ædᵞ seepkaat
cigarette lighter	**egy öngyújtót**	ædᵞ urndᵞo͞otāwt
flints	**néhány tűzkövet**	nayhaanᵞ tewzkurvæt
lighter	**egy öngyújtót**	ædᵞ urndᵞo͞otāwt
lighter fluid	**öngyújtó benzint**	urndᵞo͞otāw bænzeent
lighter gas	**öngyújtó gázt**	urndᵞo͞otāw gaast
matches	**gyufát**	dᵞoofaat
packet of …	**egy csomag …-t**	ædᵞ chawmog …-t
pipe	**egy pipát**	ædᵞ peepaat
pipe cleaners	**néhány pipatisztítót**	nayhaanᵞ peepotte͞est͞eetāwt
pipe rack	**egy pipatartót**	ædᵞ peepottortāwt
pipe tobacco	**pipadohányt**	peepoddawhaanᵞt
pipe tool	**egy pipapiszkálót**	ædᵞ peepoppeeskaalāwt
tobacco pouch	**egy dohányszelencét**	ædᵞ dawhaanᵞsælæntsayt
Do you have any …?	**Van Önöknek …?**	von urnurknæk
American cigarettes	**amerikai cigarettájuk**	ommæreeko-ee tseegorræt-taaᵞook
British cigarettes	**angol cigarettájuk**	ongawl tseegorræt-taaᵞook
menthol cigarettes	**mentolos cigarettájuk**	mæntawlawsh tseegorræt-taaᵞook

ll take 2 packets.	**2 csomaggal kérek.**	2 chawmog-gol **kayræk**
d like a carton, please.	**Egy kartonnal kérek.**	æd^Y **kortawn**-nol kayræk
A box of matches, please.	**Egy doboz gyufát kérek.**	æd^Y **dawbawz** d^{Y}oofaat kayræk

filter-tipped	**szűrőbetétes**	se̅w̅rūrbætaytæsh
without filter	**szűrő nélküli**	se̅w̅rūr naylkewlee
light tobacco	**könnyű dohány**	kurn^{Y}e̅w̅ dawhaan^Y
dark tobacco	**nehéz dohány**	næhayz dawhaan^Y

While we're on the subject of cigarettes:

Do you mind if I smoke?	**Nem zavarja, ha dohányzom?**	næm **zovvoryo** ho **daw**haan^{Y}zawm
Would you like a cigarette?	**Parancsol egy cigarettát?**	**porronchawl** æd^Y tseegorræt-taat
Have one of mine.	**Válasszon az enyémből.**	vaaloss-sawn oz æn^{Y}aym-būrl
Try one of these.	**Próbálja ki ezt.**	**praw̅**baalyo kee æst
They're very mild.	**Nagyon gyengék.**	nod^{Y}awn d^{Y}æn**gayk**
They're a bit strong.	**Egy kissé erősek.**	æd^Y **keesh**-shay ærūr**shæk**

And if somebody offers you one:

Thank you.	**Köszönöm.**	kursurnurm
No, thanks.	**Nem kérem.**	næm **kayræm**
I don't smoke.	**Nem dohányzom.**	næm **daw**haan^{Y}zawm
I'm trying to give it up.	**Le akarok szokni a dohányzásról.**	læ **okkorawk sawk**nee o dawhaan^{Y}zaashraw̅l
I've given it up.	**Felhagytam a dohányzással.**	fælhod^{Y}tom o **daw**haan^Y-zaash-shol

DOHÁNYZÓ SMOKING ALLOWED	**TILOS A DOHÁNYZÁS** NO SMOKING

SHOPPING GUIDE

Your money: banks—currency

Official foreign exchange facilities can be found at branches of the Hungarian National Bank *(Magyar Nemzeti Bank)* the National Savings Bank *(Országos Takarékpénztár—O.T.P.)* and the Hungarian Foreign Trade Bank *(Magyar Külkereskedelmi Bank),* most hotels, motels, large campsites and tourist agencies. Some department stores and speciality shops also operate currency exchange counters.

Banking hours are generally from 9 a.m. to 5 p.m., Monday to Friday, and 9 a.m. to 2 p.m., Saturday. Keep all exchange slips. Remember to take your passport with you.

At larger exchange offices some staff usually speak English.

The unit of Hungarian currency is the *Forint* (**faw**reent), abbreviated *Ft.* It is divided into 100 *fillér* (**feel**-layr). Here are the different banknotes and coins in circulation:

Banknotes: 10, 20, 50, 100, 500 and 1000 Forints.
Coins: 10, 20 and 50 fillérs; 1, 2, 5, 10 and 20 Forints.

Visitors may take any amount of foreign currency or traveller's cheques into or out of the country, but check before leaving with your home travel agency on possible currency registration requirements. The import and export of local currency is limited to Ft. 100.

Note that there are restrictions on the amount of forints that may be re-exchanged when leaving the country. Remember to keep the official exchange slips you were issued at the time of the original transaction.

Most internationally recognized traveller's cheques and credit cards are accepted by official currency exchange agencies. A considerable number of tourist-oriented establishments (hotels, restaurants, shops, etc.) also take them— just look for the signs on the door.

Where?

Where's the nearest ...?	Hol a legköze- lebbi ...?	hawl o lægkurzælæb-bee
bank	bank	bonk
exchange office	valuta beváltó hely	vollooto bævaaltāw hæ^y
Where can I cash a traveller's cheque (check)?	Hol lehet traveller's csekket beváltani?	hawl læhæt trovvæl-lærs chæk-kæt bævaaltonnee

At the counter

I'd like to change some ...	Szeretnék ... beváltani.	særætnayk ... bævaal- tonnee
Austrian schillings	osztrák shillinget	ostraak sheel-leengæt
Canadian dollars	kanadai dollárt	konnoddo-ee dawl-laart
German marks	nyugatnémet márkát	n^yoogotnaymæt maarkaat
pounds sterling	angol fontot	ongawl fawntawt
U.S. dollars	amerikai dollárt	ommæreeko-ee dawl-laart
What's the exchange rate?	Mi az átváltási árfolyam?	mee oz aatvaaltaashee aarfaw^yom
I'd like to cash a traveller's cheque (check).	Egy traveller's csekket szeretnék beváltani.	æd^y trovvæl-lærs chæk- kæt særætnayk bævaal- tonnee
Can you cash a personal cheque?	Személyes csekket elfogadnak?	sæmay^yæsh chæk-kæt ælfawgodnok
What rate of commission do you charge?	Mennyi az átváltási jutalék?	mæn^yee oz aatvaaltaa- shee yootollayk
How long will it take to clear?	Meddig tart a csekk ellenőrzése?	mæd-deeg tort o chæk æl-lænūrzayshæ
Can you wire my bank at home?	Táviratoznának a bankomnak?	taaveerottawznaanok o bonkawmnok
I have ...	Rendelkezem ...	rændælkæzæm
a credit card	hitelkártyával	heetælkaart^yaavol
an introduction	ajánló levéllel	oyaanlāw lævayl-læl
a letter of credit	hitellevéllel	heetæl-lævayl-læl
I'm expecting some money from home.	Hazulról várok átutalást.	hozzoolrāwl vaarawk aatootollaasht
Has it arrived yet?	Megjött már?	mægyurt maar

Please give me 5000 forints in large denominations and 100 forints in small change.	**5000 forintot kérek nagy címletekben, továbbá 100 forintot apróban.**	5000 **fawreentawt kayræk** nod^y **tsēēmlætækbæn taw**vaab-baa 100 **fawreentawt** **oprāwbon**
I'd like some small change.	**Aprót szeretnék.**	**oprāwt særætnayk**
Could you please check that again?	**Lenne szíves újra ellenőrizni?**	**læn-næ sēēvæsh ōō^{y}ro æl-lænūūreeznee**
Could I have an exchange slip, please?	**Kaphatnék egy elismervényt?**	**kophotnayk æd^y æleeshmærvayn^{y}t**

Depositing

I want to credit this to my account.	**Ezt az összeget szeretném a számlámra befizetni.**	æst oz **urs-sægæt særætnaym o saamlaamro bæfeezætnee**
I'd like to pay this amount into Mr. ...'s account.	**Ezt az összeget ... úr számlájára szeretném befizetni.**	æst oz **urs-sægæt ... ōōr saamlaa^{y}aaro særætnaym bæfeezætnee**
Where should I sign?	**Hol írjam alá?**	hawl **ēēryom ollaa**

Currency converter

In a world of floating currencies, we can offer no more than this do-it-yourself chart. You can obtain details of current exchange rates from any bank or tourist agency.

	£	$
50 fillér		
1 forint		
2 forint		
5 forint		
10 forint		
15 forint		
20 forint		
50 forint		
100 forint		

NUMBERS: see page 175

At the post office

The offices of the Hungarian postal authority *(Magyar Posta)* are open from 8 a.m. to 4 p.m., Monday–Friday, and from 8 a.m. to 1 p.m., Saturday. Main municipal and regional post offices work from 7 a.m. to 8 p.m., Monday–Saturday, sometimes with a skeleton service in the morning on Sundays and public holidays. Post offices handle mail, telephone, telegraphic and telex services, but not international money transfers.

In Budapest, a special international post, telegraph and telex office operates at the corner of Petofi Sándor utca and Martinelli-tér. It is open from 7 a.m. to 9 p.m., Monday-Friday, until 7 p.m., Saturday, and in the morning only on Sundays and public holidays.

Registered, airmail and express (special-delivery) services are available. Postal and telegraph charges, which are quite low compared with those practised in most western European countries, may be paid in forints.

Postage stamps are also on sale in tobacconists' shops. Mailboxes are red.

Few post office counter staff speak foreign languages.

Where's the nearest post office?	**Hol a legközelebbi postahivatal?**	hawl o lægkurzælæb-bee pawshtoheevottol
What time does the post office ...?	**Mikor ... a postahivatal?**	meekawr ... o pawshtoheevottol
open	**nyit**	n^yeet
close	**zár**	zaar
Which counter do I go to for stamps?	**Melyik ablaknál kapok bélyegeket?**	mæ^yeek obloknaal koppok bay^yægækæt
I want some stamps.	**Bélyegeket kérek.**	bay^yægækæt kayræk
I want ... 5-Ft. stamps.	**... darab 5 forintos címletet.**	... dorrob 5 fawreentawsh tsēēmlætæt

POST OFFICE

What's the postage for a letter/postcard to ... ?	Mennyibe kerül egy levél/képeslap postadíja ... ?	mæn^{Y}eebæ kærewl æd^Y lævayl/kaypæshlop pawshtoddēēyo
Great Britain the U.S.A.	Angliába az Egyesült Allamokba	ongleeaabo os æd^{Y}æsewlt aal-lommawkbo
I want to send this parcel.	Szeretném feladni ezt a csomagot.	særætnaym fælodnee æst o chawmoggawt
I'd like to send this ...	... szeretném feladni.	... særætnaym fælodnee
airmail express (special delivery)	Légipostán Expressz	laygheepawshtaan æxpræs
registered	Ajánlva	oyaanlvo
Where's the mailbox?	Hol a postaláda?	hawl o pawshtollaado
Do I have to fill in a customs declaration form?	Vámnyilatkozatot ki kell töltenem?	vaamn^{Y}eelotkawzottawt kee kæl turltænæm
Where's the poste restante (general delivery)?	Hol a «poste restante» szolgálat?	hawl o pawst ræstont sawlgaalot
Is there any mail for me? My name is ...	Van posta a részemre? ... vagyok.	von pawshto o rayssæmræ ... vod^{Y}awk

BÉLYEGEK	STAMPS
CSOMAGFELADÁS	PARCELS
TÁVIRATOK	TELEGRAMS

Telegrams

Where's the telegram counter?	Hol lehet táviratot feladni?	hawl læhæt taaveerottawt fælodnee
I'd like to send a telegram.	Táviratot szeretnék feladni.	taaveerottawt særætnayk fælodnee
May I have a form, please?	Kaphatok egy táviró-blankettát?	kophottawk æd^Y taavee-rāw-blonkæt-taat
When will the telegram be delivered?	Mikor kézbesítik a táviratot?	meekawr kayzbæshēēteek o taaveerottawt

PLACE NAMES: see page 174

Telephoning

Apart from local calls, direct dialling facilities are still the exception rather than the rule in Hungary. Among hotels, only a few five-star establishments can be reached automatically. However, modernization is proceeding apace, and each year brings an expansion of the automatic telephone network.

Local calls can be made from street pay phones. Long-distance connections are best made through your hotel switchboard operator or at a post office.

To phone abroad you'll have to ask your hotel operator to put the call through for you or go to a major post office. In Budapest you may use the convenient facilities of the international telecommunications centre at the corner of Petőfi Sándor utca and Martinelli-tér.

Where's the telephone?	**Hol a telefon?**	hawl o tælæfawn
Where's the nearest telephone booth?	**Hol a legközelebbi telefonfülke?**	hawl o lægkurzælæb-bee tælæfawnfewlkæ
May I use your phone?	**Használhatom a telefonját?**	hosnaalhottawm o tælæfawnyaat
Do you have a telephone directory for ...?	**Van ...-i telefonkönyvük?**	von ...-ee tælæfawn-kurn^{v}vewk
Can you help me get this number?	**Segítene felhívni ezt a számot?**	shægheetænæ fælheevnee æst o saamawt

Operator

Do you speak English?	**Beszél angolul?**	bæsayl ongawlool
Hello, I want Boston 123-456.	**Halló! A Boston 123-456-os számot kérem kapcsolni.**	hol-lāw. o bawstawn 123-456 awsh saamawt kayræm kopchawlnee
Can I dial direct?	**Lehet közvetlenül tárcsázni?**	læhæt kurzvætlænewl taarchaaznee

NUMBERS: see page 175

I want to place a personal (person-to-person) call.	**Személyes beszélgetést szeretnék rendelni.**	sæmay^Væsh bæsaylgæ-taysht særætnayk ræn-dælnee
A transferred-charge (collect) call, please.	**«R» beszélgetést kérek.**	"ær" bæsaylgætaysht kayræk
Please tell me the cost of the call when I'm finished.	**A beszélgetés végén legyen szíves közölni a költséget.**	o bæsaylgætaysh vaygayn læd^Væn sēēvæsh kurzurlne o kurltshayghæt

Speaking

Hello, this is ... speaking.	**Halló, itt ... beszél.**	hol-lāw eet ... bæsayl
Would you put me through to ...?	**Kapcsolná ...-t?**	kopchawlnaa ...-t
I want to speak to Mr./Mrs. ...	**... úrral/úrnövel szeretnék beszélni.**	...ōōr-rol/ōōrnurvæl særætnayk bæsaylnee
I want extension ...	**A ...-es melléket kérem.**	o ...-æsh mæl-laykæt kayræm
Is that ...?	**Ön ...?**	urn
Please speak more slowly.	**Legyen szíves, mondja lassabban.**	læd^Væn sēēvæsh mawnd^Vo losh-shob-bon

Telephone alphabet

A	**Aladár**	olloddaar	N	**Nándor**	naandawr
Á	**Ágota**	aagawto	O	**Olga**	awlgo
B	**Balázs**	bollaazh	Ö	**Ödön**	urdurn
C	**Cecília**	tsætsēēleeo	P	**Péter**	paytær
D	**Dénes**	daynæsh	Q	**Kú**	kōō
E	**Erzsébet**	ærzhaybæt	R	**Róbert**	rāwbært
É	**Éva**	ayvo	S	**Sándor**	shaandawr
F	**Ferenc**	færænts	T	**Tivadar**	teevoddor
G	**Gábor**	gaabawr	U	**Ubul**	ooboool
H	**Helén**	hælayn	Ü	**Üröm**	ewrurm
I	**Ilona**	eelawno	V	**Vilma**	veelmo
J	**József**	yaw^Vzhæf	W	**duplavé**	dooplovvay
K	**Károly**	kaaraw^V	X	**iksz**	eeks
L	**László**	laaslāw	Y	**ipszilon**	eepseelawn
M	**Mónika**	māwneeko	Z	**Zorán**	zawraan

Bad luck

Operator, you gave me a wrong number.	**Központ! Rossz számot adott meg nekem.**	kurzpawnt. rawss saamawt oddawt mæg nækæm
Operator, we've been cut off.	**Központ! Megszakadt a beszélgetés.**	kurzpawnt. mægsokkodt o bæsaylgætaysh
Would you please try again later?	**Kérem, később legyen szíves újra felhívni.**	kayræm kayshūrb lædⱽæn sēēvæsh ōōⱽro fælhēēvnee

Not there

When will he/she be back?	**Mikor lesz benn az illető?**	meekawr læs bæn oz eel-lætūr
Will you tell him/her I called? My name is ...	**Kérem, értesítse, hogy kerestem. ... vagyok.**	kayræm ayrtæshēētshæ hawdⱽ kæræshtæm. ... vodⱽawk
Would you please take a message?	**Átadná az üzenetet?**	aatodnaa oz ewzænætæt

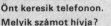

Önt keresik telefonon.	There's a phone call for you.
Melyik számot hívja?	What number are you calling?
Kérem, tartsa a vonalat.	Please hold the line.
Foglalt a vonal.	The line is busy.
Nem veszik fel.	There's no answer.
Téves számot hív.	You've got the wrong number.
A telefon nem működik.	The phone is out of order.
Az illető jelenleg nincs benn.	He/She is out at the moment.

Charges

What was the cost of that call?	**Mibe kerül a beszélgetés?**	meebæ kærewl o bæsaylgætaysh
I want to pay for the call.	**Ki szeretném fizetni a telefonbeszélgetés díját.**	kee særætnaym feezætnee o tælæfawnbæsaylgætaysh dēēyaat

The car

Filling station

We'll start this section by considering your possible needs at a filling station.

Petrol (gasoline), oil and diesel fuel are sold by the litre. Fuel generally comes in three octane ratings—98, 92, 86—and unleaded (rare). Most filling stations will change your oil and wash your car, but they are rarely equipped for handling any repairs.

Since spare parts for Western-built vehicles are extremely difficult to obtain, it's advisable at least to take a set of some basic items with you (gaskets, fan belt, etc.) when driving to Hungary. A wise precaution is to have your car thoroughly serviced before leaving home.

Where's the nearest filling station?	**Hol a legközelebbi töltőállomás?**	hawl o **læg**kurzælæb-bee turltūr-aal-lawmaash
I'd like 30 litres of ...	**30 liter ... benzint kérek.**	30 leetær ... bænzeent kayræk
98 octane	**extra**	æxtro
92 octane	**szuper**	soopær
86 octane	**normál**	nawrmaal

Fluid measures					
litres	imp. gal.	U.S. gal.	litres	imp. gal.	U.S. gal.
5	1.1	1.3	30	6.6	7.9
10	2.2	2.6	35	7.7	9.2
15	3.3	4.0	40	8.8	10.6
20	4.4	5.3	45	9.9	11.9
25	5.5	6.6	50	11.0	13.2

TIPPING: see page 1

Give me ... forints' worth of petrol (gas), please.	Kérek ... forintért benzint.	kayræk ... fawreentayrt bænzeent
Fill the tank, please.	Tele kérem.	tælæ kayræm
Please check the oil and water.	Kérem, ellenőrizze az olajszintet és a hűtővizet.	kayræm æl-lænūrreez-zæ oz awloyseentæt aysh o hewtūrveezæt
Give me a litre of oil.	Egy liter motor-olajat kérek.	æd^y leetær mawtawraw-loyot kayræk
Top up the battery with distilled water, please.	Kérem, töltse fel az akkumulátort desztillált vízzel.	kayræm turltshæ fæl oz ok-koomoolaatawrt dæsteel-laalt vēēz-zæl
Would you check the brake fluid?	Kérem, ellenőrizze a fékolajnyomást.	kayræm æl-lænūrreez-zæ o faykawloyn^yawmaasht
Please check the tire pressure.	Kérem, ellenőrizze a gumikat.	kayræm æl-lænūrreez-zæ o goomeekot
1.6 front, 1.8 rear.	1 egész 6 elöl, 1 egész 8 hátul.	æd^y ægayss hot ælurl æd^y ægayss n^yawlts haatool
Please check the spare tire, too.	Kérem a tartalék-kereket is ellenőrizni.	kayræm o tortollayk-kæ-rækæt eesh æl-lænūrreeznee

CAR—FILLING STATION

Tire pressure			
lb./sq. in.	kg./cm²	lb./sq. in.	kg./cm²
10	0.7	26	1.8
12	0.8	27	1.9
15	1.1	28	2.0
18	1.3	30	2.1
20	1.4	33	2.3
21	1.5	36	2.5
23	1.6	38	2.7
24	1.7	40	2.8

Note: In Hungary, tire pressure is measured in kilograms per square centimetre. The following conversion chart will make sure your tires get the treatment they deserve. You can just show this panel to the filling station attendant and point to the pressures you need.

NUMBERS: page 175

Can you mend this puncture (fix this flat)?	**Kérem ezt a defektes gumit megjavítani.**	kayræm æst o dæfæktæsh goomeet mægyovēētonne
Would you please change this tire?	**Kérem ezt az abroncsot kicserélni.**	kayræm æst oz obrawncha keechæraylnee
Would you please change the oil?	**Egy olajcserét kérek.**	æd^y awloychærayt kayræk
Would you clean the windscreen (windshield)?	**Lemosná a szélvédőt?**	læmawshnaa o saylvaydūr

Miles into kilometres										
1 mile = 1.609 kilometres (km)										
miles	10	20	30	40	50	60	70	80	90	100
km	16	32	48	64	80	97	113	129	145	161

Kilometres into miles													
1 kilometre (km) = 0.62 miles													
km	10	20	30	40	50	60	70	80	90	100	110	120	130
miles	6	12	19	25	31	37	44	50	56	62	68	75	81

Have you any windscreen scrapers?	**Van szélvédő tisztítójuk?**	von saylvaydūr teestēē-tāw^{y}ook
Can you sell me some antifreeze?	**Van fagyásgátló folyadékjuk?**	von fod^{y}aashgaatlāw faw^{y}oddaykyook
Could you give me small change for this?	**Adna ezért aprót?**	odno æzayrt oprāwt
Have you a road map of this area?	**Van a környékről útitérképük?**	von o kurrn^{y}aykrūrl ōōteetayrkaypewk
May I use your phone?	**Használhatom a telefonját?**	hosnaalhottawm o tælæ-fawnyaat
Where are the toilets?	**Hol a W.C.?**	hawl o vaytsay

Asking the way—Street directions

English	Hungarian	Pronunciation
Excuse me.	Elnézést.	ælnayzaysht
Do you speak English?	Beszél ön angolul?	bæsayl urn ongawlool
Could you tell me the way to …?	Elmagyarázná az utat …-ba/-be/-ra/-re?*	ælmod^yorraaznaa oz ootot …-bo/-bæ/-ro/-ræ
How do I get to …?	Hogy jutok el …-ba/-be/-ra/-re?*	hawd^y yootawk æl …-bo/-bæ/-ro/-ræ
Where does this road lead to?	Ez az út hova vezet?	æz oz ōōt hawvo væzæt
Can you show me on the map where I am?	Megmutatná ezen a térképen, hogy hol vagyok?	mægmoototnaa æzæn o tayrkaypæn hawd^y hawl vod^yawk
How far is it to … from here?	Innen milyen messze van …?	een-næn mee^yæn mæs-sæ von
How far is the next town?	Milyen messze van a legközelebbí város?	mee^yæn mæs-sæ von o lægkurzælæb-bee vaarawsh
Where can I find this address?	Hogy jutok el erre címre?	hawd^y yootawk æl ær-ræ o tsēēmræ
Where's this?	Ez merre van?	æz mær-ræ von

Nem jó irányban megy.	You're on the wrong road.
Egyenesen tovább előre.	Go straight ahead.
Balra/Jobbra van, arra lenn.	It's down there on the left/right.
Menjen az első/második keresztútig.	Go to the first/second crossroads.
A közlekedési lámpánál forduljon balra/jobbra.	Turn left/right at the traffic lights.

English	Hungarian	Pronunciation
Can you show me on the map where … is?	Megmutatná a térképen, hogy hol …?	mægmoototnaa o tayrkaypæn hawd^y hawl
Are we on the right road for …?	Jó úton vagyunk … felé?	yāw ootawn vod^yoonk … fælay

* See Grammar section for word endings.

In the rest of this section we'll be more closely concerned with driving conditions in Hungary and the car itself. We've divided it into two parts:

Part A   contains general advice on motoring in Hungary. It would be advisable to read through it in advance.

Part B   is concerned with the practical details of accidents and breakdowns. It includes a list of car parts and of things that may go wrong with them. All you have to do is to show it to the garage mechanic and get him to point to the items required.

Part A

Customs—Documentation—Other requirements

You will need the following documents in order to drive in Hungary:

● passport and visa
● valid driving licence
● car registration papers (log book)
● adequate insurance (check with your home motoring organization on latest requirements)

Motor vehicles must bear a nationality plate or sticker, clearly visible at the rear.

A red warning triangle for display on the road in case of accident or breakdown is compulsory. So is the use of safety belts in the front seats. Crash helmets must be worn by both driver and passenger of motorcycles and scooters.

Here's my ...	Tessék ...	tæsh-shayk
driving licence	a jogosítványom	o yawgawsheetvaan^yawm
insurance certificate	a biztosítási kötvényem	o beeztawsheetaashee kurtvayn^yæm
passport	az útlevelem	oz ōōtlævælæm
registration (log) book	a gépkocsim okmányai	o gaypkawcheem awkmaan^yo-ee

CUSTOMS, see also page 22

| I've nothing to declare. | **Nincs elvámolni valóm.** | neench ælvaamawlnee vollāwm |
| Where can I get a visa? | **Hol kapok vízumot?** | hawl koppawk vēēzoomawt |

Driving—Roads

In Hungary you drive on the right and pass on the left. Go carefully until you have had time to take the measure of the local drivers—the accident rate is one of Europe's highest.

Hungary's motorways (expressways) are well maintained and toll-free. Emergency telephones for use in case of breakdown or accident are located every two kilometres (about 1¼ miles) along these roads.

Other roads are well maintained but out in the countryside not always very wide. Roads are numbered.

Traffic lights have the familiar red, yellow and green colours. You'll probably notice that the yellow stays lit longer than you're used to—but nevertheless, you are supposed to wait until it changes to green before moving off. The green light flashes several times before changing to yellow. At night, traffic lights work on a single flashing yellow, advising all drivers to pay great attention at the crossroads.

You must always stop at railway level crossings. These points are indicated by flashing red and white lights. At bridges, the vehicle closest to the approach, or already on the bridge, has priority.

Pedestrian crossings are marked with white stripes and are illuminated at night. Pedestrians have absolute priority on these crossings at all times.

Winter tires or chains are not compulsory, but driving during the November–March period without them is hazardous.

For help in case of breakdown, see page 151.

Roadsigns—Signposts

Roadsigns used in Hungary are mainly the international pictographs that are also seen on roads throughout western Europe. Some of the more important signs are shown on pages 160–161. Since they are mostly self-explanatory, they are hardly ever supplemented with written notices.

When a signboard has a smaller plate under it bearing a figure in metres, this means that the directive indicated by the roadsign only becomes effective after you have covered the distance shown.

Motorways are indicated by green signs, and other main roads by dark-blue shields. Minor roads and country lanes have signposts bearing black lettering on a white background. Signposting is generally clear.

Speed limits and some other special regulations

Speed limits for cars are: 120 kilometres per hour (75 miles per hour) on motorways, 80 kph (50 mph) on other roads outside city limits and 60 kph (37 mph) within residential areas.

Buses, heavy good vehicles, cars towing caravans (trailers) and motorcycles are restricted to 90 kph (56 mph), 70 kph (43 mph) and 50 kph (31 mph), respectively, on the three types of road specified above.

At night within residential areas, drive with your sidelights only.

If you intend to drive, don't touch a drop of alcohol: the zero limit for blood alcohol content is strictly enforced. If you are caught driving under the influence of alcohol there will be no mitigating circumstances. Penalties range from a very heavy fine to loss of your driving licence, and if you have been the cause of an accident while under the influence of drink, you are likely to end up with a stiff prison sentence.

Police

The police are normally lenient with foreign drivers, but don't push your luck. They are particularly vigilant about alcohol (see above), speeding and illegal parking in urban areas.

I'm sorry, Officer, I didn't see the sign.	Sajnálom, uram, nem vettem észre a jelzőtáblát.	shoynaalawm oorom næm væt-tæm aysræ o yælzūrtaablaat
The light was green.	Zöldet mutatott a lámpa.	zurldæt mootottawt o laampo
How much is the fine?	Mennyi a büntetés?	mæn^{y}ee o bewntætaysh
Excuse me, my car has broken down.	Elnézését kérem. Meghibásodott a gépkocsim.	ælnayzayshayt kayræm. mægheebaashawdawt o gaypkawcheem

Parking

On the street, park your car in the direction of the traffic flow. Do not park at bus, tram (streetcar) or trolley-bus stops or at taxi ranks. Zigzag markings painted on the road surface and "no parking" signs indicate other areas where parking is prohibited. If your car has been parked in such a way as to impede traffic, it will be towed away by the police.

Budapest has parking meters, which take 1- and 5-forint coins, and guarded parking lots where you must purchase your ticket in advance.

Is there a car park in the neighbourhood?	Van a környéken, gépkocsi parkoló?	von o kurrn^{y}aykæn gaypkawchee porkawlāw
Excuse me, may I park here?	Elnézést, szabad itt parkolnom?	ælnayzaysht sobbod eet porkawlnawm
What's the charge for parking here?	Mennyi itt a parkolási díj?	mæn^{y}ee eet o porkawlaashee dēē^y
Excuse me, have you some forint coins for the parking meter?	Elnézést kérek, volna néhány egy-forintosa a parkoló órába?	ælnayzaysht kayræk vawlno nayhaan^y æd^{y}fawreentawsho o porkawlāw āwraabo

Part B

Accidents

This section is confined to immediate aid. The legal problems of responsibility and settlement can be taken care of at a later stage. Your first concern will be for the injured.

Is anyone hurt?	**Megsérült valaki?**	mægshayrewlt vollokkee
Don't move.	**Ne mozogjon!**	næ mawzawgyawn
It's all right, don't worry.	**Nincs semmi baj, ne aggódjon.**	neench shæm-mee boy na og-gāwd^{y}awn
Where's the nearest telephone?	**Hol a legköze-lebbi telefon?**	hawl o lægkurzælæb-bee tælæfawn
May I use your telephone? There's been an accident.	**Használhatom a telefonját? Baleset történt.**	hosnaalhottawm o tælæfawnyaat. bollæshæt turrtaynt
Call a doctor/an ambulance quickly.	**Kérem, azonnal hívjon orvost/mentőket!**	kayræm ozzawn-nol hēēvyawn awrvawsht/mæntūr kæt
There are people injured.	**Többen megsérül-tek.**	turb-bæn mægshayrewl-tæk

Police—Exchange of information

Please call the police.	**Kérem, hívja a rendőrséget.**	kayræm hēēvyo o rændūrrshaygæt
There's been an accident.	**Baleset történt.**	bollæshæt turrtaynt
It's about 3 kilometres from ...	**...-tól/-től körül-belül 3 kilométernyire.***	...-tāwl-tūrl kurrewlbælewl 3 keelawmaytærn^{y}eeræ
I'm on the Vienna—Budapest road ... of Győr.	**A Bécs—budapesti országúton vagyok Győrtől ...**	a baych boodoppæshtee awrsaagōōtawn vod^{y}awk d^{y}ūrrtūrl
north/south east/west	**északra/délre keletre/nyugatra**	ayssokro/daylræ kælætræ/n^{y}oogotro

* See Grammar section for word endings.

DOCTOR: see page 162

CAR—ACCIDENTS

Here's my name and address.	Tessék a nevem és a címem.	tæsh-shayk o nævæm aysh ó tseeemæm
Would you mind acting as a witness?	Vállalná a tanuskodást?	vaalolnaa o tonnooshkaw-daasht
I'd like an interpreter.	Kérek tolmácsot.	kayræk tawlmaachawt

B-r-e-a-k-d-o-w-n

Remember to put out a red warning triangle if the car is out of action or impeding traffic. It should be placed 50 metres behind your vehicle.

On all major roads, all year round, any driver may call for a "yellow angel"—one of the patrol cars of the Hungarian Automobile Club *(Magyar Autóklub)*. They do quick repairs at moderate prices, though they won't have any important spare parts for Western models.

This section is divided into four parts:

1 On the road
  You ask where the nearest garage is.

2 At the garage
  You tell the mechanic what's wrong.

3 Finding the trouble
  He tells you what he thinks is the trouble.

4 Getting it repaired
  You tell him to repair it and, once that's over, settle the account (or argue about it).

Phase 1—On the road

| Where's the nearest garage? | Hol a legközelebbi javítóműhely? | hawl o lægkurzælæb-bee yovveeetawmewhæ^Y |
| What's the telephone number of the nearest garage/"yellow angel" post? | Mi a telefonszáma a legközelebbi javítóműhelynek/ «sárga angyal» szolgálatnak? | mee o tælæfawnsaamo o lægkurzælæb-bee yovveeetawmewhæ^{Y}næk/ shaargo ond^{Y}ol sawlgaa-lotnok |

TELEPHONE: see page 139

Sidebar: CAR—REPAIRS

152

May I use your telephone?	Használhatom a telefonját?	hawsnaalhottawm o tælæfawnyaat
I've had a breakdown at ...	...-nál/-nél elromlott a kocsim.*	...-naal/-nayl ælrawmlawt o kawcheem
Can you send a mechanic?	Küldene egy szerelőt?	kewldænæ æd^y særælürt
Can you send a breakdown truck?	Tudna küldeni egy szervizkocsit?	toodno kewldænæ æd^y særveezkawcheet
How long will you be?	Meddig tart?	mæd-deeg tort
Shouldn't we call the police?	Nem szükséges a rendőrséget kihívni?	næm sewkshaygæsh o rændūrshaygæt keehēēvnee

Phase 2—At the garage

Can you help me?	Segítene?	shæghēētænæ
I don't know what's wrong with it.	Nem tudom, mije romlott el.	næm toodawm mee^{y}æ rawmlawt æl
I think there's something wrong with the ...	Azt hiszem, ... elromlott.	ost heessæm ... ælrawmlawt
battery	az akkumulátor	oz ok-koomoolaatawr
brakes	a fék	o fayk
bulbs	az izzók	oz eez-zāwk
cables	a vezetékek	o væzætaykæk
carburettor	a karburátor	o korbooraatawr
clutch	a kuplung	o kooploong
contact	az érintkezés	oz ayreentkæzaysh
cooling system	a hűtőberendezés	o hēwtūrbærændæzaysh
dipswitch (dimmer switch)	a reflektor-kapcsoló	o ræflæktawr-kopchawlāw
dynamo	a dinamó	o deenommāw
electrical system	az elektromos berendezés	oz ælæktrawmawsh bærændæzaysh
engine	a motor	o mawtawr
exhaust pipe	a kipuffogó	o keepoof-fawgāw
fan	a ventillátor	o vænteel-laatawr
filter	a szűrő	o sēwrūr

---

*See Grammar section for word endings.

fuel pump	az üzemanyag-szivatyú	oz ewzæmon^Yogseevot^Yōō
fuel tank	az üzemanyagtartály	oz ewzæmon^Yogtortaa^Y
gear shift	a sebességváltó kar	o shæbæsh-shaygvaaltāw kor
generator	a dinamó	o deenommāw
handbrake	a kézifék	o kayzeefayk
headlights	a fényszórók	o fayn^Ysāwrāwk
heating	a fűtés	o fēwtaysh
horn	a kürt	o kewrt
ignition system	a gyujtás	o d^Yoo^Ytaash
indicator	az irányjelző	oz eeraan^Yyælzūr
lights	a lámpák	o laampaak
backup lights	a hátrameneti lámpák	o haatrommænætee laampaak
brake lights	a féklámpák	o fayklaampaak
rear lights	a hátsóvilágítás	o haatshāwveelaaghēētaash
reversing lights	a hátrameneti lámpák	o haatrommænætee laampaak
sidelights	a városi világítás	o vaarawshee veelaaghēētaash
tail lights	a hátsóvilágítás	o haatshāwveelaaghēētaash
lines (cables)	a vezetékek	o væzætaykæk
lubrication system	a fékbetétek	o faykbætaytæk
parking brake	a kézifék	o kayzeefayk
radiator	a vízhűtő	o vēēzhēwtūr
seat	az ülés	oz ewlaysh
sliding roof	a tolótető	o tawlāwtætūr
spark plugs	a gyújtógyertya	o d^Yoo^Ytāwd^Yært^Yo
speedometer	a sebességmérő	o shæbæsh-shaygmayrūr
starter	az önindító	oz urneendēētāw
steering	a kormánymű	o kawrmaan^Ymēw
suspension	a felfüggesztés	o fælfewg-gæstaysh
transmission	a sebességváltó-áttétel	o shæbæsh-shaygvaaltāw-aat-taytæl
turn signal	az irányjelző	oz eeraan^Yyælzūr
wheels	a kerekek	o kærækæk
wipers	az ablaktörlők	oz oblokturrlūrk

LEFT	RIGHT		FRONT	REAR
BALRA	**JOBBRA**		**ELÖL**	**HÁTUL**
(bolro)	(yawbro)		(ælurl)	(haatool)

It's …

blowing	**ereszt**	æræst
broken	**eltört**	ælturrt
burnt	**kiégett**	keeaygæt
cracked	**megrepedt**	mægræpædt
defective	**hibás**	heebaash
disconnected	**szétszakadt**	saytsokkodt
dry	**száraz**	saaroz
frozen	**befagyott**	bæfod^{y}awt
jammed	**beszorult**	bæsawroolt
knocking	**kopog**	kawpawg
leaking	**folyik**	faw^{y}eek
loose	**meglazult**	mæglozzoolt
misfiring	**rossz a gyújtása**	rawss o d$^y\overline{oo}{}^y$taasho
noisy	**hangos**	hongawsh
not working	**nem működik**	næm m$\overline{ew}$kurdeek
overheating	**túlmelegszik**	t$\overline{oo}$lmælægseek
short-circuiting	**zárlatos**	zaarlottawsh
slack	**laza**	lozzo
slipping	**csúszik**	ch$\overline{oo}$sseek
stuck	**beszorult**	bæsawroolt
vibrating	**beremeg**	bæræmæg
weak	**gyenge**	d^{y}ængæ
worn	**elkopott**	ælkawpawt

The car won't start.	**Nem indul.**	næm eendool
It's locked and the keys are inside.	**Be van zárva és a kulcsok belül vannak.**	bæ von zaarvo aysh o koolchawk bælewl von-nok
The battery is flat.	**Az akkumulátor kimerült.**	oz ok-koomoolaatawr keemærewlt
The fan belt is too slack.	**A ventillátor-szíj nagyon laza.**	o vænteel-laatawr s$\overline{ee}{}^y$ nod^{y}awn lozzo
I want my car serviced and lubricated.	**Karbantartást és zsírzást kérek.**	korbontortaasht aysh zh$\overline{ee}$rzaasht kayræk
The idling needs adjusting.	**Az alapjáratot be kell állítani.**	oz ollopyaarottawt bæ kæl aal-l$\overline{ee}$tonnee
The pedals need adjusting.	**A pedált szükséges beállítani.**	o pædaalt sewkshaygæsh bæaal-l$\overline{ee}$tonnee
The steering wheel is vibrating.	**A kormánykerék beremeg.**	o kawrmaan^{y}kærayk bæræmæg
The wipers are smearing.	**Az ablaktörlők maszatolnak.**	oz oblokturrl$\overline{u}$rk mossottawlnok

Now that you've explained what's wrong:

How long will it take to repair?	**Meddig tart a javítás?**	mæd-deeg tort o yovvēē-taash
Can you give me a ride into town?	**Elvinne a városba?**	ælveen-næ o vaarawshbo
Could you get me a taxi?	**Hívna nekem egy taxit?**	hēēvno nækæm æd^y toxeet
Is there a hotel nearby?	**Van a környéken szálloda?**	von o kurn^{y}aykæn saal-lawdo

Phase 3—Finding the trouble

If you don't know what's wrong with the car, it's up to the mechanic to find the trouble. You can ask him what has to be repaired by handing him the book and pointing to the Hungarian text below.

Kérem, tekintse végig a következő, ábécé sorrendben összeállított listát és mutasson rá a meghibásodott tételre. Ha az ügyfele a hiba okát is tudni kívánja, válassza ki a megfelelő kifejezést a következő listából (eltört, zárlatos stb.).*

adagoló	injection pump
akkumulátor	battery
akkumulátor cellák	battery cells
automata sebességváltó	automatic transmission
betét	lining
csapágy	bearing
csapszeg	stems
csatlakozó	connection
desztillált víz	distilled water
dinamó	dynamo, generator
dugattyú	piston
dugattyú gyűrű	piston ring
elosztó kábel	distributor leads

---

* Please look at the following alphabetical list and point to the defective item. If your customer wants to know what's wrong with it, pick the applicable term from the next list (broken, short-circuited, etc.).

érintkezési pont	contact
felfüggesztés	suspension
felfüggesztő gyűrű	suspension ring
felfüggesztő rugó	suspension spring
fék	brakes
fékdob	brake drum
fékpofa	brake shoes
féktárcsa	brake disc
fogastengely	rack and pinion
fogazás	teething
főcsapágy	main bearing
főtengely	camshaft
függesztőmű	stabilizer
gyertya	spark plug
gyertyakábel	plug leads
gyújtás	ignition
gyűrű	ring
hajtómű	transmission
henger	cylinder
hengerfej	cylinder head
hengerfej tömítés	cylinder head gasket
hűtőberendezés	cooling system
illesztés	joints
indító motor	starter motor
karburátor	carburettor
kardánház	crankcase
kardántengely	crankshaft
kardán vezérlés	universal joint
kábel	cable
kondenzátor	capacitor
kormány	steering column
kormánymű	steering system
kuplung	clutch
kuplung pedál	clutch pedal
lengéscsillapító	shock absorber
légrugózás	pneumatic suspension
légszűrő	air filter
membrán	diaphragm
motor	engine
motorház	engine block
olajszivattyú	oil pump
olajszűrő	oil filter
radiátor	radiator
reflektor kapcsoló	dipswitch (dimmer switch)
rugók	springs
sebességváltó	gearbox

szelep emelő	tappet
szeleptest	valve
szivattyú	pump
szűrő	filter
tengely	shaft
termosztát	thermostat
úszó	float
üzemanyag szivattyú	petrol (gas) pump
üzemanyag szűrő	petrol (gas) filter
ventillátor	fan
ventillátor szíj	fan belt
villamos berendezés	electrical system
vízszivattyú	water pump

A következő lista azokat a kifejezéseket tartalmazza, amelyek a hibákat és a kijavítás módját magyarázzák meg.*

alacsony	low
áteresztés	blowing
beállítani	to adjust
becsiszolni	to grind in
befagyott	frozen
beszorult	jammed, stuck
csúszás	sliding
defekt	puncture
elégett	burnt
elgörbült	deformed, bent, warped
elkopott	chipped, worn
eltört	broken
feltölteni	to charge
folyás	leaking
gyenge	weak
gyors	quick
gyújtáshibás	misfiring
hegeszteni	to weld
hibás	defective
holtjáték	play
kicserélni	to change, replace
kiegyensúlyozni	to balance
kiereszteni	to bleed
kiégett	blown
kiszerelni	to strip down
kiugrott	cracked

* The following list contains words which describe what's wrong as well as what may need to be done.

CAR—REPAIRS

kopogás	knocking
laza	slack, loose
magas	high
meghúzni	to tighten
meglazítani	to loosen
megrozsdásodott	corroded
piszkos	dirty
rezgés	vibration
rövid	short
száraz	dry
széntelieníteni	to decarbonize
szétment	disconnected
túlmelegedés	overheating
újrabélelni	to reline
üres	empty
zárlatos	short-circuited
zsírozni	to grease

Phase 4—Getting it repaired

Have you found the trouble?	**Megvan a hiba?**	mægvon o heebo
Is it serious?	**Komoly?**	kawmaw^y
Can you repair it?	**Meg tudják javítani?**	mæg tood^{y}aak yovvēētonnee
Can you repair it at once?	**Meg tudják rögtön javítani?**	mæg tood^{y}aak rurgturn yovvēētonnee
What's it going to cost?	**Mennyibe kerül?**	mæn^{y}eebæ kærewl
Do you have the necessary spares?	**Van alkatrészük hozzá?**	von olkotrayssewk hawz-zaa

What if he says "no"?

Why can't you do it?	**Miért nem tudják megjavítani?**	meeayrt næm tood^{y}aak mægyovvēētonnee
Is it essential to have that part?	**Feltétlenül szükséges az az alkatrész?**	fæltaylænewl sewkshaygæsh oz oz olkotrayss
How long is it going to take to get the spare parts?	**Meddig tart beszerezni az alkatrészeket?**	mæd-deeg tort bæsæ-ræznee oz olkotrayssækæt

| Where's the nearest garage that can repair it? | Hol a legközelebbi szerviz, ahol meg tudják javítani? | hawl o lægkurzælæb-bee særveez ohawl mæg tood^yaak yovvēētonnee |
| Can you fix it so that I can get as far as …? | Rendbe tudják annyira hozni, hogy …-ig eljuthassak vele? | rændbæ tood^yaak on^yeero hawznee hawd^y …-eeg ælyoot-hosh-shok vælæ |

If you're really stuck, ask if you can leave the car at the garage. Don't forget to empty it of valuables. Contact the Hungarian Automobile Association or hire another car.

Settling the bill

Is everything all right?	Minden rendben?	meendæn rændbæn
How much do I owe you?	Mennyivel tartozom?	mæn^yeevæl tortawzawm
Do you accept traveller's cheques (checks)?	Traveller's csekket elfogadnak?	trovvæl-lærs chæk-kæt ælfawgodnok
Can I pay with this credit card?	Fizethetek ezzel a hitelkártyával?	feezæt-hætæk æz-zæl o heetælkaart^yaavol
Do you accept foreign money?	Külföldi valutát elfogadnak?	kewlfurldee vollootaat ælfawgodnok
I have to change some money.	Pénzt kell váltanom.	paynzt kæl vaaltonnawm
Thanks very much for your help.	Köszönöm szépen a segítségét.	kursurnurm saypæn o shæghēētshaygayt

But you may feel that the workmanship is sloppy or that you're paying for work not done. In that case, get the bill itemized. If necessary have it translated before you pay.

| I'd like to check the bill first. | Először szeretném ellenőrizni a számlát. | ælūrssurr særætnaym æl-lænūrreeznee o saamlaat |
| Will you itemize the work done? | Részleteznék az elvégzett munkát? | rayslætæznayk oz ælvaygzæt moonkaat |

Some international road signs

No vehicles

No entry

No overtaking
(passing)

Oncoming tra
has priority

Maximum
speed limit

No parking

Caution

Intersectio

Dangerous bend
(curve)

Road narrows

Intersection
with secondary
road

Two-way tra

Dangerous hill

Uneven road

Falling rocks

Give way
(yield)

Main road,
thoroughfare

End of
restriction

One-way traffic

Traffic goes
this way

Roundabout
(rotary)

Bicycles
only

Pedestrians
only

Minimum
speed limit

Keep right
(left if symbol
reversed)

Parking

Hospital

Motorway
(expressway)

Motor
vehicles only

Filling
station

No through
road

162

Doctor

Frankly, how much use is a phrase book going to be to you in case of serious illness or injury? The only phrase you need in such an emergency is:

| Get a doctor quickly! | Kérem, azonnal hívjon orvost! | kayræm ozzawn-nol hēēvyawn awrvawsht |

But there are minor aches and pains, ailments and irritations, that can upset the best planned trip. Here we can help you—and, perhaps, the doctor.

Some doctors may speak a little English. At any rate, they are likely to know enough medical terminology in English for your needs. But suppose there's something the doctor cannot explain because of language difficulties? We've thought of that. As you'll see, this section has been arranged to enable you and the doctor to communicate. From page 165 to page 171, you'll find your part of the dialogue on the upper half of each page—the doctor's is on the lower half.

The whole section is divided into three parts: illness, wounds, nervous tension. Page 171 is concerned with prescriptions and fees. The phrases on pages 172 and 173 will be of help to you at the dentist's or the optician's.

General

Can you get me a doctor?	Tudna hívni orvost?	toodno hēēvnee awrvawsht
Is there a doctor here who speaks English?	Van angolul beszélő orvosuk?	von ongawlool bæsaylūr awrvawshook
Where's the surgery (doctor's office)?	Hol az orvosi rendelő?	hawl oz awrvawshee rændælūr
What are the surgery (office) hours?	Mikor rendel?	meekawr rændæl
Could the doctor come to see me here?	Kihívható az orvos hozzám?	keehēēvhottāw oz awrvawsh hawz-zaam

PHARMACY: see page 108

The Hungarian National Health Service, widely known by its abbreviation *Sz. T. K.* (**æstaykaa**), or the special emergency squad *Mentők* (**mænt̄ūrk**) provide all necessary help, including hospitalization, in case of emergency. Medical standards are in general very high. Most doctors and dentists also have private practices, and many foreigners go to Hungary to enjoy private medical and dental care at relatively low cost.

Symptoms

Use this section to tell the doctor what's wrong. Basically, what he'll require to know is:

What?	(ache, pain, bruise, etc.)
Where?	(arm, stomach, etc.)
How long?	(have you had the trouble)

Before you visit the doctor find out the answers to these questions by glancing through the pages that follow. In this way you'll save time.

Parts of the body

ankle	**boka**	bawko
appendix	**vakbél**	vokbayl
arm	**kar**	kor
artery	**ütőér**	ewt̄ūr-ayr
back	**hát**	haat
bladder	**hólyag**	h̄aw^yog
blood	**vér**	vayr
bone	**csont**	chawnt
bowels	**has**	hosh
breast	**mell**	mæl
cheek	**arc**	orts
chest	**mellkas**	mælkosh
chin	**áll**	aal
collar-bone	**kulcs-csont**	koolch-chawnt
ear	**fül**	fewl
elbow	**könyök**	kurn^yurk
eye	**szem**	sæm
face	**arc**	orts
finger	**ujj**	oo^y

foot	**lábfej**	laabfæ^y
forehead	**homlok**	hawmlawk
genitals	**nemi szervek**	næmee særvæk
gland	**mirigy**	meereed^y
hair	**haj**	hoy
hand	**kéz**	kayz
head	**fej**	fæ^y
heart	**szív**	seev
heel	**sarok**	shorrawk
hip	**csípő**	cheepur
intestines	**belek**	bælæk
jaw	**állkapocs**	aalkoppawch
joint	**ízület**	eezewlæt
kidney	**vese**	væshæ
knee	**térd**	tayrd
knee-cap	**térdkalács**	tayrdkollaach
leg	**láb**	laab
lip	**ajak**	oyok
liver	**máj**	maa^y
lung	**tüdő**	tewdur
mouth	**száj**	saa^y
muscle	**izom**	eezawm
neck	**nyak**	n^yok
nerve	**ideg**	eedæg
nervous system	**idegrendszer**	eedægrændsær
nose	**orr**	awr
rib	**borda**	bawrdo
shoulder	**váll**	vaal
skin	**bőr**	burr
spine	**hátgerinc**	haatgæreents
stomach	**gyomor**	d^yawmawr
tendon	**ín**	een
thigh	**comb**	tsawmb
throat	**torok**	tawrawk
thumb	**hüvelyk**	hewvæ^yk
toe	**lábujj**	laaboo^y
tongue	**nyelv**	n^yælv
tonsils	**mandula**	mondoolo
urine	**vizelet**	veezælæt
vein	**ér**	ayr
wrist	**csukló**	chooklaw

LEFT/ON THE LEFT SIDE	RIGHT/ON THE RIGHT SIDE
BAL/A BALOLDALON	**JOBB/A JOBB OLDALON**
(bol/o **bol**lawldollawn)	(yawb/o yawb **awl**dollawn)

DOCTOR

PATIENT
Part 1—Illness

I'm not feeling well.	**Rosszul érzem magam.**	rawss-sool ayrzæm moggom
I'm ill.	**Beteg vagyok.**	bætæg vod^yawk
I've got a pain here.	**Itt fáj valami.**	eet faa^y vollommee
I've got a fever.	**Lázas vagyok.**	laazosh vod^yawk
I've got a ...	**Fáj a ...**	faa^y o
backache	**hátam**	haatom
headache	**fejem**	fæ^yæm
sore throat	**torkom**	tawrkawm
stomachache	**gyomrom**	d^yawmrawm
I've been vomiting.	**Hánytam.**	haan^ytom
I'm constipated.	**Szorulásom van.**	sawroolaashawm vawn

DOCTOR

DOCTOR
Első rész—Betegség

Mi a panasza?	What's the trouble?
Hol fáj?	Where does it hurt?
Milyen fájdalmat érez?	What kind of pain is it?
tompa/éles/lüktető állandó/változó	dull/sharp/throbbing constant/on and off
Mióta érzi így magát?	How long have you been feeling like this?
Tűrje fel az ingujját.	Roll up your sleeve, please.
Kérem vetkőzzön le (derékig).	Please undress (down to the waist).

PATIENT

I feel dizzy.	Szédülök.	saydewlurk
I feel faint.	Gyengének érzem magamat.	d^yængaynæk ayrzæm moggommot
I feel shivery.	Ráz a hideg.	raaz o heedæg
I feel nauseous.	Hányingerem van.	haan^yeengæræm von
I've got ... degrees temperature.	... fok lázam van.	... fawk laazom von
I've got (a/an) ...		
asthma	Asztmás vagyok.	ostmaash vod^yawk
bronchitis	Bronhitiszem van.	brawnheeteessæm von
cold	Meg vagyok fázva.	mæg vod^yawk faazvo
cough	Köhögök.	kurhurgurk
cramps	Görcsölök.	gurrchurlurk
diarrhoea	Megy a hasam.	mæd^y o hoshom
earache	A fülem fáj.	o fewlæm faa^y
haemorrhoids	Aranyerem van.	orron^yæræm von
hayfever	Szénanáthám van.	saynonnaat-haam von
heartburn	Gyomorégésem van.	d^yawmawraygayshæm von

DOCTOR

Kérem, feküdjön le ide.	Please lie down over there.
Nyissa ki a száját.	Open your mouth.
Sóhajtson mélyeket.	Breathe deeply.
Köhögjön kérem.	Cough, please.
Megmérem a vérnyomását/a lázát.	I'll take your blood pressure/ temperature.
Először van ilyen állapotban?	Is this the first time you've had this?
Adok egy injekciót.	I'll give you an injection.
Vér/Széklet/Vizelet mintára van szükségem.	I want a specimen of your blood/stools/urine.
... napig ágyban kell maradnia.	You must stay in bed for ... days.

PATIENT

hernia	Sérvem van.	shayrvæm von
indigestion	Gyomorrontásom van.	d^{V}awmawr-rawntaashawm von
an itch	Viszketegségem van.	veeskætægshaygæm von
nosebleed	Vérzik az orrom.	vayrzeek oz awr-rawm
palpitations	Szívdobogásom van.	s$\overline{ee}$vdawbawgaashawm von
period pains	Menstruálok.	mænshtrooaalawk
rash	Kiütéses vagyok.	keeewtayshæsh vod^{V}awk
rheumatism	Reumás vagyok.	ræoomaash vod^{V}awk
shivers	Ráz a hideg.	raaz o heedæg
stiff neck	Nyakmerevedésem van.	n^{V}okmærævædayshæm von
sunstroke	Napszúrásom van.	nops$\overline{oo}$raashawm von
ulcer	Fekélyem van.	fækay^{V}æm von
It's nothing serious, I hope.	Remélem, semmi komoly.	ræmaylæm shæm-mee kawmaw^V
Is it contagious?	Fertőző?	fært$\overline{u}$rz$\overline{u}$r
I'd like you to prescribe some medicine for me.	Kérem írjon fel a részemre néhány orvosságot.	kayræm $\overline{ee}$ryawn fæl o rayssæmræ nayhaan^V awrvawsh-shaagawt

DOCTOR

Semmi komoly.	It's nothing serious.
Önnek ...	You've got ...
ételmérgezése	food poisoning
gyomorhurutja van	gastritis
.. gyulladása van	inflammation of ...
hólyaggyulladása	cystitis
homloküreggyulladása van	sinusitis
influenzája van	flu
ízületi gyulladás	arthritis
középfültő gyulladása van	inflammation of the middle ear
megfázásos hasmenése	gastric flu
tüdőgyulladása van	pneumonia
vakbélgyulladása	appendicitis
veseköve van	biliary colics
Önnek szakorvoshoz kell mennie.	I want you to see a specialist.

PATIENT

I'm a diabetic.	**Cukorbeteg vagyok.**	tsookawrbætæg vod^yawk
I've a cardiac condition.	**Szívbántalmaim vannak.**	sēēvbaantolmo-eem von-nok
I had a heart attack ... years ago.	**... évvel ezelőt szívrohamom volt.**	... ayv-væl æzælūrt sēēvrawhommawm vawlt
I'm allergic to ...	**Allergiás vagyok ...-ra/-re.***	ol-lærgheeaash vod^yawk ...-ro/-ræ
This is my usual medicine.	**Ezt a gyógyszert szoktam szedni.**	æst o d^yāwd^ysært sawktom sædnee
I need this medicine.	**Erre a gyógyszerre van szükségem.**	ær-ræ o d^yāwd^ysær-ræ von sewkshaygæm
I'm expecting a baby.	**Terhes vagyok.**	tærhæsh vod^yawk
I'm in my ... month.	**A ...-dik hónapban vagyok.**	o ...-deek hāwnopbon vod^yawk
Can I travel?	**Utaznom szabad?**	ootoznawm sobbod

DOCTOR

Milyen adag inzulint kap?	What dose of insulin are you taking?
Injekcióban, vagy szájon át?	Injection or oral?
Hogy kezelik jelenleg?	What treatment are you having?
Milyen gyógyszert szed?	What medicine are you taking?
Általában mennyit szed?	What's your normal dose?
(Enyhe) szívrohama volt.	You've had a (mild) heart attack.
...-t Magyarországon nem használjuk. Ez hasonló.	We don't use ... in Hungary. This is similar.
Mikorra esedékes a szülés?	When is the baby due?
...-ig nem utazhat.	You can't travel until ...

---

* See Grammar section for word endings.

PATIENT

Part 2—Wounds

Could you have a look at this ...?	**Megvizsgálná ezt a ...?**	mægveezhgaalnaa æst o
bite	**harapást**	horroppaasht
blister	**hólyagot**	hāw^yoggawt
boil	**kelést**	kælaysht
bruise	**zúzódást**	zōōzāwdaasht
burn	**égést**	aygaysht
cut	**vágást**	vaagaasht
graze	**horzsolást**	hawrzhawlaasht
insect bite	**rovarcsípést**	rawvorchēēpaysht
lump	**csomót**	chawmāwt
rash	**kiütést**	keeewtaysht
sore	**sebet**	shæbæt
sting	**csípést**	chēēpaysht
swelling	**daganatot**	doggonnottawt
wound	**sebet**	shæbæt
I can't move ...	**Nem tudok mozogni**	næm toodawk
It hurts.	**a ... Fáj.**	mawzawgnee o ... faa^y

DOCTOR

2. rész—Sebesülés

(Nem) fertőzőtt.	It's (not) infected.
Porckorongsérve/Isiásza van.	You've got a slipped disc/sciatica.
Meg kell önt röntgeneztetnem.	I'd like you to have an X-ray.
Ez ...	It's ...
eltört/kiugrott	broken/dislocated
elszakadt/kificamodott	torn/sprained
Izomrándulása van.	You've pulled a muscle.
Antiszeptikumot/ Fájdalomcsillapítót adok Önnek.	I'll give you an antiseptic/a painkiller.
Tetanusz ellen már oltották?	Have you been vaccinated against tetanus?
Kérem, hogy ... nap múlva jöjjön vissza.	I'd like you to come back in ... days.

PARTS OF THE BODY: see page 163

PATIENT

Part 3—Nervous tension

I'm in a nervous state.	Ideges vagyok.	eedægæsh vod^yawk
I'm feeling depressed.	Depressziós a hangulatom.	dæpræs-seeāwsh o hongoolottawm
I'm suffering from anxiety.	Izgatott vagyok.	eezgottawt vod^yawk
I can't eat.	Nem tudok enni.	næm toodawk æn-nee
I can't sleep.	Nem tudok aludni.	næm toodawk olloodnee
Can you prescribe ...?	Felírna valami ...?	fælēērno vollommee
an antidepressant	depresszió elleni szert	dæpræs-seeāw æl-lænee sært
some sleeping pills	altatót	oltottāwt
a tranquillizer	nyugtatót	n^yoogtottāwt
I don't want anything too strong.	Kérem, ne adjon túl erős orvosságot.	kayræm næ odyawn tōōl ærūrsh awrvawsh-shaagawt

---

DOCTOR

3. rész—Idefeszültség

Ön idegfeszültségben. szenved.	You're suffering from nervous tension.
Pihenésre van szüksége.	You need a rest.
Milyen gyógyszert szedett eddig?	What pills have you been taking?
Naponta hányat?	How many a day?
Mióta érzi így magát?	How long have you been feeling like this?
Felírok néhány tablettát.	I'll prescribe some pills.
Adok Önnek nyugtatót/ altatót.	I'll give you a tranquillizer/ some sleeping pills.
Ezzel kihúzza amíg hazaér.	This will see you through until you get home.

PATIENT

Prescription and dosage

What kind of medicine is this?	**Ez milyen orvosság?**	æz mee^Yæn awrvawsh-shaag
How many times a day should I take it?	**Naponta hányszor szedjem?**	noppawnto haan^Ysawr sæd^Yæm
Must I swallow them whole?	**Egészben kell lenyelnem?**	ægaysbæn kæl læn^Yæl-næm

Fee

How much do I owe you?	**Mennyivel tartozom?**	mæn^Yeevæl tortawzawm
Do I pay you know or will you send me your bill?	**Most fizessek, vagy elküldi a számláját?**	mawsht feezæsh-shæk vod^Y ælkewldee o saamlaa^Yaat
May I have a receipt for my health insurance?	**Kaphatok egy elismervényt a biztosítóm részére?**	kophottawk æd^Y æleeshmærvayn^Yt o beeztawsheetāwm rayssayræ

DOCTOR

Gyógyszerfelírás és adagolás

Ebből az orvosságból ... kávéskanállal szedjen.	Take ... teaspoons of this medicine.
.. tablettát vegyen be minden ...-ik órában egy pohár vízzel.	Take ... pills with a glass of water every ... hours.
minden étkezés előtt	before each meal
minden étkezés után	after each meal
reggelente/esténként	in the morning/at night
mikor fájdalmai vannak	in case of pain
... napig	for ... days

Tiszteletdíj

Tudna most fizetni?	Can you pay me now, please?
Elküldöm Önnek a számlát.	I'll send you the bill.

DOCTOR

NUMBERS: page 175

Dentist

Can you recommend a good dentist?	Ajánlana egy jó fogorvost?	oyaanlonno æd^y yāw fawgawrvawsht
Can I make an (urgent) appointment to see Doctor ...?	(Sürgősen) mikor kereshetem fel doktor ...-t?	(shewrgūrshæn) meekawr kæræshhætæm fæl dawktawr ...-t
Can't you possibly make it earlier than that?	Nem lehetne hamarabb?	næm læhætnæ hommorrob
I've a toothache.	Fáj a fogam.	faa^y o fawgom
I've an abscess.	Tályogos a fogam.	taa^yawgawsh o fawgom
This tooth hurts.	Ez a fogam fáj.	æz o fawgom faa^y
at the top at the bottom in the front at the back	fent lent elöl hátul	fænt lænt ælurl haatool
Can you fix it up temporarily?	Ideiglenesen rendbe tudná hozni?	eedæeeglænæshæn rændbæ toodnaa hawznee
Please give me a local anaesthetic.	Kérem, adjon helyi érzéstelenítést.	kayræm od^yawn hæ^yee ayrzayshtælænēētaysht
I don't want it extracted.	Nem akarom kihúzatni.	næm okkorrawm keehōōzotnee
I've lost a filling.	Kiesett egy tömítésem.	keeæshæt æd^y turmēētayshæm
The gum is ...	... az ínyem.	... oz ēēn^yæm
bleeding sore	Vérzik Sebes	vayrzeek shæbæsh

Dentures

I've broken my denture.	Eltörtem a műfogsoromat.	ælturrtæm o mēw̄fawgshawrawmot
Can you repair this denture?	Meg tudná javítani?	mæg toodnaa yovvēētonnee
When will it be ready?	Mikor lesz kész?	meekawr læss kayss

Optician

Where can I find an optician?	Hol találok egy optikust?	hawl **tollaalawk** æd^y **awpteekoosht**
I've broken my glasses.	Eltörtem a szemüvegemet.	ælturrtæm o **sæmewvæ-gæmæt**
Can you repair them for me?	Meg tudná javítani?	mæg **toodnaa yovvēē-tonnee**
When will they be ready?	Mikor lesz kész?	meekawr læss kayss
Can you change the lenses?	Ki tudja cserélni az üvegeket?	kee **tood**^{y}o **chæraylnee oz ewvægækæt**
I'd like tinted lenses.	Színes üveget szeretnék.	sēēnæsh **ewvægæt særætnayk**
I'd like to have my eyesight checked.	Szeretném megvizsgáltatni a szememet.	særætnaym **mægveezh-gaaltotnee o sæmæmæt**
I'm short-sighted/long-sighted.	Rövidlátó/Távolbalátó vagyok.	rurveedlaatāw/taavawlbo-laatāw **vod**^{y}awk
I'd like a spectacle case.	Egy szemüvegtartót kérnék.	æd^y **sæmewvægtortāwt kayrnayk**
I've lost a contact lens.	Elvesztettem az egyik kontakt üvegemet.	ælvæstæt-tæm oz æd^{y}eek **kawntokt ewvægæmæt**
I've hard/soft lenses.	Kemény/Puha lencséim vannak.	kæmayn^y/pooho **læn-chayeem von-nok**
Could you give me another lens?	Tudna másik lencsét adni?	toodno **maasheek læn-chayt odnee**
Have you got some liquid for contact lenses?	Van kontakt len-cséhez szem-cseppjük?	von **kawntokt lænchayhæz sæmchæpyewk**
A small/large bottle, please.	Egy kis/nagy üveggel kérek.	æd^y **keesh/nod^y ewvæg-gæl kayræk**
I'd like a pair of sunglasses.	Egy napszemüveget kérek.	æd^y **nopsæmewvægæt kayræk**
May I look in a mirror?	Megnézhetem magam a tükörben?	mægnayz-hætæm **moggom o tewkurrbæn**
I'd like a pair of binoculars.	Egy távcsövet kérnék.	æd^y **taavchurvæt kayr-nayk**
How much do I owe you?	Mennyivel tartozom?	mæn^{y}eevæl **tortawzawm**

Reference section

Hungarian cities

Budapest	boodoppæsht
Debrecen	dæbrætsæn
Győr	d^{Y}ūrr
Pécs	paych
Szeged	sægæd

Countries

Austria	Ausztria	ooostreeo
Belgium	Belgium	bælgheeoom
Canada	Kanada	konnoddo
Czechoslovakia	Csehszlovákia	chæhslawvaakeeo
East Germany	Német Demokratikus Köztársaság	naymæt dæmawkrottee-koosh kurztaarshoshaag
England	Anglia	ongleeo
Finland	Finnország	feenawrsaag
France	Franciaország	frontseeo-awrsaag
Great Britain	Nagybritánia	nod^{Y}breetaaneeo
Hungary	Magyarország	mod^{Y}orawrsaag
Ireland	Írország	ēērawrsaag
Italy	Olaszország	awlossawrsaag
Japan	Japán	yoppaan
Netherlands	Hollandia	hawl-londeeo
New Zealand	Újzéland	ōō^{Y}zaylond
Poland	Lengyelország	lænd^{Y}ælawrsaag
Scotland	Skócia	shkāwtseeo
Soviet Union	Szovjetunió	sawvvyætooneeāw
Sweden	Svédország	svaydawrsaag
Switzerland	Svájc	shvaa^{Y}ts
United States	Egyesült Államok	æd^{Y}æshewlt aal-lommawk
Wales	Vélsz	væls
West Germany	Nyugatnémetország	n^{Y}oogotnaymætawrsaawg
Yugoslavia	Jugoszlávia	yoogawslaaveeo

... and continents

Africa	Afrika	ofreeko
Asia	Ázsia	aazheeo
Australia	Ausztrália	ooostraaleeo
Europe	Európa	æeorāwpo
North America	Északamerika	ayssokkommæreeko
South America	Délamerika	daylommæreeko

Numbers

0	nulla	**nool**-lo
1	egy	æd^y
2	kettő	**kæt**-tūr
3	három	**haa**rawm
4	négy	nayd^y
5	öt	urt
6	hat	hot
7	hét	hayt
8	nyolc	n^{y}awlts
9	kilenc	**kee**lænts
10	tíz	tēēz
11	tizenegy	**tee**zænæd^y
12	tizenkettő	**tee**zænkæt-tūr
13	tizenhárom	**tee**zænhaarawm
14	tizennégy	**tee**zæn-nayd^y
15	tizenöt	**tee**zænurt
16	tizenhat	**tee**zænhot
17	tizenhét	**tee**zænhayt
18	tizennyolc	**tee**zæn-n^{y}awlts
19	tizenkilenc	**tee**zænkeelænts
20	húsz	hōōss
21	huszonegy	**hoo**ssawnæd^y
22	huszonkettő	**hoo**ssawnkæt-tūr
23	huszonhárom	**hoo**ssawnhaarawm
24	huszonnégy	**hoo**ssawn-nayd^y
25	huszonöt	**hoo**ssawnurt
26	huszonhat	**hoo**ssawnhot
27	huszonhét	**hoo**ssawnhayt
28	huszonnyolc	**hoo**ssawn-n^{y}awlts
29	huszonkilenc	**hoo**ssawnkeelænts
30	harminc	**hor**meents
31	harmincegy	**hor**meentsæd^y
32	harminckettő	**hor**meentskæt-tūr
33	harminchárom	**hor**meentshaarawm
40	negyven	**næd**^{y}væn
41	negyvenegy	**næd**^{y}vænæd^y
42	negyvenkettő	**næd**^{y}vænkæt-tūr
43	negyvenhárom	**næd**^{y}vænhaarawm
50	ötven	**urt**væn
51	ötvenegy	**urt**vænæd^y
52	ötvenkettő	**urt**vænkæt-tūr
53	ötvenhárom	**urt**vænhaarawm
60	hatvan	**hot**von
61	hatvanegy	**hot**vonnæd^y

62	hatvankettő	hot**v**onkæt-tūr
63	hatvanhárom	hot**v**onhaarawm
70	hetven	hætvæn
71	hetvenegy	hætvænæd**y**
72	hetvenkettő	hætvænkæt-tūr
73	hetvenhárom	hætvænhaarawm
80	nyolcvan	n**y**awltsvon
81	nyolcvanegy	n**y**awltsvonnæd**y**
82	nyolcvankettő	n**y**awltsvonkæt-tūr
83	nyolcvanhárom	n**y**awltsvonhaarawm
90	kilencven	keelæntsvæn
91	kilencvenegy	keelæntsvænæd**y**
92	kilencvenkettő	keelæntsvænkæt-tūr
93	kilencvenhárom	keelæntsvænhaarawm
100	egyszáz	æd**y**saaz
101	százegy	saazæd**y**
102	százkettő	saazkæt-tūr
103	százhárom	saazhaarawm
110	száztíz	saaztēēz
120	százhúsz	saazhōōss
130	százharminc	saazhormeents
140	száznegyven	saaznæd**y**væn
150	százötven	saazurtvæn
160	százhatvan	saazhotvon
170	százhetven	saazhætvæn
180	száznyolcvan	saazn**y**awltsvon
190	százkilencven	saazkeelæntsvæn
200	kettőszáz	kæt-tūrsaaz
300	háromszáz	haarawmsaaz
400	négyszáz	nayd**y**saaz
500	ötszáz	urtsaaz
600	hatszáz	hotsaaz
700	hétszáz	haytsaaz
800	nyolcszáz	n**y**awlts-saaz
900	kilencszáz	keelænts-saaz
1000	egyezer	æd**y**æzær
1100	ezeregyszáz	æzæræd**y**saaz
1200	ezerkettőszáz	æzærkæt-tūrsaaz
1300	ezerháromszáz	æzærhaarawmsaaz
2000	kétezer	kaytæzær
5000	ötezer	urtæzær
10,000	tízezer	tēēzæzær
50,000	ötvenezer	urtvænæzær
100,000	százezer	saazæzær
1,000,000	egymillió	æd**y**meel-leeāw

rst	első	ælshūr
econd	második	maashawdeek
hird	harmadik	hormoddeek
ourth	negyedik	næd^{Y}ædeek
ifth	ötödik	urturdeek
ixth	hatodik	hottawdeek
eventh	hetedik	hætædeek
ighth	nyolcadik	n^{Y}awltsoddeek
inth	kilencedik	keelæntsædeek
enth	tizedik	teezædeek
undredth	századik	saazoddeek
housandth	ezredik	æzrædeek
nce	egyszer	æd^{Y}sær
wice	kétszer	kaytsær
hree times	háromszor	haarawmsawr
alf	fél	fayl
alf of ...	a ... fele	o ... fælæ
quarter	egy negyed	æd^Y næd^{Y}æd
third	egy harmad	æd^Y hormod
pair of ...	egy pár ...	æd^Y paar
dozen	egy tucat	æd^Y tootsot
alf a dozen	féltucat	fayltootsot
he 19th century	a tizenkilencedik század	o teezækeelæntsædeek saazod
n the 20th century	a huszadik században	o hoossoddeek saazodbon
low old are you?	Hány éves?	haan^Y ayvæsh
'm 26.	26 éves vagyok.	26 ayvæsh vod^{Y}awk
When's your birthday?	Mikor van a születésnapja?	meekawr von o sewlætayshnopyo
was born in ...	...-ban/-ben születtem.	...-bon/-bæn sewlætætæm
986	ezerkilencszáznyolcvanhat	æzærkeelænts-saaznYawltsvonhot
997	ezerkilencszázkilencvenhét	æzærkeelænts-saazkeelæntsvænhayt
998		

Time

**tizenkettő óra múlt
tizenöt perccel**
(**teezz**ænkæt-tū̄r **ā̄wro**
mō̄ōlt **teezz**ænurt
pærts-tsæl)

**egy óra múlt húsz
perccel**
(æd^y **ā̄wro** mō̄ōlt
hō̄ōss pærts-tsæl)

fél négy*
(fayl nayd^y)

**négy óra harmincöt
perc**
(nayd^y **ā̄wro** hormeen-
tsurt pærts)

**hat óra lesz húsz
perc múlva**
(hot **ā̄wro** læs hō̄ōss
pærts **mō̄ōlvo**)

háromnegyed hé
(haarawmnæd^yæd
hayt)

**öt perc múlva
kilenc óra**
(urt pærts **mō̄ōlvo**
keelænts **ā̄wro**)

tíz óra
(tē̄ēz **ā̄wro**)

**tizenegy óra múl
öt perccel**
(**teezz**ænæd^y **ā̄wro** mō̄ō
urt **pærts**-tsæl)

---

* literally "half *to* four".

Date Line

Eastern European Time

Central European Time

Western European Time (G.M.T.)

Atlantic Time

Eastern Time

Central Time

Mountain Time

Pacific Time

Alaska Time

Countries which have adopted a time differing from that in the corresponding time zone. Note that also in the USSR, official time is one hour ahead of the time in each corresponding time zone. In summer, numerous countries advance time one hour ahead of standard time.

When?

What time is it?	**Hány óra?**	haan^y aw̄ro
It's ...	**... óra van.**	... aw̄ro von
Excuse me. Can you tell me the time?	**Bocsánat. Megmondaná hogy hány óra van?**	bawchaanot. mǣgmawndonnaa hawd^y haan^y aw̄ro von
At what time does ... open?	**Mikor nyit a/az ...?**	meekawr n^yeet zaar o/oz
At what time does ... close?	**Mikor zár be a/az ...?**	meekawr zaar bæ o/oz
At what time does it begin?	**Mikor kezdődik?**	meekawr kæzdūr̄deek
At what time does it end?	**Mikor van vége?**	meekawr von vaygæ
I'll meet you at ... tomorrow.	**Holnap ... órakor találkozunk.**	hawlnop ... aw̄rokkawr tollaalkawzoonk
At what time will you be there?	**Mikor lesz ott?**	meekawr læs awt
At what time should I be there?	**Mikorra jöjjek?**	meekawr-ro yur^y-yæk
Can I come at ...?	**Jöhetek ... -kor?**	yurhætæk ...-kawr
9 o'clock half past 2	**9-kor fél-3-kor**	9-kawr fayl 3-kawr
I'm sorry, I'm late.	**Sajnálom, hogy elkéstem.**	shoynaalawm hawd^y ælkayshtæm
after	**utánna**	ootaan-no
before	**előtte**	ælūr̄t-tæ
early	**korán**	kawraan
on time	**pontosan**	pawntawshon
in time	**időben**	eedūr̄bæn
late	**későn**	kayshūr̄n
noon/midnight	**délben/éjfélkor**	daylbæn/ay^yfaylkawr
hour	**egy óra**	æd^y aw̄ro
half an hour	**félóra**	faylaw̄ro
quarter of an hour	**egy negyed óra**	æd^y næd^yæd aw̄ro
minute	**perc**	pærts
second	**másodperc**	maashawdpærts

Days

What day is it today?	**Ma milyen nap van?**	mo mee^yæn nop von
It's ...	... **van.**	... von
Sunday	**Vasárnap***	voshaarnop
Monday	**Hétfő**	haytfūr
Tuesday	**Kedd**	kæd
Wednesday	**Szerda**	særdo
Thursday	**Csütörtök**	chewturrturk
Friday	**Péntek**	payntæk
Saturday	**Szombat**	sawmbot
in the morning	**reggel**	ræg-gæl
at noon	**délben**	daylbæn
in the afternoon	**délután**	daylootaan
in the evening	**este**	æshtæ
at night	**éjjel**	ay^y-yæl
at midnight	**éjfélkor**	ay^yfaylkawr
the day before yesterday	**tegnapelőtt**	tægnopælūrt
yesterday	**tegnap**	tægnop
today	**ma**	mo
tomorrow	**holnap**	hawlnop
the day after tomorrow	**holnapután**	hawlnoppootaan
the day before	**az előző nap**	oz ælūrzūr nop
the next day	**a következő nap**	o kurvætkæzūr nop
two days ago	**két nappal ezelőtt**	kayt nop-pol æzælūrt
in three days' time	**három nap múlva**	haarawm nop mōōlvo
last week	**a múlt héten**	o mōōlt haytæn
this week	**ezen a héten**	æzæn o haytæn
next week	**a jövő héten**	o yurvūr haytæn
birthday	**születésnap**	sewlætayshnop
day	**nap**	nop
holiday	**ünnepnap**	ewn-næpnop
holidays	**szabadság**	sobbodshaag
month	**hónap**	hāwnop
week	**hét**	hayt
week-end	**hétvége**	haytvaygæ
working day	**munkanap**	moonkonnop
year	**év**	ayv

* Note that, except when they appear at the beginning of a sentence, the names of days and months are not capitalized in Hungarian.

REFERENCE SECTION

Months

January	január*	yonnooaar
February	február	fæbrooaar
March	március	martseeoosh
April	április	aapreeleesh
May	május	maa^yoosh
June	június	yōōneeoosh
July	július	yōōleeoosh
August	augusztus	ooogoostoosh
September	szeptember	sæptæmbær
October	október	awktāwbær
November	november	nawvæmbær
December	december	dætsæmbær

since June	június óta	yōōneeoosh āwto
in August	augusztusban	ooogoostooshbon
3 months ago	3 hónappal ezelõtt	3 hāwnop-pol æzælūrt
last month	a múlt hónapban	o mōōlt hāwnopbon
next month	a következõ hónapban	o kurvætkæzūr hāwnop-bon
the month before	az elõzõ hónapban	oz ælūrzūr hāwnopbon
the following month	a következõ hónapban	o kurvætkæzūr hāwnopbon

Letter headings are written thus:

Budapest, May 24, 19..   **Budapest 19.. május 24**

Seasons

spring	tavasz	tovvoss
summer	nyár	n^yaar
autumn	õsz	ūrss
winter	tél	tayl

in spring	tavasszal	tovvos-sol
in summer	nyáron	n^yaarawn
in autumn	õsszel	ūrs-sæl
in winter	télen	taylæn

---

* Note that the names of days and months are not capitalized in Hungarian.

Public holidays

January 1	**Újév**	New Year's Day
April 4	**A felszabadulás ünnepe**	Liberation Day
May 1	**A munka ünnepe**	Labour Day
August 20	**Az alkotmány napja**	Constitution Day
November 7	**A forradalom ünnepe**	Revolution Day
December 25	**Karácsony első napja**	Christmas Day
December 26	**Karácsony második napja**	Boxing Day
Movable:	**Húsvét hétfő**	Easter Monday

The year round

Here are the average monthly temperatures in Fahrenheit and centigrade for some centres in Hungary:

	Budapest		Lake Balaton		Mountains	
	°F	°C	°F	°C	°F	°C
January	34	1	37	3	18	− 8
February	34	1	32	0	14	−10
March	46	8	48	9	32	0
April	52	11	55	13	43	6
May	59	15	61	16	50	10
June	66	19	68	20	57	14
July	68	20	75	24	59	15
August	66	19	73	23	55	13
September	61	16	64	18	50	10
October	54	12	59	15	48	9
November	37	3	45	7	28	− 2
December	36	2	39	4	21	− 6

Common abbreviations

áll.	állami	state
ált.	általános	general
bek.	bekezdés	paragraph
B.N.V.	Budapesti Nemzetközi Vásár	Budapest International Fair
Bp.	Budapest	Budapest
db/drb.	darab	piece
d.e.	délelőtt	a.m.
d.u.	délután	p.m.
et.	elvtárs	comrade
évf.	évfolyam	year
f.é.	folyó év	this year
f.h.	folyó hó	this month
fmh	feltételes megállóhely	request stop
főv.	fővárosi	metropolitan
fsz.	földszint	ground floor
gk.	gépkocsi	car
gy.v.	gyorsvonat	express train
hat.eng.	hatóságilag engedélyezett	licensed
IBUSZ	Idegenforgalmi Ügynökség	Ibusz Tourist Agency
kb.	körülbelül	approximately
K.B.	Központi Bizottság	Central Committee
KEOKH	Külföldieket Ellenőrző Országos Központ	Foreigners' Registration Office
Közért	élelmiszerüzlet	food shop trust
LE	lóerő	horsepower
MALÉV	Magyar Légiforgalmi Vállalat	Hungarian Airlines
MÁV	Magyar Államvasutak	Hungarian State Railways
M.N.B.	Magyar Nemzeti Bank	Hungarian National Bank
M.T.I.	Magyar Távirati Iroda	Hungarian Telegraphic Services
p.u.	pályaudvar	railway station
röv.	rövidítés	abbreviation
s.k.	sajátkezüleg	in one's own hand
stb.	és a többi	etc.
szt.	szent	saint
távb.	telefon	telephone
T.c.	Tisztelt Cím!	Sir, Madam (polite, written)
u.	utca, út	street
u.a.	ugyanaz	the same, idem
u.n.	úgynevezett	so called
v.á.	vasútállomás	railway station

Conversion tables

Centimetres and inches

To change centimetres into inches, multiply by .39.

To change inches into centimetres, multiply by 2.54.

	in.	feet	yards
1 mm	0.039	0.003	0.001
1 cm	0.39	0.03	0.01
1 dm	3.94	0.32	0.10
1 m	39.40	3.28	1.09

	mm	cm	m
1 in.	25.4	2.54	0.025
1 ft.	304.8	30.48	0.305
1 yd.	914.4	91.44	0.914

(32 metres = 35 yards)

Temperature

To convert centigrade into degrees Fahrenheit, multiply centigrade by 1.8 and add 32.

To convert degrees Fahrenheit into centigrade, subtract 32 from Fahrenheit and divide by 1.8.

Metres and feet

The figure in the middle stands for both metres and feet
e.g., 1 metre = 3.28 ft. and 1 foot = 0.30 m.

Metres		Feet
0.30	1	3.281
0.61	2	6.563
0.91	3	9.843
1.22	4	13.124
1.52	5	16.403
1.83	6	19.686
2.13	7	22.967
2.44	8	26.248
2.74	9	29.629
3.05	10	32.810
3.35	11	36.091
3.66	12	39.372
3.96	13	42.635
4.27	14	45.934
4.57	15	49.215
4.88	16	52.496
5.18	17	55.777
5.49	18	59.058
5.79	19	62.339
6.10	20	65.620
7.62	25	82.023
15.24	50	164.046
22.86	75	246.069
30.48	100	328.092

REFERENCE SECTION

Other conversion charts

Weight conversion

The figure in the middle stands for both kilograms and pounds, e.g., 1 kilogram = 2.205 lb. and 1 pound = 0.45 kilograms.

Kilograms (kg.)		Avoirdupois pounds
0.45	1	2.205
0.91	2	4.409
1.36	3	6.614
1.81	4	8.818
2.27	5	11.023
2.72	6	13.227
3.17	7	15.432
3.62	8	17.636
4.08	9	19.841
4.53	10	22.045
6.80	15	33.068
9.06	20	44.089
11.33	25	55.113
22.65	50	110.225
34.02	75	165.338
45.30	100	220.450

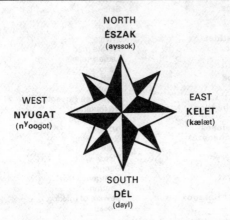

NORTH
ÉSZAK
(ayssok)

WEST
NYUGAT
(nʸoogot)

EAST
KELET
(kælæt)

SOUTH
DÉL
(dayl)

REFERENCE SECTION

What does that sign mean?

You're sure to encounter some of these signs or notices on
your trip:

A bejáratot kérjük szabadon hagyni	Do not block the entrance
Átjárás tilos	Trespassers will be prosecuted
Bejárat	Entrance
Belépés díjtalan	Admission free
Dohányzó	Smoking allowed
Eladó	For sale
Elfogyott	Sold out
Érintése tilos	Do not touch
Fáradjon be	Enter without knocking
Fel	Up
Felvilágosítás	Information
Férfi W.C.	Men's toilets
Foglalt	Reserved, occupied
Forró	Hot
Halálveszély	Danger of death
Hideg	Cold
Húzni	Pull
Kérem, csengessen	Please ring
Kiadó	To let
Kiárusítás	Sale
Kijárat	Exit
Le	Down
Magánterület	Private
Magánút	Private road
Női W.C.	Ladies' toilets
Nyitva	Open
Pénztáros	Cash desk
Szabad	Vacant
... kiadó	... for hire (to rent)
Szemetelni tilos	No littering
... tilos	... prohibited
Tilos a belépés	No entry
Tilos a dohányzás	No smoking
Tólni	Push
Várjon kérem	Please wait
Veszély	Danger
Vészkijárat	Emergency exit
Vigyázat	Caution
Vigyázat! Harapós kutya	Beware of the dog
Zárva	Closed

REFERENCE SECTION

Emergency

By the time the emergency is upon you it's too late to turn to this page to find the Hungarian for "Call the police". So have a look at this short list beforehand—and, if you want to be on the safe side, learn the expressions shown in capitals.

Be quick	**Gyorsan**	d^yawrshon
Call the police	**Hívja a rendőrséget**	hēēvyo o rændūūrshaygæt
CAREFUL	**ÓVATOSAN**	āwvottawshon
Come here	**Jöjjön ide**	yur^y-yurn eedæ
Come in	**Szabad**	sobbod
Consulate	**Konzulátus**	kawnzoolaatoosh
Danger	**Veszély**	væsay^y
Embassy	**Nagykövetség**	nod^ykurvætshayg
FIRE	**TŰZ**	tēwz
GET A DOCTOR	**HÍVJON ORVOST**	hēēvyawn awrvawsht
Get help quickly	**Hozzon gyorsan segítséget**	hawz-zon d^yawrshon shæghēētshaygæt
Go away	**Távozzék**	taavawz-zayk
HELP	**SEGÍTSÉG**	shæghēētshayg
I'm ill	**Beteg vagyok**	bætæg vod^yawk
I'm lost	**Eltévedtem**	æltayvædtæm
Keep your hands to yourself	**Ne fogdosson**	næ fawgdawsh-shawn
Leave me alone	**Hagyjon békét**	hod^yyawn baykayt
Lie down	**Feküdjön le**	fækewdyurn læ
Listen	**Figyeljen**	feed^yælyæn
Look	**Nézzen körül**	nayz-zæn kurrewl
Look out	**Vigyázat**	veed^yaazot
POLICE	**RENDŐRSÉG**	rændūūrshayg
STOP	**MEGÁLLNI**	mægaalnee
Stop, or I'll scream	**Hagyjon békét, vagy kiáltok**	hod^yawn baykayt vod^y keeaaltawk
Stop that man	**Állítsák meg azt az embert**	aal-lēētshaak mæg ost oz æmbært
STOP THIEF	**FOGJÁK MEG TOLVAJ**	fawgyaak mæg tawlvoy

Emergency telephone numbers:

Ambulance	04	**Mentők**
Fire	05	**Tűzoltók**
Police	07	**Rendőrség**

CAR ACCIDENTS: see page 150

REFERENCE SECTION

Index

INDEX

Quick reference page

Yes/No.	**Igen/Nem.**	eegæn/næm
Please.	**Kérem.**	kayræm
Thank you.	**Köszönöm.**	kursurnurm
Excuse me.	**Bocsásson meg.**	bawchaash-shawn mæg
I'm sorry.	**Sajnálom.**	shoynaalawn
Waiter/Waitress, please!	**Pincér/Pincérnő, kérem!**	peentsayr/peentsayrnūr kayræm
How much is that?	**Mennyibe kerül?**	mæn^{y}eebæ kærewl
Where are the toilets?	**Hol a W.C.?**	hawl o vaytsay

Toilets

FÉRFI W.C.	**NŐI W.C.**
(fayrfee vaytsay)	(nūree vaytsay)

Please, could you tell me ...?	**Kérem, meg tudná mondani, hogy ...?**	kayræm mæg toodnaa mawndonnee hawd^y
where/when/why	**hol/mikor/miért**	hawl/meekawr/meeayrt
What time is it?	**Hány óra van?**	haan^y āwro von
Help me, please.	**Segítene kérem.**	shæghēētænæ kayræm
Where's the ... consulate/embassy?	**Hol ... Konzulátus/ Nagykövetség?**	hawl ... kawnzoolaatoosh/ nod^{y}kurvætshayg
American British Canadian	**az amerikai az angol a kanadai**	oz ommæreeko-ee oz ongawl o konnoddo-ee
What does this mean?	**Ez mit jelent?**	æz meet yælænt
I don't understand.	**Nem értem.**	næm ayrtæm
Do you speak English?	**Beszél angolul?**	bæsayl ongawlool